The Concord Theatre

The

CONCORD THEATRE

And Concord's Love Affair with the Movies

PAUL E. BROGAN

Foreword by Barry Steelman

PLAIDSWEDE PUBLISHING
Concord, New Hampshire

Designed and composed at Hobblebush Design, Concord, New Hampshire (www.hobblebush.com)
Printed in the United States of America

ISBN:978-1-7323648-4-4
Library of Congress Control Number: 2019939035

Cover design by Alan Jesseman and Hobblebush Design

Published by:

PLAIDSWEDE PUBLISHING
P.O. Box 269 · Concord, New Hampshire 03302-0269
www.plaidswede.com

For Theresa Cantin, who lived her dream,
and for Alan Jesseman, who urged me to share it.

Contents

Acknowledgments

THIS STORY WOULD BE IMPOSSIBLE TO TELL without the support of so many, some who shared their own stories with me for inclusion in this book. At the top of that list would be Theresa Cantin, herself. During the thousands of hours we spent together at the Concord Theatre, she shared stories that she'd never shared with anyone outside of her immediate family. She would half-jokingly tell me that "One day I hope you'll share them in a book." I was at the theater almost every evening between the summer of 1967 and 1975. In the two hours between the start of the first show and the start of the second, we talked endlessly about a variety of topics. Between 1975 and 1994, when the theater shut its doors, I was still a presence several nights a week and on the phone with Theresa frequently.

I once told a story comparing my talks about the movies with Theresa as being similar to someone who loved the Boston Red Sox and had the chance to spend thousands of hours talking with Ted Williams. This book reflects my conversations with Theresa. I didn't know her as a competitive theater owner or as a tenant, but as a friend who had lived an extraordinary life both as a business owner who happened to be a woman and as a survivor who faced incredible odds and never gave up. I also knew her as someone who never lost her joy and delight in the movies.

The archives of the Concord Monitor were an amazing source of information about Concord's movie history and I appreciate the Monitor allowing me permission to use select pictures in this book. In the days before pictures could be easily taken with a handheld device, there were not many pictures taken of Concord's theaters, especially their interiors. Special thanks to the Concord Public Library for its excellent Concord Room as well as the availability of information on microfiche going back hundreds of years. I've voiced the opinion previously but it bears repeating—The Concord Public Library and its staff are second to none.

While publicly speaking about the Concord Theatre, I heard from scores of individuals with warm and personal memories of the theater and Theresa. They often provided confirmation as to what happened on particular occasions.

A special thank you also to Michael Von Redlich for permission to use his photo and very special thanks to James Webber and Robert Pingree for sharing their memories of the Concord Theatre. A tip of the hat also to Tony Schinella, former editor of Concord Patch. Tony shared some memories for this book but even more importantly encouraged me to share stories about the Concord Theatre back in 2011 when Concord Patch was in its infancy. I am also grateful to Tony for permission to use several photographs he took of the theater. Lynn Colby, thanks for your friendship and memories of the theater.

Grateful thanks and appreciation to Bill Gordon for permission to use some of the pictures he took inside the Concord Theatre in 2018. Jim and Wendy Spain also provided some background information into the history of the Norris Bakery. Thank you both. Thank you to Dana Wormald and the Concord Monitor for permission to use the photograph on the book cover. A tip of the hat, also, to these Monitor reporters, past and present for their invaluable contributions. Thank you Mike Pride, Bob Hohler, Tom Keyser, Felice Belman and Ray Duckler.

Barry Steelman has occupied a very special place in our community for the last 52 years. During that time he has unfailingly shared his love, passion and knowledge of film with tens of thousands of fortunate individuals. He deserves the sobriquet, "Mr. Movie," and I have always been a bit in awe of him. He seemed the ideal individual to write the forward to this book and I am sincerely grateful that he agreed.

There are so many unsung heroes who I talk about in the book—names that won't be familiar to many readers but all of whom played important roles in bringing the magic of the movies to Concord. They are the theater owners, theater managers and the projectionists who skillfully watched for the cue marks and most of the time left an audience unaware that a reel change had occurred. These folks include Barry Steelman, Jacob Conn,

Frank K. Eldridge, Ernie Mayo, Brad Callahan, Merton Tolman, Arthur Dame, Lawrence Bunker, Lionel Irwin, Maurice Cantin, Tom Tolman and James Kenison to name but a few.

A very special thank you to Paul Constant, Theresa's nephew. When I started working at the theater in the summer of 1967, Paul was a seven-year-old ball of energy who would help me clean the auditorium after the last show of the evening ended. In the years after he became a successful businessman, husband and father. One thing that never changed was his devotion to his aunt, Theresa. Nicki Clarke, the executive director of the Capitol Center for the Arts, my thanks. Joe Gleason, from the Capitol Center for the Arts, thank you for making the vision that the CCANH has for the former Concord Theatre, so alive, real and exciting and for sharing all of those public chats we have done. Angie Lane, you're going down the path that Theresa helped to clear, as the E.D. of a much-loved local independent film venue.

Thank you to Dick Osborne, Jim Milliken and the Concord Historical Society. This organization does so much to help preserve the rich history and heritage of Concord, New Hampshire.

Steve Duprey, a mere thank you barely encompasses the gratitude I feel for you and your unrelenting mission to make sure the Concord Theatre didn't disappear into a pile of dust.

Special gratitude to George Geers and his Plaidswede Publishing here in Concord. When I initially approached George about doing the book, he could not have been more encouraging. He has helped to nurture this project with the perfect blend of honesty, nudging and genuine enthusiasm. I am proud to have this book go out under the banner of Plaidswede. Sincere appreciation to my editor and Kirsty Walker of Hobblebush Design

My loving thanks to my mom who drove me to all of those exhibitor screenings on behalf of the Concord Theatre and for making all of those delicious Christmas cookies that Theresa treasured each year. Thank you to my spouse, Alan Jesseman, who sat enthralled as I told stories about my 27-year association with the Concord Theatre. He made me realize that the history I had been a part of needed to be shared and that I was the person who needed to share it.

Foreword

PAUL BROGAN HAS ORCHESTRATED a very personal account about movie theater employee/manager/owner Theresa Cantin. It is a chronicle primarily based on Paul's recollections, empowered by innumerable conversations with Theresa (and other personalities involved), access to her business records and, of course, lots of dutiful research.

The book spans decades of motion picture exhibition in Concord, New Hampshire—which includes venues that have come and gone, all of Theresa's competition, and several theaters in nearby communities.

It is the story of a woman—and that distinction is an important factor—whose affection for movies kept her thoroughly engaged, even when some discouraging aspects of film distribution often outweighed the genuine rewards the industry provided.

I entered the scene in 1967, operating a single screen theater (initially for a Boston-based circuit) named Cinema 93 on Loudon Road. Learning about the other area theaters, I quickly realized the owner of the Concord Theatre was the toughest competitor, having survived thirty-plus years of duking it out with two potent corporations (the Maine/New Hampshire and SBC Management). And she did not soften during the next 27 years.

There was no socializing between us, but there was no hostility either. Perhaps a mutual admiration and understanding of the situations we found ourselves existing in would best describe our relationship.

Maybe someday, if I ever retire and find some spare time, I'll summon up tales of my involvement in this crazy business.

Until then, please turn the page and discover what Paul is generously offering.

Barry Steelman

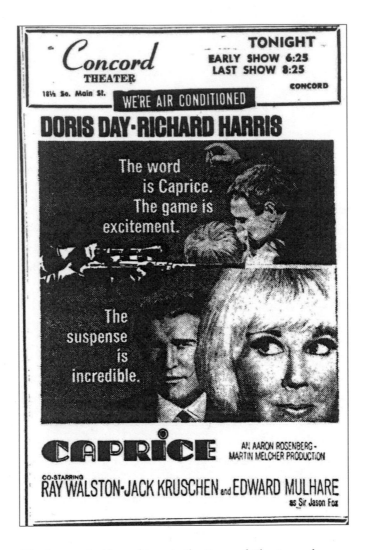

*The feature that brought me to the Concord Theatre and a new
career path was a film that Doris Day almost disowned.*

Preface

MOTION PICTURES OFFICIALLY ARRIVED in Concord, New Hampshire, in February of 1897. I didn't come along until more than 50 years later and while I was a regular moviegoer as a child, I didn't start my so-called career at the movies until Friday, June 23, 1967. That was the night that the latest Doris Day film, *Caprice,* opened at the Concord Theatre at 18 ½ South Main Street.

I'd been to the Concord Theatre many times previously, seeing everything from a reissue of the Disney classic, *Pinocchio,* to the Doris Day musical, *Jumbo,* to Sidney Poitier's Oscar-winning performance in *Lilies of the Field.* I had even gone there several years earlier, in 1962, to see a Bert I. Gordon sword and sorcery epic entitled *The Magic Sword.*

As I entered the upper lobby for that long-forgotten film, I was amazed at seeing what I was certain to be the sword from the film, on display in the concession stand. It sure looked real to my young eyes, and I was impressed that the Concord Theatre seemed to have been able to obtain the prop from the film.

Now as I walked in on that warm and humid late June evening, I had a lightness to my step because I was going to see Doris Day's new film— against her wishes.

Doris Day and I had become pen pals after I had seen her, at the Concord Drive-In Theatre, in a family film entitled, *Please Don't Eat the Daisies* some seven years earlier.

As was often the custom, our family had loaded up the "beach wagon," the name given to our station wagon, with air mattresses in the back for my sister and I to sleep on after the first feature had concluded. A cooler with homemade lemonade and four bags of home-popped popcorn had also accompanied us. The Brogan family was frugal when it came to needless spending on concession items.

I had loved *Daisies* and in those days before there were zip codes, I had written a long and rambling letter to Doris Day, addressing it to her in Hollywood, California. Somehow it had managed to reach her and she responded with a warm and thoughtful note to "Master Paul Brogan." She also sent her home address to ensure that future correspondence made it directly to her. In the years since there had been numerous exchanges between us.

In response to my clearly over enthusiastic letter about seeing her latest film, *Caprice*, she had advised me to ". . . skip it. Save your allowance for something better. This one isn't very good . . . *Caprice* was one of several films that her husband/manager/agent, Martin Melcher, had signed her to do without her consent. He received a co-producer credit for each film as well as a $50,000 fee for "delivering his wife." It seemed that at times he didn't care what kind of project his wife might ultimately be subjected to as long as the money kept rolling in.

Never one to take advice from a movie star, I was in line on opening night to see the first show at 6:25. I also planned to remain for the 8:25 screening. The Concord Theatre had never objected to an audience member remaining to see a picture during the next showing, unless it appeared the next showing would be a sell-out.

As I exited the auditorium about 10:20, I stopped at the box-office counter in the upper lobby to let theater owner Theresa Cantin know that I'd enjoyed the movie.

"Would you like to see it again?" she asked.

For a second, I wasn't sure what she meant since the second and final show of the evening had just concluded. I remember feeling a little confused and I am certain that was reflected on my face.

She continued on, "Paul Bissonnette, who has been working here, closing up each night, for the last year or so is leaving. His family is moving to Manchester and I'm looking for someone to take his place."

Within five minutes we'd agreed that I would start the next night. Over the course of the next 27 years, I was rarely absent, until the theater closed its doors in September of 1994.

While I didn't technically "work there" for all of those years, I was a regular presence, often volunteering my time and frequently stepping into the projection booth as needed in an emergency. A Monday rarely went by in which Theresa and I didn't talk on the phone, no matter where I might be. We'd talk endlessly about pictures, pictures and more pictures. She would often say to a salesman who had attempted to sell her a film, "I need to speak with my associate, Mr. Brogan, and I'll then get back to you."

More than anything, however, we became close and trusted friends. Having spent virtually every day of her life, from the time she was 19, at the theater, Theresa didn't have a lot of time to make friends, outside of her close-knit family. In the days when shows had run continuously starting at noon until late into the evening, Theresa was in the ticket booth much of that time. Later at night she was reconciling the books and preparing the newspaper ads. Theresa did know, with certainty, the meaning of friendship and when you became a friend of Theresa, you were friends for life.

This book is the story of that theater—The Concord Theatre—and that remarkable woman, Theresa Cantin. It is also the story of the important role that the movies played in Concord, both as a source of great social interaction but also as an economic generator. Thousands and thousands of people in Concord attended a movie each week at one of the city's many theaters and each of those theaters had a story to tell.

The Concord Theatre showed films longer than any other movie theater in Concord's history—61 years. From October of 1933 until September of 1994, images flickered on the silver screen.

To the best of my ability, I have dutifully researched the facts which I am sharing as part of the narrative. I don't profess to say this is the ultimate historical in-depth look at each of these film emporiums and the people associated with them. I have tried, nevertheless, to make it entertaining, informative and fun. The kind of book that anyone can enjoy leafing through even if the movies are not their cup of tea.

I was fortunate to have a front row seat for 27 years to the machinations that went on at the Concord Theatre and can therefore share more detail from those experiences since I witnessed them first-hand.

It is my hope that through these stories about these amazing individuals, readers will understand why there are still so many people who maintain warm and nostalgic memories about the places where they saw films. I hope, too, to bring to life some of the people who helped to make the magic on those silver screens possible.

The Concord Theatre

Chapter One

THE MOVIES HAVE INTRIGUED, confused, bewildered, stirred anger, mesmerized and delighted millions since their inception. It was much the same story for the citizenry of Concord, New Hampshire, after getting off to a somewhat slow start.

The Concord Monitor reports that on November 16, 1896, a "paltry turnout of 100 people comes to the 1,100 seat White's Opera House on Park Street in Concord for the first motion picture which is to be shown on Edison and Dow's Rayoscope. The Rayoscope doesn't work, and the crowd goes home disappointed." It wouldn't be until February 8, 1897 that the first movie would finally play Concord.

The site was once again White's Opera House and "the show included bathers at Rahway, N.J., a watermelon-eating contest, a mounted policeman stopping a runaway horse and a three-minute boxing matching featuring Gentleman Jim Corbett. The *Monitor* reviewer reported that, "There is nothing fake about it," adding that "the pictures are vivid and truthful".

In no time at all, "Moving Pictures" as they became known at the time, were popular attractions at White's and would also become popular, when shown, at the nearby Phenix Hall at 40 North Main Street. Built to replace the original Phenix Hall which had burned in a fire in 1893, the new hall seated nearly 500. While not a regular moving picture theater, it frequently showed films in the early years of the 20th century. It was also utilized for speeches and other events including theatrical productions, boxing matches and dances.

The opening of the Concord City Auditorium in November of 1904, brought yet another venue into the city where stage presentations and lectures could be presented. It also provided yet another place for motion pictures to be shown, which they were eventually in the 1920s after the loss of White's Opera House in a tragic fire.

In May of 1908, the *Concord Monitor* noted, "Unable to keep up with the Concord City Auditorium for live shows, manager Ben White of White's Opera House begins showing continuous motion pictures and illustrated songs every day but Sunday. Admission is a dime for adults and a nickel for children. The songs are by Fred Rushlow. The venture will prove an immense success".

White's proudly advertised that they were showing movies by installing a large, lighted sign on the side of the building saying "Moving Pictures." While they continued to intermittently have live productions, movies became their staple until a fire destroyed the building in 1920.

By 1908 it seemed like everybody was mad about the movies as indicated by another piece in the newspaper. "Fire Chief William Green sets out for the movies at Phenix Hall, but even though the same show played at the nearby Opera House for more than a year, the Phenix is filled. There are plans to convert yet another building in the Durgin block into a theater."

When Conn's Theatre opened on School Street in Concord on October 14, 1912, it was the first theater designed to be a movie theater. Conn's would show some stage presentations and vaudeville to accompany films, but it was not for nothing that they advertised themselves as "Concord's Theatre, De Luxe".

Movies changed on Monday, Wednesday and Friday and the vaudeville presented changed on Mondays and Thursdays.

Captain Jacob Conn was the man behind the theater that had his name. Conn began business in Concord in 1898 with borrowed capital of $2.50, according to *The Granite State Monthly*. When the old Durgin silverware factory was destroyed by a fire in 1911, Captain Conn became the owner of the land and the remnants of the building that had been on the land. Conn worked nights and Sundays on his tailoring business in Concord, spending the remaining time cleaning up the debris on the property he now owned. In June of 1911 the cornerstone was laid for his theater. Conn's Theatre, from the day it opened, became a very popular spot in the community. It continued showing motion pictures as the Conn until 1920 by which time Conn had left the area to pursue business ventures in Rhode Island. Among the motion pictures theaters that he opened in the Providence area were the Olympia, which opened on September 5, 1926, and the Metropolitan, which opened on August 25, 1932.

Conn also owned and operated a radio station, WCOT, in Providence and ran for mayor of that city in 1928. Reportedly, Conn used his radio station to defame his opponents. In 1928 the station's license was revoked for failure to serve public interest and on the ground "that false statements and defamatory language had been broadcast over the station." Jacob Conn also wrote a 1933 movie entitled, *Found Alive,* which failed. The November 3, 1932, issue of *Boxoffice Magazine* reported that Conn had filed for bankruptcy, listing liabilities at more than $940,000 and assets at just under $1.5 million. "The principal creditors are banks, financiers and contractors on the new theatre which closed recently."

On July 19, 1920, a story appeared in the *Concord Monitor* regarding the School Street Theater. That was, of course, the location of Conn's Theatre. The piece noted that redecorating was going on and was expected to be completed in approximately a month's time. In fact it took a little longer than that, but on Thursday, September 16, 1920, the former Conn's Theatre did reopen, announcing itself as the Sterling.

The Sterling's opening film attraction was *The Mollycoddle* starring the immensely popular Douglas Fairbanks. An added attraction was a Harold Lloyd comedy as well as "Weekly News" and *Topics of the Day.* David Schmidt and the Sterling Orchestra would also play, live, selections from the musical show, *Irene.* Tickets were priced at 17 cents for adults and 11 cents for children. There was no indication that the Sterling had anything to do with Jacob Conn and a couple of years later in 1922, they announced that it was "Under New Management." It closed in December of 1922.

Cohn's Theatre,
Concord, N. H.

Conn's Theatre, which opened on School Street in Concord in 1912. Named for the owner, Captain Jacob Conn, the theater name is misspelled on the postcard as Cohn's.

The Star Theatre, which was situated on Pleasant Street,
opened in 1915 and played movies until December 1951.

Although Conn had talked of opening another theater in Concord—this time on Pleasant Street and dubbing it the Palace—it did not happen. A theater did rise, however, on Pleasant Street, opening on November 24, 1915 and calling itself the Star Theatre. An ad in the *Concord Monitor* strenuously noted, "THE STAR THEATER HAS NO CONNECTION WITH ANY OTHER THEATER IN CONCORD, NH"

Boasting more than 1,000 seats and a balcony, one of the first attractions at the Star was Geraldine Farrar in the opera, *Carmen*. The ads also stated, "With a full Orchestra and the Musical score as it was played at Boston Symphony Hall." The Star also heavily promoted its cost, which was almost $50,000 and that "It is second to no theater in the entire state".

E.J. Caron, the Star manager, also made sure the public knew the Star was "The Photo Playhouse De-Luxe of New Hampshire".

The day that the Capitol Theatre on South Main Street in Concord opened, was a real event in Concord and one that everyone wanted to be a part of. Nearly 3,000 people filled both performances on opening day, January 31, 1927. What they saw inside amazed them and even left a few speechless. Referred to as "The Wonder Theater," matinee prices for adults were 25-35 cents, depending on where you sat. In the evening it cost 35-50 cents and children were always 10 cents. The 50-cent seats were reserved, and you could call to make a reservation for one of them as a convenience.

What the audience saw inside, however, was almost as good as the show on the large stage and on the screen. You knew the moment you walked into the enormous auditorium that you were someplace special. The ceiling, with its four chandeliers, seemed to stretch on toward heaven. There was an army of ushers ready and eager to escort you to a seat and the Capitol Theatre was the talk of the town for days after. Everyone who'd not yet been inside, wanted to know, from those who had been, what the experience had been like.

Silent movies were still in vogue and Arthur Martel, the reported "Organ Wizard," manned the Mighty Wurlitzer whose sound filled the vast hall. He provided background music for the films showing but also performed an organ recital, the likes of which nobody in Concord had heard before outside of Boston. Before the start of the feature film, audiences were treated to 5 live vaudeville acts followed by a feature film, in this case Reginald Denny starring in *The Cheerful Fraud*.

Arthur Martel was a Boston-based organist and a highly respected musician. *The Etude*, a music-oriented publication for many years, reported in their July, 1920 issue:

Arthur Martel, a Boston organist, *has just signed a ten years' contract with a movie syndicate for ten thousand dollars per annum—the highest salary ever paid to a movie organist.*

One could only assume that the salary he was paid by the time the Capitol Theatre opened seven years later, was considerably more.

For many who attended during the first weeks, it mattered little what was showing on the screen. They all wanted to partake in the experience of going to the Capitol Theatre. The Twenties were still roaring and no one could foresee that about 2 ½ years later, the Great Depression would crush optimism, hope and the lives of so many with its relentless grip. While there was talk about something called "Talking pictures," it seemed as though should it happen, it would be a fad, if anything. But by the end of 1927, Al Jolson's *The Jazz Singer* had opened and would begin to completely change the way that movies were presented.

In 1929, Frank K. Eldridge, who had been the manager of the Keith Memorial Theatre in downtown Boston, became the manager of the Capitol Theatre. He would remain in that position until the mid-1960s when he retired.

The first time I was taken, as a youngster, to the Capitol Theatre was more than thirty years after it had opened. The movie I saw was Disney's *Old Yeller* and while I joined in with the hundreds of sobbing viewers during parts of the film, my most pronounced memory of that afternoon was walking into that vast hall and being stunned into silence, quite an accomplishment for a little child. I couldn't believe that Concord had such a place and even after all the years and the thousands of films that had been played, the theater still had a majestic magic to it. It would be a few more years before I saw my first film in wide-screen at the Capitol and that was *Ben Hur*. After they installed its Cinemascope screen in 1954, the Capitol Theatre could truthfully boast of having the largest movie screen north of Boston.

In all of New Hampshire, only the State Theatre, which opened in Manchester in November of 1929, could be seen as possibly being even more lavish than the Capitol. The State had 2,100 seats. Their Cinemascope screen, however, was not as large as the one that eventually graced Concord's Capitol Theatre.

The Capitol Theatre as it appeared in 1937, 10 years after opening.

For nearly a half century, the Capitol Theatre or "The Cap" as it was referred to by locals, held sway as a reminder of what a great "Movie Palace" was. While most of the ushers vanished in the 1950s and it became more and more difficult to fill the many seats in the large movie house (the balcony was frequently chained off and not used), she still held her head high.

During the last decade of showing films the heat in the theater sometimes didn't work. In the meantime, audiences didn't seem to hesitate to flock to some of the more modern multiplex theaters. However, when it was reported in the 1990s that the Capitol might be demolished or turned into something else, the people of Concord rallied, as they have in the past and continue to do. As a result, the theater was not only saved but turned into a performing arts center that is the envy of many communities throughout America.

The Concord Theatre arrived 6 ½ years after the Capitol Theatre opened. Although the drive-in theaters would arrive in the greater Concord area in the early 1950s, it would be 34 years between the opening of the Concord Theatre and the opening of the next indoor theater in Concord. Cinema 93, which opened its doors for the first time in April of 1967, is featured elsewhere in this book.

By 1979, the first multiplex theater had reached Concord and would force both the Concord Theatre and Cinema 93 to up their game. For nearly twenty years after the arrival of the first multiplex, Cinema 93 flourished by offering something for everyone and doing it as well or better than theaters in large cities were able to do. The Concord Theatre chugged along, managing to keep its doors open seven days a week with mostly first-run films. A second multiplex cinema, currently known as the Regal, arrived in the mid-1990s by which time the Concord Theatre had closed and was, unfortunately, in its last years.

The next real cinema milestone for Concord was the 2007 arrival of Red River Theatres in downtown Concord. Unlike the two multiplex cinemas that were located on Loudon Road, miles from the heart of the city, Red River returned motion pictures to downtown Concord helping to bring a new energy to a city trying to reinvent itself.

It seems appropriate that the original downtown effort was spearheaded by Barry Steelman. After the closure of his Cinema 93 (the owners of the mall where the theater had been located for more than thirty years did not renew his lease, instead having other plans for the site). Barry brought his prospering video business to the former Star Theatre location in downtown Concord and began a plan to return movies to the downtown. The group of volunteers who banded together with him named the organization after the classic 1948 western, *Red River*. John Wayne had been the star of the film. In the story, a journey that is considered impossible is undertaken with a successful end result.

Opening in the fall of 2007, Red River, with its three screens, made an immediate impact upon the community and showed, once again how a uniting spirit and dedication could be found within the City of Concord. Like the project to save the Capitol Theatre and a similar project to restore the Concord City Auditorium some years earlier, the spirit of the local community came together with a successful end result. Over the past twelve years, Red River has provided opportunities for audiences to see new films, art and foreign films, view film classics and experience diverse film festivals. Public support continued when Red River converted its 35mm projectors to modern systems no longer requiring the use of film as well as the addition of Dolby Digital Surround Sound. Even more recently the screening room was converted into a more comfortable viewing theater.

On a stiflingly hot July morning in 2018, I sat down and chatted with Red River's effusive Executive Director Angie Lane. I shared stories with her about Theresa Cantin and the struggles she had faced as a trailblazing woman running a first-run independent movie theater some seven decades earlier. I asked Angie what some of the pluses were about being an independent theater in a world where the multiplex cinemas seemed to rule.

"When people come to Red River, they see their friends. They connect and talk and share the movie experience. We're a part of an exciting and diverse downtown and customers feel that energy when they come to see a movie."

We talked about the many distinct touches that set Red River aside, in much the same way that the Concord Theatre and Cinema 93 were immediately defined. Whether you walked into the Concord in 1940 or 1970 or 1990, the familiar face of Theresa Cantin was there to greet you and sell you a ticket. Likewise at Cinema 93, you saw Barry and you saw his distinctive father, Arthur, as well as other members of the staff who spent years work-ing there.

Angie continued, "You can walk into the Regal Cinemas and from week to week see a different face selling the tickets, or at the concession stand. It's hard to establish any level of personal connection. At Red River, you see the same people, the same faces and many of the same customers. You are instantly brought into a certain comfort zone that only enhances the complete moviegoing experience."

Somehow it seems only appropriate that more than 120 years after movies first flickered on the screen in Concord at the downtown White's Opera House they continue to bring eager and curious audiences into the city's downtown. The notion of an independent movie theater that was first a part of Concord's downtown area in 1912 with the opening of Conn's Theatre, is still, 107 years later, alive and thriving at Red River Theatres.

Chapter Two

IF I WERE GOING TO FILM A MOVIE about the life of Barry Steelman, the face and heart of Concord's legendary Cinema 93, I would have once upon a time cast James Stewart in the role. Today I would probably cast Tom Hanks. Why? Because both actors represent a unique quality on the screen. They're regular people who often have had to fight against tremendous odds to achieve something and they are usually successful in their mission. They play characters who usually have the audience rooting for them and with whom the audience can identify. That is so much a part of the appeal of Barry Steelman.

Although not a Concord native, he has been such an integral part of Concord for so many years that we feel as though he has always been here. Certainly few, if any other people, myself included, know and understand how the movies work and what makes a movie a classic better than Barry does. He has his finger on the pulse of the community and knows what people would like and what might turn them off. Sometimes he has gone ahead and taken a risk, hoping that in the process he can expand their horizons and enable them to try something a little bit different than their regular cinema taste.

My feelings about Barry Steelman and about Cinema 93, can be summed up more aptly by this blog I wrote in 2017 as a tribute to the 50th anniversary of the opening of Cinema 93.

To those of us who have lived in Concord for a long time as well as those of us with long memories, Friday, April 28, meant something special. It was exactly 50 years ago on a Friday that also happened to be April 28, back in 1967, that Cinema 93 opened its doors for the first time.

The gleaming new theater, located in what was then known as the King's Shopping Plaza, was the first new indoor theater to open in Concord since

October of 1933, when the Concord Theatre opened. The first attraction at Cinema 93 was "In Like Flint," a film in the popular spy genre—this one starring James Coburn. While the film may be forgettable, a first visit to Cinema 93 was not. The ad in the "Concord Monitor" noted the modern setting and comfortable seating as well as the concession stand and projection system. It also noted that reservations could be taken to guarantee you seating. "Concordians" by the thousands made the trek across the river to give the new film emporium a once over.

Clearly they liked what they saw because for some thirty years, Cinema 93 would be a very popular destination, not only for local residents but those from out of town who heard of the theater's reputation for showing an amazing cross-section of films for every taste. I know I have very fond memories of hundreds of film viewings during those 30 plus years.

What really distinguished Cinema 93, however, was the manager, later owner, Barry Steelman. Barry loves movies—all kinds—and his knowledge of films is second to none. From the first attraction, Barry wanted the people who attended his theater to have the best possible experience and when he became owner, wanted to make sure that film types, previously not shown in Concord with any degree of regularity, were given a chance. In doing so, he developed a passionate and loyal audience.

Cinema 93 played a great mix of popular hits over the years including the made in New Hampshire, "On Golden Pond," a film that Barry worked on. Others like "The Graduate," "Bonnie and Clyde" and others, became classics. You also had the opportunity to be exposed to foreign fare as well as rarely seen classics from Hollywood's Golden Era. Long before there were videos or DVDs or Turner Classic Movies, Cinema 93 was the place to go to find out why movies mattered.

Barry started a video rental center in the theater's lobby with a wide array of hard to find films. Even better, Barry made himself available to help you find that title that was on the tip of your tongue but you could not remember. As long as you had a little information—cast or plot or time frame as to when it came out—Barry was able to not only give you the title, but considerable background information to make the viewing experience all the better.

Sadly, Cinema 93 was forced to close in the late 1990s—not due to a decrease in attendance but due to planned changes in the shopping plaza. Appropriately enough, Barry relocated and expanded his video operation to the old Star

Theatre on Pleasant Street in Concord. Most of us never thought of renting a film elsewhere, so complete was his selection.

Cinema 93 was a community experience. You always ran into friends or made new friends through the shared experience of seeing a film together. It was a destination stop and one of many reasons to consider locating to Concord. Fortunately, Barry Steelman remains a vital and active part of our community. He is the programming specialist at Concord's independent Red River Theatre and brings an amazing group of films deserving to be seen. He also continues to share his knowledge and passion with new generations of moviegoers.

Something remarkable occurred on Friday, April 28, 1967, and it resonates even more today than it did half a century ago. Thanks for the memories, Cinema 93, and kudos to you Barry Steelman for sharing your passion.

Barry's story would certainly read like the screenplay of a Frank Capra classic, and everyone who knows Barry realizes that he's a long way from "calling it a wrap."

Born in Burlington, Vermont, Barry attended high school in Rutland. His father, an imposing figure who was a fixture at Cinema 93, worked for Standard Oil of New Jersey. When Barry was in his late teens, the family relocated to Allenstown, New Hampshire.

Barry always loved the movies. Westerns were his favorites but he treasured the time he spent in a movie theater watching the images on the screen.

Barry was only in his early 20s when he began operating his first movie theater. The Empire in Manchester was located on Massabesic Street and had been closed for some years. He opened the theater in June of 1966 and remained there for about a year. Films were only shown at the Empire on weekends and the titles included *A Hard Day's Night* and *Help*, both starring the Beatles. He also played other available titles including many second-run movies that had played elsewhere in Manchester but did better than he had expected as repeats.

He applied for a job as a manager at a new cinema opening in Concord, New Hampshire. Although he was initially turned down, he eventually got the job and Cinema 93 on Loudon Road opened on April 27, 1967. For more than 30 years, Cinema 93 would be a destination spot in Concord and earned a reputation far outside the city limits as a place where you could see just about anything. The strip mall where Cinema 93 was located also contained an IGA Foodliner, a King's Department Store, Deering Restaurant, a Hallmark card shop and one or two other businesses. Some of them changed over the course of 30 years, but Cinema 93 remained a staple.

In an interview with Amy Diaz in *Hippo Press*, Barry noted that *Dances with Wolves* was the biggest thing that played at Cinema 93. There were many other films that have become Hollywood classics that also played there. These would definitely include *Bonnie and Clyde, The Graduate, El Norte, My Dinner with Andre, Star Wars* and *On Golden Pond,* which was filmed in New Hampshire. Barry had the pleasure of working on that production while it was being filmed in the summer of 1980.

Barry is a visionary and he is always looking beyond the next mountain to scale. That became especially true after he bought Cinema 93 in 1974. As the owner, he had a great deal more latitude in what played at the theater than he'd had when he was the manager. While he had to make a living in order to support his family and thus needed to play some films with commercial potential to achieve that, he wanted to also play a more interesting assortment of lesser known pictures.

Despite a thirty-year difference in their ages, Barry and Theresa were similar in many ways. Neither was driven by a desire to amass a fortune through motion picture exhibition. As the owner of the theater, you have a more personal investment in your place of business. It was important to each of them that each and every ticket buyer have a good experience when viewing a film. With an increasing number of entertainment options available by the 1970s and 80s, developing loyalty and a good relationship with a customer became all the more important.

Barry actively discussed increasing Cinema 93's ability to show films by adding an additional space and was at the forefront of recognizing the value of video, when he began renting video tapes in the lobby of Cinema 93. Some theaters would have considered such rentals as being in direct competition with their business of showing movies. Barry thought otherwise and the selection of tapes that he had available brought many people to Cinema 93 who had never been there before.

As the video business swelled, and it did, you could eventually rent anything from a classic Hollywood film from the 1930s to foreign titles from every country, to the more recent Hollywood blockbusters. A stop at Cinema 93 to rent a video was a regular habit for my mom and dad for many years.

Cinema 93, after opening in 1967, became one of the city's most enduring success stories for more than 30 years, thanks to the skill, knowledge and talent of Barry Steelman.

When Cinema 93 closed its doors in the latter 90s, there was a genuine sense of sadness among many. For anyone who knew Barry well or understood how he felt about movies, there was a sense of hope and optimism, however, that the closure was only a temporary blip. His video business continued to thrive and Barry was on premises almost all of the time, ready and eager to answer questions from his customers. He'd offer suggestions, if asked, about a good title to rent for a particular occasion, and he could identify many films merely from a description offered by a prospective renter. All of this he did with the same modesty and graciousness that had earned him a sterling reputation in the community.

A couple of years after Theresa's passing and after the Concord Theatre building had been sold, Barry went inside with an eye toward bringing it back to life. Having been urged by many of his longtime customers, he recognized the value of a downtown movie theater while also realizing the challenges such an undertaking would involve. There was a genuine buzz of excitement within the area when word got out that something might be happening.

Red River a 1948 film classic that starred John Wayne and Montgomery Clift had been one of Barry's favorite films. It opened in Concord, N.H., on Wednesday, December 8, 1948 at the Capitol Theatre. In 1990 the film was selected for preservation by the National Film Registry as being "culturally, historically, or aesthetically significant." It remains a masterpiece directed by Howard Hawks but even more so, its message continues to resonate today. A group of individuals facing what seem like insurmountable odds and not allowing anything to stand in the way of their completing their cattle drive from Texas to Kansas.

It only seemed right to title the venture that Barry and a group of supporters undertook to bring movies back to downtown Concord after that classic film.

Like the characters in *Red River*, there were many obstacles that had to be overcome but ultimately motion picture exhibition did return to Concord's Main Street after an absence of nearly thirteen years. Red River Theatres became an instant hit with movie lovers who were starved for the variety of films that the multiplexes seemed unwilling to gamble on. Better still, Barry Steelman was right there as a part of the team that had made it succeed.

While Barry isn't the E.D. some would have wanted him to be, his role at the theater has great influence upon what is seen. The "Barry Touch" is evident with the choice of classic films often shown in the screening room. His valuable input also helps to shape the film festivals shown and in so many other ways. His presence in the lobby brings the perfect transition from Concord's movie past to the present and unlimited future. Barry will hopefully continue to be a major force in making people want to experience all types of film.

Theresa Cantin admired Barry. She spoke of him with genuine admiration and respect. Yes, they were competitors in trying to secure the very best films from a gradually diminishing list as new theaters arrived. No doubt there were clashes although I never heard Theresa say anything but good things about Cinema 93 and its owner. It isn't often that a city of 30-40,000 people gets to have even one independent movie theater which attempts to bring a cross section of quality films that are not determined by box-office grosses. In Concord's case, there were two such exhibitors. They were from different generations for sure but in their hearts they shared the same desire, putting their customers first and giving them their money's worth. Red River has carried on that tradition and generations of Concord residents are all the better for Theresa, Barry and his dream that mushroomed into Red River Theatres.

The Norris Bakery building on South Main Street. In 1933 the building would be transformed into the Concord Theatre.

Chapter Three

THERESA CANTIN WAS BORN IN MANCHESTER, New Hampshire, on December 15, 1913. She was the first child born to Wenceslas and Emma (Noel) Cantin. A son, Maurice A. Cantin would follow in 1915 and another daughter, Rena H. Cantin (later Constant) in 1919. Several years later in 1925, another daughter would be born and they baptized her Laurence, although most knew her by the name Laurie. Wenceslas had been born in Quebec and Emma was from Lynn, Massachusetts. They settled in Manchester, New Hampshire, where Wenceslas built a good reputation and business as a contractor and builder.

The Cantin family was passionate about its Catholic faith. There were parishioners of St. Anthony's in Manchester, and Theresa attended Parochial School at St. Anthony's until she was ten years of age. Theresa next entered a convent school in Boscawen, remaining there as a boarder. Although she later admitted that she felt as though she were in a jail, she ultimately felt that some good had come from the experience.

For any Catholic family of faith, it was hoped that a child would either become a nun or a priest. In Theresa's case she was encouraged to follow a vocation but she was uncertain about. The time spent at the convent deepened her religious fervor but also made her realize that the religious life was not for her. Blessed with a surprisingly rich and vibrant contralto voice which often silenced those around her into a sense of awe as she sang beloved Catholic music in church or school, Theresa even gave thought to pursuing a singing career.

Any dreams she might have held, however, became secondary to family responsibility. In 1928, when she was 14, Theresa was called back home. Her mother, who was 36 at the time, had never fully recovered, physically, from the birth of her fourth child and third daughter, Laurie, in 1925. She had become increasingly frail and was unable to care for her three children or to even carry out the regular day-to-day necessities of running a home. At 14, Theresa became the person who ran the home, did the cooking, cleaning and tended to her three siblings, as well as helping to care for her invalid mother. Late at night, Theresa would spend two hours daily studying and teaching herself much of what she would have learned had she been able to return to school.

Maurice was 13, Rena was 9 and Laurie was 3 years of age when Theresa was called home. Theresa's father told her many years later that she had single-handedly saved the Cantin family by never questioning why she had to put her own life and dreams on hold. For the rest of her life, Theresa believed in the value of family and always did whatever she could do for those she loved, even to her own detriment.

Her mother's health never recovered, and Emma Cantin rarely if ever left the house, succumbing to various illnesses at the age of 52 in July of 1944.

On the rare occasions when Theresa had a few hours of time in which she was not needed at home, she found a new escape from her 18-hour days—the movies.

Talking films were just starting to become the norm in 1929 when Theresa walked into downtown Manchester and into the State Theatre on Elm Street. The new movie palace, and indeed it was a palace boasting more than 2,000 seats and a lavishness that made anyone entering it feel as though they had stepped into a royal residence. Here Theresa sat in wonder and watched the images before her on the screen. For a brief hour or two she was able to laugh, cry or simply find herself caught up in a story. It became a weekly habit for her and sometimes she was even able to see a second film during a week. Her brother Maurice, who was 14, would sometimes volunteer to watch their mother and youngest sisters so that Theresa could get away for a little while. Maurice never forgot how hard Theresa worked throughout her life and while he didn't verbalize his gratitude and appreciation, he would sometimes just hug her tight and that expressed all of his feelings.

The Cantin family had a strong work ethic and Wenceslas Cantin worked as hard as anyone. Although he had workers, he believed in leading by example and working alongside his crew for as many hours as it took to complete the work. He wanted to make a good living for his family and to make sure his ailing wife and four children were well provided for. Fortunately when the Great Depression hit in late 1929, his business continued to thrive and much of the money he had made was kept safely at home and not in banks. He lost some of his money that had been invested but not enough to cause the level of devastation that many unfortunately felt.

Theresa made sure that her brother and sisters were able to attend school and helped provide as stable a home life as was possible.

In 1932 Wenceslas was approached by Joseph E. (J.E.) Charbonneau, a businessman who had experience with theaters. In 1930 he had begun managing the Colonial Theatre in Nashua, which had previously been closed for a year. Charbonneau was successful at what he did and was also amiable and knowledgeable. He was interested in expanding his movie exhibition experience into Concord, the state's capital. At the time Concord had only two regular first-run movie theaters—the Capitol and the Star. Both were part of the Maine and New Hampshire Theatres Company and the city was without any independent movie theater. Charbonneau had studied the community and felt that an additional theater would do very well.

Cantin was very interested in what Charbonneau had to say. He liked his energy, knowledge about movie exhibition and obvious belief that this venture would work. Cantin was even more impressed when Charbonneau suggested they team up on a joint venture—50/50, with Cantin also doing the necessary work to convert the site he had in mind into a movie theater.

The Norris Bakery on South Main Street in Concord had sat empty for a number of years. The building, which had been constructed almost seventy-five years earlier, played an important role during the Civil War in the early 1860s. Hard bread which was commonly known as "Hard Tack" by the troops was made at the Norris Bakery. In addition, the bakery also provided molasses cookies which were sold to the troops at six cookies for a quarter.

Once a bustling and thriving business, times had changed for the bakery in the 1920s and the building was available for sale, for the right price. The two gentleman and prospective business partners traveled to Concord where they toured the building with Cantin outlining some ideas he had as they walked around. This venture would require a major amount of construction work to be viable since there was no building that could be converted into the auditorium portion of a theater. There would need to be construction to make that a reality.

When Wenceslas came home that evening and shared his discussion with his daughter Theresa, he saw a visible spark within her light up. The notion of her family being involved with a movie theater was something that her then 19-year-old self liked. She urged her father to give serious consideration to Mr. Charbonneau's offer, and Wenceslas did. Within days the two had reached a decision to move forward and the former Norris Bakery was purchased and work began.

Theresa told me more than 40 years later that she believed this turn of events in the Cantin family life was a gift from God for her having never questioned why she'd had to put her own needs on hold. She also noticed how relieved and how much happier her father seemed to be as he took on the work involved. In the past he had never been one to talk in detail with the family about his business dealings. All of that changed as he gladly shared details about the transformation happening in Concord. In the summer of 1933 he invited Theresa to join him on a trip to Concord to inspect the progress.

For just a brief second Theresa was a little disappointed when she saw the theater. It didn't have the chandeliers and lavishness that she'd seen at the State Theatre and some other theaters she had gone to in Manchester. It also didn't have a marquee and wouldn't for some years. However, her tinge of disappointment quickly evaporated as she walked through the place and it settled in her mind that her father was half owner of the theater.

On the journey home to Manchester, Theresa asked her father whether she might work at the theater when it opened. "I'd be happy just to sell tickets and greet the customers," she enthusiastically said in making her case.

"I don't see why not" was Wenceslas' response. "It might also help you learn some business practices which are always good for a girl to know." Cantin also felt it would be good to have the presence of a family member on the site to look after his investment. He had every plan to continue his thriving Manchester business and was not about to give that up for the theater. However his daughter clearly loved the idea of being a part of the movie house and he approved.

Theresa told her mother all about her future job when they arrived home. Emma smiled at her daughter and squeezed her hand, giving her approval, as Theresa began a new chapter in her life. She continued to do much of the housework, cooking and making sure her two sisters made it to school each day. Maurice was, by now, much more independent and able to look after himself. Wenceslas also had someone come in to help care for his wife as necessary.

The opening attraction at the Concord Theatre in 1933.

Chapter Four

THE CONCORD THEATRE opened on Wednesday, October 18, 1933. There wasn't any fanfare. There were no klieg lights, no ribbon-cutting ceremony and no officials declaring it "Concord Theatre Day!" It was as though the theater quietly slipped into town, not wanting to create a stir, instead wishing to simply start the business of entertaining customers.

That same day the Capitol Theatre was preparing to open with Katharine Hepburn and Douglas Fairbanks Jr. in *Morning Glory*. The film would earn Miss Hepburn the first of her four Academy Awards as Best Actress. On stage were "Five Big Acts" to accompany the feature. Around the corner on Pleasant Street at the Star Theatre were "5 Units of Entertainment." Unit number 1 was the main feature *The Solitaire Man*, Unit number 2 was a Vitaphone musical entitled, *Seasoned Greetings*. Unit number 3 was a so-called "Novelty" entitled *Strange as It Seems*, Unit number 4 was another "Novelty" entitled, *Grand National Sweepstakes* and the final unit was a *Silly Symphony Cartoon*. In neighboring Penacook, the Palace Theatre was showing George Arliss as *Voltaire*.

On its opening day, the Concord was playing its show only in the evening, at 7 and at 9 p.m. The same program would also run on Thursday, Friday and Saturday. Admission for children was 10 cents for all shows, and for adults the price was 20 cents in the afternoon and 25 cents in the evening. Performances beginning on Thursday were continuous daily from 12:30 p.m. until 10:30 p.m.

The opening program was headlined by the Monogram film, *The Sweetheart of Sigma Chi* starring legendary swimming star Buster Crabbe and Mary Carlisle. There was also a "Port o' Call" entitled, *The Seventh Wonder*, together with an "organlogue," a comedy and a Mickey Mouse cartoon. Buster Crabbe was known to millions as winner of a bronze medal at the 1928 Olympics and a gold medal at the 1932 Olympics for his swimming.

Theresa Cantin worked in the box office that evening as she would thousands of times in the future. Theresa also followed a piece of advice her father had given to her only days before the theater opened. "Connect with the customers," he advised. "Establish a relationship with them. Get to know the people that return over and over again and make their purchase of a ticket something personal. Make sure to let them know you appreciate their making a choice to come to our theater." Theresa followed that advice throughout her 61 years at the South Main Street spot that was her domain. In no time at all she became the face of the Concord Theatre and if for some reason she was busy elsewhere in the building when a regular showed-up to buy a ticket, they'd enquire about her absence out of concern.

One of Theresa's favorite memories of the early years was the numerous occasions in which she had to put up the "Sold-Out" sign. That first evening the theater was open, it went up for both performances much to the delight of Theresa and her father as well as their business partner. Local film lovers were clearly eager to sample the wares at the opening of the new downtown movie house.

Movies, radio and an occasional stage show or lecture, were the main sources of entertainment, not only for the residents of the capital city but for millions all over the country. The Great Depression was at a nadir and after nearly four years of the Depression, it didn't show any sign of disappearing or even improving in the near future. The one glimmer of hope was Franklin D. Roosevelt.

Roosevelt had been inaugurated the previous March and he was instituting an aggressive series of programs designed to help lift the country out of the depth of despair. Everyone wanted to believe that better days were ahead. In the meantime, the movies provided an escape and a chance to temporarily forget the realities of what was happening.

Concord had a population of just over 25,000 at the time and the railroad industry still provided employment to a great number of individuals in the city. The railroad station was an imposing structure that dominated a large area, a block east of Main Street, the city's main thoroughfare. Streetcar tracks were still visible on many streets in the community. Streetcar service had only recently been discontinued.

Monogram Pictures, the studio responsible for the opening feature film, *The Sweetheart of Sigma Chi*, had only been in business for two years. Between 1931 and 1953, it produced and released hundreds of low-budget motion pictures. In the Hollywood scheme of things, they were known as a "Poverty Row Studio." It shared this distinction with Republic Pictures. Monogram and Republic would provide the bulk of motion picture product for the fledgling Concord Theatre for the first decade or more of its existence. While these studios sometimes had known stars appearing in their films, they could not boast of having the star power of major studios. MGM, the leader in Hollywood at the time, was quick to claim it had, "More Stars than there are in the Heavens!"

Mr. Charbonneau did not have any expectations that the Concord Theatre would be playing films made by MGM, Fox, Paramount or Warners. He knew that the films being made by those studios would most certainly end up playing at either the Capitol Theatre, Star Theatre or in some cases at both. It was not unusual to have a film that did great business at the Capitol then play a second-run at the Star. This provided an opportunity for those who might have missed it at the Capitol to see it. In the days of split weeks, when a film bill would change two and sometimes three times in a week, it was often impossible for every interested patron to see the picture within those few days.

The Concord Theatre did not initially have a concession stand. Many theaters did not. What they did have were ushers who would eagerly tear the ticket you'd purchased from Theresa and, if necessary, show you to your seat. Working as an usher at a local movie theater was the dream job for many teenage boys and Theresa recalls having a waiting list of interested individuals.

Mr. Cantin did not involve himself in the booking of films for the theater. He was extremely busy with his own business but would listen to what Theresa had to say in the evening when she returned home from work. Theresa realized after several months of asking Mr. Charbonneau whether they could play a Garbo film or perhaps one of Marlene Dietrich's movies made by Paramount, that there was little likelihood of that happening. Mr.

Charbonneau regularly went to Boston for meetings and would respectfully but sternly tell Theresa that the programs they were showing at the
Concord were more than satisfactory.

When she had an afternoon off from working, Theresa would regularly
take in a film at one of the other local theaters. She was especially fond of
the MGM films that played at the Capitol Theatre and she became friendly
with the Capitol Theatre staff who would joke with her that she was only
there to "case the joint."

Fortunately there were enough audiences to go around to all of the
Concord theaters. Eager to escape the ongoing recession, Concord audiences, like audiences all over the country, flocked to the movies to forget
the woes that seemed almost ready to smother the joy out of everyday
life. While Theresa may have yearned to see some of the stars she gazed
at upon the Capitol Theatre's screen at the Concord, she was grateful that
thousands of locals lined up to purchase a ticket from her every week.

While the majority of films booked at the Concord were from
Monogram and Republic and were usually westerns, serials and comedies,
periodically a film from England was booked with a surprising degree of
success. There was a small but dedicated group of Concord residents who
would turn up each time Jessie Matthews, Gracie Fields or Anna Neagle
were advertised as the stars of a film at the Concord.

Jessie Matthews was a major star in England and there was often talk of
Hollywood bringing her to this country to dance in a film with Fred Astaire.
It never happened, but her British musicals, often released by Gaumont
British, were popular for a day or two in Concord. One in particular, *Head
Over Heels in Love* which played in early 1937, did especially well.

Anna Neagle had the longest film career of the three ladies—nearly 30
years. For several years in the mid to late 40s, she was voted in Great Britain
as their top box-office drawing star. When the Concord Theatre announced
the January 1938 engagement of her film, *Victoria the Great*, they did so with
a seriousness befitting the story of Queen Victoria. The ad read:

> "There WAS a reason for a hold-over at the Radio City Music Hall and a
> hold-over at the Keith Memorial in Boston. By all means see "Victoria the
> Great" one of the greatest films in motion picture history."

More than 3,000 people heeded that advice and attended the movie easily rivalling the kind of attendance many Hollywood A-Pictures were drawing at the Capitol or Star.

Gracie Fields was beloved in England and known in other parts of the world for her comedic timing and her memorable voice, which was skillfully used for singing comic numbers but could also do full justice to a serious piece of music. The Concord Theatre played several of her movies including *We're Going to Be Rich* which opened in November of 1938. More than 30 years later, Theresa could still do a flawless imitation of Fields singing her hit song from that film, *Walter, Walter Lead Me to the Altar.* She would always reduce me to tears of laughter whenever she'd launch into the song.

Theresa was a big fan of singer-actress Jeanette MacDonald and would usually take a couple of hours off from work whenever a new MacDonald film arrived at the Capitol Theatre. Miss MacDonald was under contract to MGM for much of her career, and Theresa knew that the Concord Theatre stood little to no chance of ever playing one of her films, even in second-run.

In 1965 soon after Jeanette MacDonald's passing, Capitol Theatre Manager Frank K. Eldridge told me that MacDonald, with or without frequent co-star Nelson Eddy, had been a phenomenal box-office draw for the Capitol Theatre. In fact, he noted, "when we played *Maytime* back in 1937, we had the biggest crowd we'd ever had for a split-week—over 12,000 paid attendees which was about half the city's population at the time . . ."

Maytime did indeed play the Capitol, opening on April 11, 1937, for a five-day run, which was highly unusual at a time when most theaters in Concord played a film for either two, three or four days.

According to the film trade publication, *Film Daily*, in its Year Book for 1938, at the beginning of the year New Hampshire had 111 movie theaters with a total seating of 63,365. During 1938, 29 theaters closed in the state. At year's end, there were 82 movie theaters with a total of 49,153 seats. In noting the three theaters showing motion pictures in Concord, the Capitol had 1,423 seats, while the Star had 1,073 and the Concord had 500. The population of the State of New Hampshire was approximately 485,000 at the time.

Fortunately by late 1938, five years after the theater had opened, Mr.

Charbonneau, being busy with other responsibilities, would allow Theresa to occasionally book a title that was more to her liking. These films usually filled the less popular weekly slots. The theater was running three separate programs during the split week at this time. The Wednesday and Thursday slot was usually considered the lowest attended showings. At almost 25, Theresa considered this booking opportunity to be a major step forward.

In early November of 1938, while the Capitol Theatre was playing the latest MGM musical opus, *The Great Waltz* (The 1972 remake would play the Concord Theatre), the Concord opened a British film that appealed to a similar audience. *Moonlight Sonata* starred the world-famous pianist, Paderewski and ran 86 minutes. Theresa promoted the film extensively, not only with ads in the newspaper but by contacting the local piano teachers as well as several local schools. To her delight, the film brought in more than double what they paid for it. Even better, a great many new faces were spotted buying tickets. The following month she would try a similar tactic with the highly acclaimed French film, *The Mayerling* starring Charles Boyer and Danielle Darrieux. Shown in its original French with subtitles, the motion picture attracted a larger audience than similar Hollywood-made love stories were attracting. When the film was remade more than thirty years later, starring Omar Sharif, Catherine Deneuve, James Mason and Ava Gardner, the Concord would once again play the story.

Westerns with names like Ken Maynard, Johnny Mack Brown and Tex Ritter continued to be the bread and butter for the Concord Theatre. Once in a while one of the stars of the westerns would make a personal appearance at the Concord Theatre. This was a means of generating additional box office sales for its pictures but also provided great publicity for the theater. The audience that would attend was usually made up mostly of children who would hoot and holler for their favorite.

In 1983, Theresa would tell *Concord Monitor* columnist, Tom Keyser, about one of those appearances.

Tex Ritter, father of the late popular television actor, John Ritter, came to the Concord to perform and to talk to the audience about his latest western opus, scheduled to open at the Concord Theatre. All four performances were filled to capacity. The pay agreement with Ritter was a 50/50 split of all ticket sales.

After the performance Ritter came to Theresa for his share and she gave him the $ 300.00 that was owed him. He looked somewhat aghast until she explained to him that while they had filled all four shows, the tickets were mostly at children's prices and the average ticket price was about 25 cents. The total box office take therefore was $ 600.00 of which he was entitled to half. Ritter told her, "This is the lowest gross I ever picked up anywhere."

Throughout the 1930s and much of the 40s, the Concord Theatre did not have a marquee. Theresa Cantin purchased the marquee in the late 1940s and it became a downtown landmark. (Photo Courtesy of Theatre Historical Society of America.)

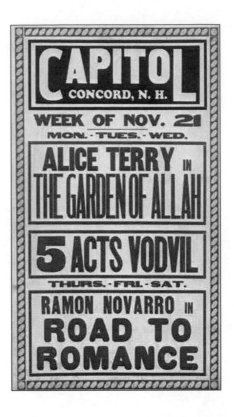

This placard for the Capitol Theatre was typical of the placards distributed by the Capitol, Star and Concord Theatre. For many decades, into the 1960's, hundreds of these placards were displayed throughout the Concord area in businesses including barber shops and grocery stores. (Imaged by Heritage Auctions, HA.com.)

Chapter Five

A GREAT MANY PEOPLE were relieved when the 1930s ended and the 1940s started. The 30s had been a difficult decade for many people, mostly due to the Great Depression. Despite growing fears about the situation in Europe, there was a cautious hope that America might not find itself involved in another war. The *Concord Monitor* reported, daily, about the worsening situation across the sea and a growing number of local residents began to feel that something needed to be done to help our friends abroad.

Locally, the Concord projectionists' union had named a new slate of officers for 1940. Bradley (Brad) Callahan was named the new president. Ernest (Ernie) Mayo was named as the business agent. Aldis Kirk was named financial officer while Gerald Hogle was named the treasurer. Assuming the position of recording secretary was Frank Gay. These gentlemen were among the local projectionists that kept the pictures on the screens of theaters in the Concord area. Others at the time included Paul King and Lewis Hill. Thirty years later, at the end of the 60s, Brad Callahan and Ernie Mayo were still active local projectionists. Callahan worked at the Capitol Theatre for many years and became manager in the mid 1960s when longtime manager Frank Eldridge retired.

During 1940, the Concord Theatre closed for a week at the end of June and in early July, to undergo a major inside painting as well as some general sprucing up. It also seemed appropriate in light of the planned stage presentation starring popular screen actor, Tex Ritter. Scheduled for one day only (July 23, 1940), it generated a great deal of excitement in the community. Ritter would be appearing with *His Musical Tornadoes* and the Concord Theatre ad noted that "Positively no children's tickets will be sold in the evening." That guaranteed sold-out afternoon performances, and the adults managed to fill the theater in the evening at slightly higher prices (35 cents plus 4 cent tax).

That same summer the Concord played a British film entitled, *21 Days Together* starring Laurence Olivier and Vivian Leigh. In their ads they incorrectly spelled Olivier's first name as Lawrence.

There was major movie news in Manchester in the summer. On June 30 the Mammoth Drive-In opened adjacent to Pine Island Amusement Park. It could hold 400 cars and a few curiosity seekers from Concord ventured south, returning with a mix of opinions and comments. It would be over a decade before drive-in movies arrived in the Concord area. In the meantime, the Rex Theatre opened in Manchester on Amherst Street. Today, the concept of stadium seating in a movie theater is somewhat common. It was not in 1940, and the Rex boasted that it was the only movie theater in New Hampshire with stadium seating. In one of their first ads in the *Concord Monitor*, it promoted its feature attraction in a rather direct way: "See Marihuana exposed in *Assassin of Youth*".

Locally during that summer, you could drop by the A & P on Park Street and buy lobster for twenty-nine cents a pound. You could also stop at Concord Buick over on Beacon Street and purchase a used car in good condition. For $845.00 you could get a 1940 Packard, and for only $ 45.00 you could leave owning a 1937 Ford half-ton pick-up. President Roosevelt toured the Portsmouth Naval Yard to check on the progress of five submarines that were in the process of being constructed.

The Capitol Theatre tried something new—The First Frigidaire-Spry Cooking School, which was held on Thursday, July 11 at 1 p.m. There was an opportunity to win a Frigidaire Electric Range and the school was presented by Concord Hardware and Plumbing Supply Co. A goodly number of ladies showed-up.

Lionel A. Irwin, who owned the Palace Theatre in neighboring Penacook, stepped down from running the 400-seat theater, noting he wanted to work on his golf game. His wife took over the theater and began making major changes. During the summer of 1941, she installed a Western Electric Mirrophonic Sound system as well as a new screen. In the process, Assistant Manager Arthur Dame left his position at the Palace for a similar position at the Concord Theatre, where he would remain for two years before returning to the Palace.

Right down the street from the Concord Theatre, Endicott Furniture was offering great deals on a new "Modern Bedroom Suite." You could own the complete set for $59. Endicott Furniture first opened in 1925 and today, nearly a hundred years later, it continues to be a vibrant and important part of downtown Concord.

While the Capitol was playing films such as *The Great Lie* with Bette Davis and *Ziegfeld Girl* with James Stewart, Judy Garland, Hedy Lamarr and Lana Turner, the Concord was screening one of Gene Autry's biggest hits, *Back in the Saddle Again*. The film was named for the 1939 hit recording of the same name, which became Autry's theme song. The song also earned him his second Gold Record. Theresa recalled that it was by far the most successful Autry western the Concord had ever played. Much of it was probably due to the songs performed in the film. In addition to the title song, Autry also sang, *I'm An Old Cowhand* and *You Are My Sunshine*. Like most Autry westerns made by Republic, *Back in the Saddle Again* was filmed in about two weeks and cost just under $90,000 to make.

Over at the Star, *Topper Returns* was skillfully combining chills and laughter, as the third film in the popular series, which later served as the basis for a popular 1950s television series. The walls of the Concord shook with laughter a few days later at the antics of Judy Canova in *Sis Hopkins* and the co-feature featuring the Three Stooges. Theresa said she was always amazed at the huge following that Canova had in Concord and how much people liked her "Hillbilly antics." "She could fill this place," Theresa remarked years later.

The Concord was filled to overflowing for a different and more sobering reason on May 20 and 21, 1941. The theater held a two-day benefit of five shows each day, under the auspices of the committee for British War Relief. The benefit was a great success, drawing not only the local audience that regularly attended the British films shown at the Concord, but a number of individuals drove up from Manchester and over from Portsmouth to attend. A very pleased Mr. Charbonneau presented a check, exceeding $1,000, to British War Relief.

At the end of August, the Concord presented what it called, *The Great Walt Disney Festival of Hits*. There were five attractions advertised, including a feature film (*Snow White and the Seven Dwarfs*) together with selected *Donald Duck, The Three Little Pigs, The Ugly Duckling* and *Ferdinand the Bull*. With the start of a new school year hovering over them, kids by the thousands lined up. It would be the last summer in which a certain sweet innocence held sway over the land. Life was about to change for everyone.

For the Cantin family, one of the highpoints of 1941 was the marriage of Maurice Cantin to Lucille Roy. Theresa was thrilled for her brother. Maurice and Lucille had a son, Michael, and were happily married until Maurice died in 1997.

In early December of 1941, Concord residents were doing what they'd done for many years before. They scurried around the many downtown stores seeking bargains or just the right gift to share with a loved one for the coming Christmas holiday. At Waite Auto Supply on Warren Street, you could purchase your new snow tires, and it was urging you to make the switch to Goodrich. On North Main Street at Hardy & McSwiney, for the affordable price of $4.50, you could get a union suit for the man in your life, to help keep him warm during the cold New Hampshire winter. At Concord's most elite store—Harry G. Emmons, the pneumatic tubes that sent the transactions from the counter to the upstairs credit office, were whooshing overtime.

The war in Europe was on everyone's mind, although there remained an optimism that it would never reach America's shores. Still, there was a sense of fear or impending doom in the back of everybody's mind, no matter how much you tried to get caught up in the spirit of the season.

On Sunday, December 7, 1941, Concord audiences had some good choices of what to see at the local movie house. The Capitol Theatre was opening the latest Thin Man mystery from MGM, starring William Powell and Myrna Loy. The fourth installment of the popular series was entitled, *Shadow of the Thin Man*. At the Star Theatre on Pleasant Street, you could enjoy Loretta Young and *The Men in Her Life*. The Concord Theatre promised you laughs galore with the latest Abbott and Costello comedy entitled, *Hold That Ghost*. In featured roles were the hugely popular singing trio, The Andrews Sisters, performing their massive hit, *Boogie Woogie Bugle Boy*. By the end of that Sunday, however, the world had changed, and the attack on Pearl Harbor would send America into another World War.

Theresa was selling tickets when a man rushed through the doors to tell her what he'd heard. She made a decision to stop the show in order to tell those in the audience the tragic news. Without consulting Mr. Charbonneau, who was not in the theater at the time, Theresa made the decision to refund the ticket price to all of those who wanted to leave to go home or to be with their loved ones. After refunding about 50 tickets the program continued for those who wished to remain. The Concord Theatre closed earlier than usual in the evening and the Cantin family gathered to discuss the impact the war could have on their personal and professional lives.

When discussing that day nearly thirty years later, Theresa could still recall every detail of what happened. It was fixed in her mind as it would be in the minds of millions of others. The fear and uncertainty as well as the realization that what she had read about that was occurring across the sea might soon be happening in her beloved USA. As happened in tens of thousands of other communities across the country, the people of Concord answered the call and enlisted in huge numbers. Once the shock of Pearl Harbor had begun to lessen, there was a patriotic fervor that enveloped the city.

For several days the movie business in Concord was virtually nil. While everyone regained their bearings and decided how to move forward, the movies were not foremost in their mind. For the first time in the Concord Theatre's eight-year history, nobody came to two showings on two separate evenings. However, within a week, business was booming as life resumed and people welcomed a few hours of escape from the harsh realities that were swirling around them and that they were reading about in the newspaper or hearing on the radio. The movies also gave anxious family members a little respite from the fears and worries they faced with respect to those who were leaving to serve their country.

Two and a half weeks later, on Christmas, all three theaters reported full houses. The Capitol was playing the musical, *Birth of the Blues* with Bing Crosby and Mary Martin, while the Star had Rosalind Russell in *Design for Scandal*. The Concord Theatre was appealing to the family trade with a film entitled, *Reg'lar Fellers* whose cast included Carl "Alfalfa" Switzer from the *Our Gang/Little Rascals* shorts. The co-feature was a Buck Jones western. Jones was popular with Concord audiences and would tragically die, less than a year later, in the Coconut Grove fire in Boston. Jones was only 50 and was one of 492 victims. Like the hero he played on the screen, it was reported that Jones was a hero in real life, too. Reportedly he had escaped the blaze but went back inside to save others and died while doing so.

Chapter Six

THE SOBERING TRUTH about World War II sunk in as 1942 began in Concord. The local New Year celebrations that had always been spirited, often resulting in a number of arrests for citizens who became a little too excited, were much more muted. It had begun to sink in that the conflict might not be one that was quickly and easily won once the United States had entered the war. There were increasing numbers who believed it might go on for many years.

The movie business rebounded in January of 1942 after the slump following the bombing of Pearl Harbor and America's entry into the war. It wasn't that people didn't want to confront the truth but rather that they sought an escape from the daily bombardment in the news. The newspapers, magazines and radio were filled with bulletins and stories about what was happening around the world and the patriotism of Concord's people was sometimes tested when the news was less than optimistic and when casualties and injuries became a part of the story.

In previous years, a conversation starter often revolved around the never predictable weather in New Hampshire. That opener now became a rarity as people greeted one another in a somewhat more somber way, asking about any family members or friends who might be serving their country. People pulled together in a way that they'd never done before, and going to the movies with hundreds of other members of the community became an important shared experience. Often the main features were preceded by news and newsreels of the growing conflict. It was not unusual to hear members of the audience sobbing softly as thoughts of loved ones who were away fighting, overwhelmed them.

Laughter has always been acclaimed as one of the best medicines and one has only to glance at the 1942 Quigley Poll of the top-ten box-office attractions that year to realize how true that sentiment might be. Abbott and Costello were ranked as the top drawing stars that year. They were even ranked ahead of Clark Gable who came in at number two. Abbott and Costello comedies might have been silly, but Concord audiences howled with delight and filled the Capitol, Star and Concord Theatres whenever the duo appeared. By 1943, they'd been pushed into the number three spot—still an enviable position—but the G.I.'s favorite pin-up gal, Betty Grable, would lead the list with comic Bob Hope coming in second. A Grable musical, displaying her famous gams and all tied up with Technicolor was a surefire draw. Grable's studio, 20th Century Fox, even insured her famous legs for $1 million dollars. Bob Hope, whether hitting the road with Bing Crosby and Dorothy Lamour, accompanied by her sarong, or by himself, was the perfect antidote for keeping morale high. Hope was often on the radio or touring and entertaining the soldiers and his name would forever remain linked with our brave troops.

Bing Crosby would be the top-ranked star on the poll in the years 1944-1947, inclusive with stars Hope, Grable, Greer Garson, Van Johnson and Ingrid Bergman occupying slots near the top. Musicals and lighthearted fare as well as compelling drama and films that had a message, were what the public especially liked. For the younger moviegoer, westerns continued to dominate as well as serials which managed to hold the interest of thousands of area boys for weeks at a time. Gene Autry and Roy Rogers held the top two spots on the list of top-ten western stars, and from 1943 until the end of the decade, Rogers would place in the number one spot. This was partially due to Autry leaving films for several years during the war, after he had enlisted. Autry wanted to serve the country he loved so much and in doing so proved to be an inspiration to many.

The average ticket price to go to the movies in 1942 was 27 cents. That would increase to an average of 29 cents in 1943. A mother and her two children could enjoy an evening out at the movies for just under a dollar.

The Hollywood version of the war was often designed to provide hope and, indeed, these films did. Mostly true and factual, they often had members of the military as special advisers on the production to ensure accuracy. Immediately after Pearl Harbor, dozens of films went into production in which the military figured prominently.

In January of 1942, Concord and the rest of the world were shaken by the passing of actress Carole Lombard, the wife of Clark Gable. She died in a plane crash while returning from a War Bond Rally. She was 33 and her death made front page headlines in newspapers everywhere.

On January 24, 1942, New Hampshire Governor Blood announced regulations and orders of conduct in case of an air raid or blackouts. Theaters were to remain open in these instances and not to disrupt or stop the motion picture being shown. In addition, theaters were to admit, free of charge, anyone seeking refuge in the case of an air raid or blackout.

All three downtown theaters were busy in January playing a variety of film fare that was greeted enthusiastically by a nervous public, uncertain as to what would happen next. The Capitol Theatre played the Alfred Hitchcock film, *Suspicion*, which would win lead actress Joan Fontaine an Oscar. The uproarious *The Man Who Came to Dinner* brought roars of laughter and Greta Garbo starred opposite Melvyn Douglas in the MGM comedy, *Two-Faced Woman*. Nobody knew at the time that this would be the final screen appearance for the 36-year-old Garbo. Despite dozens of offers over the next four decades, she never appeared in another motion picture.

Tarzan in the form of Johnny Weissmuller swung through the trees in MGM's fifth film in the series, *Tarzan's Secret Treasure* co-starring Maureen O' Sullivan as Jane. While *How Green Was My Valley* was creating a sensation at the Capitol, the Star played a romantic comedy called *Skylark* as well as the latest in the MGM Doctor Kildaire series.

The Concord Theatre had a full schedule that included repeats of such popular recent hits as *Sun Valley Serenade* which introduced the catchy *Chattanooga Choo Choo* and *A Yank in the R.A.F.* as well as a Deanna Durbin musical and "Weekend in Havana" with Alice Faye. Republic and Monogram kept the schedule filled with everything from John Wayne in *Lady for a Night* co-starring Joan Blondell to a couple of Gene Autry "oaters" as westerns were sometimes referred to.

The most popular film of the year and the eventual Academy Award winner as Best Picture, was MGM's *Mrs. Miniver*. Its story packed every kind of emotion and told inspiringly the story of a family in England and how they dealt with the war.

The year's top- ten money-making films in 1942 were:

Rank	Title	Studio
1.	*Mrs. Miniver*	MGM
2.	*Yankee Doodle Dandy*	Warner Bros.
3.	*Random Harvest*	MGM
4.	*Road to Morocco*	Paramount
5.	*Reap the Wild Wind*	Paramount
7.	*Somewhere I'll Find You*	MGM
8.	*Holiday Inn*	Paramount
9.	*Casablanca*	Warner Bros.
10.	*Wake Island*	Paramount

None of the titles in the top-ten played the Concord Theatre as a first-run. In fact all ten titles had their local opening at the Capitol Theatre.

Greer Garson became one of the most beloved stars, especially with Concord audiences, as the result of her performances in *Mrs Miniver* and *Random Harvest*. Even in the 1960s when she would appear in a film such as MGM's *The Singing Nun* or Disney's *The Happiest Millionaire,* a loyal following turned out in force. James Cagney won an Oscar for his portrayal of George M. Cohan in *Yankee Doodle Dandy* and its fervent patriotic and tuneful story brought comfort to millions. *Road to Morocco* was the third in a popular series of comedies with music that starred Bing Crosby, Bob Hope and Dorothy Lamour. The series, which began in 1940 would continue into the early 60s. Cecil B. DeMille brought lavish adventure and escapism to the screen in *Reap the Wild Wind*. *Holiday Inn* introduced *White Christmas* as sung by Bing Crosby who would forever be associated with the song. By Christmas of 1942, everyone in Concord was singing it too. *Somewhere I'll Find You* was Gable's last film until he returned from the war, and *Casablanca* became a classic while *Wake Island* was a hugely popular action, drama war propaganda film.

By the end of the year, fully a quarter of the films playing seemed to be variations on a military theme and the public could not seem to get enough of them. It seemed to reassure them of the strength of might of their country and there was often audible applause at the end of the picture.

Two of the best-received films to play the Concord Theatre in 1942 had military storylines. *Eagle Squadron* from Universal and starring Robert Stack was a huge success when it played in December. The picture's slogan in some of the ads read: "Men with Wings/Women of War." In 1942 it seemed as though the slump in business that would often occur between Thanksgiving and Christmas, didn't happen. Audiences clearly wanted to be entertained, in-between doing their shopping for family, friends and those serving their country. Another great success starred John Wayne in his first war film—*Flying Tigers*. It became the biggest money-making film for Republic Pictures, up to that time.

Gene Autry starred in a pair of popular films, among the last to be released until he would return from the service several years later. The Concord Theatre advertised its December play date of Monogram's *Down Texas Way* as "The last time to see Buck Jones." The film opened mere weeks after the popular cowboy star had perished in the Coconut Grove Fire in Boston. In the film Jones played a character named Buck Roberts and, in actuality, had completed three additional films in that series prior to heading to Boston. Those titles eventually made their way to Concord.

The Capitol Theatre had a great success with the film *Wake Island* as well as the first release of what would become a Disney classic—*Bambi*. Sonja Henie skated in *Iceland* and Fred Astaire and Rita Hayworth made beautiful music together (courtesy of Jerome Kern) in *You Were Never Lovelier*. What was announced as "RKO Vodvil" gave local audiences some interesting stage personalities in addition to a movie for both Thanksgiving and Christmas. At the Star were westerns, two-reel comedies, serials, second-run films after the Capitol and an occasional first-run film that had not played "The Cap" as it was referred to. Two of those—*Eyes in the Night* and MGM's *Seven Sweethearts* did very well.

There were certainly times during the war years in which it seemed as though all three theaters in town were playing a movie with a war or patriotic theme. Audiences, however, couldn't seem to get enough of them. During one week, for instance, the Concord was playing *True to the Army* while the Capitol was playing the inspiration British film, *In Which We Serve*. Over at the Star, Laurel and Hardy were doing their bit for the war effort in a comedy entitled, *Air Raid Wardens*. Even the Palace in Penacook was stirring patriotism with a showing of *Yankee Doodle Dandy*.

Other titles in the spring and summer of 1943 that helped local audiences channel their love of country included *Air Force*, *Prelude to War*, *Crash Dive* and *Desert Victory*. Even the beloved detective, Sherlock Holmes got into the action. *Sherlock Holmes in Washington* took the detective and Doctor Watson out of 1890s London and into Washington, D.C., in 1943. No one questioned how this had been facilitated.

In May of 1943, the Concord Theatre was turned over, for a day, to the Margaret Pillsbury General Hospital for its *May Merriment* fundraiser. The Star, in the meantime, had all its curtains fireproofed. Then Manager Lenwood Durepo also noted that with the exception of his projectionists, he had no staff that had been there over a year. It seemed everyone had run off to enlist.

The Capitol Theatre had itself entirely fireproofed and Concord Fire Chief William T. Happny attempted to "burn the place down" to prove the fireproofing had been effective. Longtime Capitol Theatre Manager Frank Eldridge's son, also named Frank, enlisted in the United States Navy. J. Marcel Charbonneau, son of the co-owner of the Concord Theatre, also enlisted in the Army.

The Concord Theatre suffered a number of staff changes in quick succession in 1943. Three Assistant Cashiers left in a matter of several weeks troubling Theresa who was the day-to-day manager of the theater. All three, Flora, Millie and Adelaide, told her they loved working for her but didn't appreciate Mr. Charbonneau interfering with their duties on a regular basis and usurping what Theresa had asked them to do.

Theresa tried to be diplomatic about it, telling them that the Charbonneaus were in the process of moving from North Spring Street to North Main and that Mr. Charbonneau was probably stressed because of the move. Arthur K. Dame, who had been assistant manager at the Palace Theatre in Penacook, working for Lionel A. Irwin, had come to the Concord in the same position. While working at the Palace, Arthur had met Vaulien P. Shaw, the proprietress of a local beauty salon. They were married in 1939. Arthur and Theresa had quickly become friends and great co-workers when he began working at the Concord Theatre for a slightly higher wage. However, when he also tendered his resignation and returned to the Palace, citing the same reasons as the cashiers, Theresa knew that the matter would need to be addressed with her father. Fortunately she and Arthur remained good friends for the rest of her life. When he and his wife Vaulien took over the Scenic Theatre in Pittsfield some years later, they continued the friendship.

On September 27, 1943, all three downtown Concord Theaters as well as the Palace in Penacook, joined forces in a united effort for the war. The four theaters offered free admission to holders of war bond purchase certificates. The effort proved to be very successful.

The managers of all four theaters had an amiable relationship. Theresa was closest with Mr. Eldridge and his wife, Jennie. Mrs. Eldridge was a frequent customer at the Concord Theatre and she and Theresa would occasionally have lunch together in downtown Concord.

In 1943 the New Hampshire Legislature passed a law permitting theaters to open on Sunday at 1 p.m. instead of 6 p.m. This was subject to local approval. In the November election later that year, voters approved Sunday afternoon movies in the communities of Concord, Manchester and Somersworth.

Chapter Seven

ON MAY 8, 1945, THE *CONCORD MONITOR* headline screamed, "V-E Day Proclaimed by Truman," and while there was cautious optimism everywhere about the possibility of the war ending soon, after three and a half years, nobody was taking anything for granted. The *Monitor*, however, also ran dozens of ads from local merchants, saluting our troops. Concord's beloved Italian restaurant, Angelo's headlined its ad, "Well Done, Boys!!" Amidst the enthusiasm was also a sense of regret that Franklin Delano Roosevelt, who had died less than a month before, was not alive to share in this step toward peace.

The Concord Theatre was showing a Loretta Young and Alan Ladd film entitled, *And Now Tomorrow* while advertising a return engagement of the suspense thriller, *Gaslight*. The Capitol had *Bring on the Girls* but most audiences were highly anticipating the theater's next attraction—MGM's *National Velvet*. *Velvet* would make Elizabeth Taylor a star. Meanwhile at the Star, *Betrayal from the East*, a story about a Japanese spy ring operating in the United States, was receiving passing notice. Theresa recalled business being way off that evening as celebrations popped up all around town.

By V-J Day on Sept. 2, 1945, there was a genuine sense that there would be peace in the world and that never again would there be such a war. Theresa remembered that day being quiet at the movies but that the next day, there seemed to be a decided frenzy of people wanting to be out and about, running into friends and seeing movies with a crowd. The Concord was showing a repeat engagement of a very popular 1944 MGM film, *Mrs. Parkington* starring Greer Garson and Walter Pidgeon. The Capitol had Bette Davis in *The Corn is Green* and was widely promoting its next attraction, *Wilson*, the story of President Woodrow Wilson. At the Star there were *Radio Stars on Parade* and Sonja Henie, still skating up a storm and this time in *It's a Pleasure.*

It has been said innumerable times that 1939 is considered to be Hollywood's greatest year. The sheer volume of films that went on to become classics, including *Gone With the Wind,* might support such a claim. However, despite the many remarkable film titles released in that year, it was not the year in which the most people headed off to see a movie. That title would easily belong to 1946. Research has shown that more than 80 million people, which represented 57 percent of the population, went to a movie every week. It was not necessarily that better films were being made, although there was certainly not a shortage of good films for every taste. It had more to do with the tremendous sense of relief that everyone felt over the conclusion of the war. It probably also had to do with a desire to return to normalcy and getting together with family or friends to take in a movie was certainly normal for many people.

When meeting with the manager of the Capitol Theatre, Frank Eldridge, in the 1950s, after the Star Theatre had closed, Theresa and Mr. Eldridge compared notes about the year 1946. Mr. Eldridge had figures from the Star Theatre and when the three theaters attendance for 1946 was added together, they were stunned to realize that just under one million tickets had been sold to those attending the movies in Concord. At an average price of 34 cents per ticket, the Capitol had sold more than 435,000 tickets while the Star had sold nearly 300,000. The Concord was third with 230,000 tickets. The Concord's figure was especially gratifying since, with 499 seats, they had far less than the more than 1,000 at the Star and the approximately 1,400 at the Capitol. For the Concord, that represented over 4,400 tickets sold per week for an average of 25 film showings weekly.

Certainly, in 1946 the Concord Theatre seemed to play a good cross-section of attractions, appealing to every kind of person residing in Concord. During the war years, Theresa had increased her responsibilities at the theater. She had taken a more active role in selecting what was shown. She managed the house, did the bookkeeping and supervised the ushers and staff. From all reports the ushers loved working with her and Theresa maintained friendships with many of them. Johnny Nyhan had worked for the Star Theatre until 1939 when he began working as an usher at the

Concord Theatre. He worked at the theater for several years and loved the work. In the 50s, 60s, 70s and 80s, he continued to drop by to say hello or to catch a movie, often with his daughter Susan.

While MGM still seemed reluctant to allow the Concord Theatre to play first-run releases, most of the second-run films they allowed to be shown there were A pictures and still found a good-sized audience wishing to stop in to sample the offerings. *Son of Lassie* and *The Thin Man Goes Home* played the Concord at a time when the Capitol was playing a grown-up Shirley Temple in *Kiss and Tell* or other smash hits like *Rhapsody in Blue*, *Leave Her To Heaven*, *The Harvey Girls* and *Love Letters*.

Monogram and Republic continued to provide a majority of titles for first-run attractions but there were also an increased number of British titles that continued to appeal to a limited but growing local audience. In 1946 Monogram also founded Allied Artists which would distribute some of its better quality productions. They recognized that just seeing the name Monogram was a put-off for some potential audience members. In 1946 the average picture produced by one of the major studios averaged about $800,000 in costs. A typical film shot on the Monogram lot averaged about $90,000. The first film made under the Allied Artists aegis cost just over $1 million. Future releases under that banner were sometimes shot in color and always had better production values.

Playing a Republic film could sometimes come with a steep price— Vera Hruba Ralston. She was a former ice skater who came to this country and signed a contract with Republic. The head of Republic, Herbert Yates, was infatuated with Ralston, who was about 40 years younger than he was. Reportedly she became his mistress and eventually his wife after he left his wife and children for her. He also cast her in leading roles in films for which she was not suited causing actors like John Wayne to scream, "NO MORE!!" after being forced to work with her on more than one occasion. Yates was sued by the shareholders of Republic for using studio assets to promote his wife. She was also named "The Worst Actress of All Time" in a book entitled, *The Golden Turkey Awards*.

Movies were certainly not the only form of entertainment in the Capital City. The Phenix Hall, which had once sporadically shown motion pictures, was a popular spot in the evening, especially on weekends. For 50 cents plus

10 cents tax, you could enjoy the music of Don Drouin and his Orchestra while dancing. On Washington's Birthday, for 83 cents plus 17 cents in tax, you could dance the evening away while benefiting the American Legion— Post 21. Tickets were available at Angelo's or Edward Fine, a popular cloth- ier. There was also boxing at the Phenix Hall, but that cost $1.50 plus a 30 cent tax.

Theresa's sister Rena (sometimes spelled Rina) got married in 1946 to Joseph Leo Constant. An amiable and easygoing man, Leo, as he was more commonly known around the theater, would often help out at the the- ater when there was something needing to be fixed or repaired. He spent many years working for Concord Group Insurance. Rena and Leo had two sons—Peter, born in 1951, and Paul, born in 1960.

By early in 1947, the boom and sense of goodwill that had permeated much of 1946, had begun to calm. Life was returning to normal and people were once again facing day to day challenges. The movies continued to promote hours of great entertainment but Theresa and the Cantin family began to realize that things could not just be allowed to continue as they had during the war years.

During the first months of 1947, the Concord found itself playing titles like, *Secrets of a Sorority Girl, The Searching Wind, Devil Bat's Daughter, Beauty and the Bandit* and *Plainsman and the Lady* starring the aforemen- tioned Vera Hruba Ralston. While it was true that they occasionally played a second-run film from one of the major studios that did very well (*Ziegfeld Follies* for instance), Theresa would find herself embarrassed at church when someone would ask what was showing that week.

Roy Rogers and Dale Evans in a first-run like *Roll On Texas Moon* or the Bowery Boys in *Spook Busters* could still pack the matinees and early eve- ning show, but the Capitol and Star always seemed to grab anything with a semblance of quality. *Blue Skies* and *The Razor's Edge* filled the Capitol, including the balcony, while *The Big Sleep, A Stolen Life* with Bette Davis and Rita Hayworth's *Gilda* kept the staff at the Star busy.

Theresa felt the theater, while doing very well, was often looked down upon because it played mostly films from Monogram and Republic and when it did play a film from one of the "majors," it was usually second-run. While Theresa loved and appreciated the loyalty and continued support of the crowds that came to see the serials, westerns and comedies, she wanted to bring in a new audience while not neglecting those who always showed-up week after week.

Mr. Charbonneau no longer took a day to day active role in the theater. Theresa sold the tickets, did the bookkeeping, managed the daily operations including the staff and projectionists, and booked most of the films from the limited selections that were available to the Concord. She remained unfailingly polite and respectful to Mr. Charbonneau, and discussed any major decisions that she wanted to make with him. She also reported, daily, the income from ticket sales. To the end of her life, Theresa always referred to him as "Mr. Charbonneau".

An agreement was finally made in the spring of 1947 and a price set for the Cantin family to purchase Mr. Charbonneau's share of the enterprise. The June 7, 1947, issue of *Boxoffice* noted:

"J.E. Charbonneu, owner and operator of the Concord, Concord, N.H., for many years, has disposed of the property to Theresa Cantin, who has been booking and managing the house for some time. Charbonneau will retire from active business."

Theresa immediately began calling representatives for the various film distribution companies to inform them of the changes that had taken place. Several were barely respectful when she informed them that the Concord was interested in showing some of their pictures and would continue to be a first-run house. The salesman from MGM asked her, "Do you realize you're a woman trying to do a man's job?" Theresa informed him that she'd been in the business for almost 14 years and understood what people liked to see and wanted to see. "I can do this job," she told him and anyone else who seemed incredulous. She also assured both Republic and Monogram that the Concord would continue to play their pictures in addition to expanding the options to include first-runs from the majors.

It took a few months before someone would give her a chance but RKO finally gave in to her insistence and pleas that the Concord Theatre could bring in big numbers on a quality film.

After taking over the theater from the family's partner, Theresa booked this Oscar-winning film, destined to become a classic. For the theater, it changed its future course.

Chapter Eight

THE BEST YEARS OF OUR LIVES opened at the Concord Theatre on Wednesday, September 28, 1947. The theater touted the fact that it was "Under New Management" and ads noted that the film was the "First 3 hour film since *Gone With the Wind*" Although it had taken nearly a year since the film first opened in November of 1946 for it to reach Concord, it seemed to be well worth the wait. The newly installed marquee made note of the Best Picture Oscar win by the film, and the lights and neon lit up that piece of Main Street reinforcing that changes had been made at the Concord Theatre.

Although it had been two years since World War II had ended, the war had affected Concord deeply and those who lined up to see this film could identify with the story, its elements and with many of the characters. Hundreds of those who enlisted from Concord and the surrounding towns had either died in the war or returned home injured. Few were able to simply step back into the life they had known. Much had happened during the years they were off fighting, and *The Best Years* brilliantly captured the trauma, pain, and adjustments everyone had to make.

There were three screenings a day with the feature being played at 2:06, 5:12 and 8:17. The theater's regular admission prices were adjusted for this one "event movie." Adult tickets for matinee were 74 cents including tax, in the evening the adult cost was $ 1.20 including tax. The admission price for children was 50 cents at all performances. Every performance during the four day run was sold-out, with nearly 6,000 people purchasing tickets.

When customers began to arrive, it was apparent to Theresa who had been there before and who had not. In a twist, first-timers strolled in and headed up the long lobby to the upper box office. Customers who had been coming to the theater for years were initially confused by the closed lower box office that they'd been used to stopping at. When they eventually arrived at the upper box office and spotted Theresa, their comment was usually a variation of, "What happened?"

To those she knew well enough, Theresa would tell the story about having become lodged in the lower box office one evening. After telling her father about the problem, Wenceslaus wasted no time in installing the counter in the upper lobby that would become the selling point for tickets for the next 47 years. Theresa loved having the box office closer to the auditorium area since it enabled her to watch and listen to the films, making sure the sound was adequate and the picture was sharp and clear.

For Theresa Cantin and her family, playing *The Best Years of Our Lives* was about much more than the minimal profit they saw after paying the costs associated with the film including extensive advertising expenses. It was the reality that the Concord Theatre had played one of the most acclaimed films in motion picture history up to that time. It was also about the fact that hundreds of individuals who had never set a foot inside of the Concord Theatre during its nearly 14 years of being in business, showed up and seemed pleasantly surprised at what they discovered. The theater had regularly sold out westerns with Gene Autry and Roy Rogers as well as films featuring the Bowery Boys or the Three Stooges. The difference with this film release was that the Concord Theatre would not now be as easily dismissed as a theater that played junk or inferior pictures.

Theresa and her family realized after the closing of *The Best Years of Our Lives* that they would not suddenly begin getting all of the films they wanted to play from the so-called "Majors" like MGM, Warners, Fox and Paramount. She knew that the theater would continue to largely play the releases from Monogram and Republic as well as some British releases. What mattered the most, however, was the ability they would now have in being able to negotiate for these quality titles. They would now be able to show the film companies the nearly $6,000 gross they had taken in during a four-day period for an Oscar winning hit.

When Theresa would attempt to book Grade-A films, she was inevitably asked, "What have you played recently that would qualify as a hit from one of the top five?" Most of the salesmen looked down their noses at Monogram and Republic and so it seemed that no matter how well she might have done with their product, it didn't weigh heavily in her favor when trying to make a deal.

In the weeks following *Best Years*, the Concord returned to more typical fare—a heavy dosage of Monogram and Republic releases including, in November of 1947, a Monogram remake of *The Sweetheart of Sigma Chi*, the first film to play the Concord in 1933. This new version didn't attract very many but a second-run of Paramount's Bob Hope-Dorothy Lamour comedy, *My Favorite Brunette*, did better than many first-run films. It did well enough that MGM, still the most prestigious of all studios, allowed the Concord to play their major re-release of the 1938 film, *The Great Waltz*.

On December 14, 1947, the Concord Theatre once again scored a major coup when Warner Brothers gave them a gift—the first area showing of *Life with Father*, a major color hit based on the long-running play and a popular book. Starring William Powell, Irene Dunne and Elizabeth Taylor among others, it was booked for four days and sold-out every performance. Admission prices were increased to 90 cents for adults at matiness and $1.25 in the evening with children admission for all shows being 50 cents. It didn't deter anyone from enjoying one of the most popular films of 1947.

Gene Autry and his horse Champion were back on the screen for the Concord's Christmas picture, *Saddle Pals*, and business was typically good for Autry. The Concord didn't do anything special for New Year's Eve as some theaters did. The Capitol gave you an evening of "VODVIL" and the latest MGM film, *Green Dolphin Street*, for the price of one dollar. You also had the choice of going to the City Auditorium and seeing just vaudeville for half a buck.

The huge success of both *Best Years* and *Life With Father* made it easier in 1948 to obtain second-run showings of films from the major studios to play in-between the usual westerns and Bowery Boys comedies.

During the early months of 1948, the Capitol Theatre played a great many films that were destined to become among the top-ten moneymakers of 1948. *Green Dolphin Street, My Wild Irish Rose, Good News, Captain from Castile, Daisy Kenyon, The Road to Rio* and *The Treasure of the Sierra Madre*, all kept the ticket sellers busy at the Capitol. The Star also continued to have a healthy helping of hits or successful second-runs with films that had done well at the Capitol. The Concord also did well but with a series of smaller films, most forgotten with the passage of time. In the meantime, Theresa continued to pursue the next big one.

The theater's original box-office advised attendees to purchase their tickets at the upper box office which Theresa's father had installed in the late 1940s. (Photo courtesy of Bill Gordon, photographer.)

A national reissue of the 1942 Oscar-nominated *The Jungle Book* was especially popular with a younger crowd at the Concord. *The Wicked Lady* from Arthur Rank Productions did nicely and there was even an MGM title in those early months of the year—*The Secret Heart*, but it had already played the Capitol a year or so earlier. *Bowery Buckaroos* with the Bowery Boys delivered what it had to in order to please their rabid Concord fans and Wild Bill Elliott scored a western bullseye with *The Fabulous Texan*. There were also several Gene Autry and Roy Rogers titles and their enormous fanbase in Concord and surrounding towns, packed the house.

In the 1970s while talking about those days in the late 40s, Theresa said that she often wondered whether those western films that poured out of Republic and Monogram with such regularity were actually just the same film with a different title. "The sets all looked the same and so did the clothes and they always had the same supporting characters. If they weren't the same film, then they must have had an assembly line set up to churn them out with a few minor changes."

In late February of 1948, the theater announced a special one day only showing of Laurence Olivier's *Henry V* on March 3. The United Artists release would screen only twice—at 2:30 and at 8:30. In an unusual move, the Concord Theatre made tickets available in advance either by mail or at the box office. Matinee prices were 90 cents to $1.20 depending on seat location. In the evening the seat prices ranged from $1.20 to $1.80. Every seat for the two performances was filled.

Soon after, Theresa visited a bank and secured financing for the purpose of putting a concession stand into the theater. The stand would be in the upper lobby, near the upper box office and across from the Ladies Room. A new popcorn machine was purchased with a modern kettle. In the concession stand was a glass case inside of which were displayed about six different types of candy that were for sale. Fresh popcorn was available for five cents in a bag. Theresa immediately began a habit that would remain for the life of the theater. She would begin popping the corn a few minutes prior to opening the doors to the theater in the evening. In that way, when customers walked in, the aroma of fresh-popped corn would greet them. When speaking to me about twenty years later, she estimated that no less than half of the people attending a movie would purchase a popcorn.

The concession stand was designed with a heavy sliding door that could be closed when the concession stand was not open. Decorated with a lovely mirror on the outside of the sliding door, it blended with the lobby area giving the appearance that it was the wall. Throughout the years customers would often wander in the lobby area trying to find the concession stand until being told it was closed with a nod toward the closed door.

Theresa closed the theater on Good Friday and would also begin a policy, that year, of closing on Christmas Eve. The Saturday before Easter, while the Star Theatre was advertising, "Our Balcony has been reseated," the Concord Theatre ran a notice at the bottom of its advertisement in the newspaper.

NOTICE

STARTING EASTER SUNDAY

Because this theater enters a new policy of playing nothing but the finest in first run product, we are forced to increase our admission from 35 cents to 40 cents. This applies only on the first part of the week. Weekend admission will remain at 35 cents. All matinees 26 cents. No changes for Juniors and Children.

One of the first films to play under the hoped-for first run policy was an abysmal failure on all levels. *Song of My Heart* from Symphony Films and promising "forbidden romance" and "the thrill of Soul-stirring music" to the music of Tchaikovsky, played to virtually empty houses, Theresa recalled many years later. She laughed as she remarked, "The film was so badly made that it made those things we played from Monogram, Republic and Eagle Lion look like masterpieces. . . ."

The Concord would continue to navigate the waters between select first-run pictures and some repeats when necessary. RKO Pictures which was the distribution arm for films made by Walt Disney, even let her play a pair of animated Disney films—*Fun and Fancy Free* in April of 1948 and as part of a major reissue, *Bambi* in June of 1948. In the 1950s and 60s when Disney films, including live action, were breaking records, the Concord Theatre was usually ignored in favor of the Capitol. RKO was no longer distributing Disney films by that time and it didn't seem to matter that the Concord had brought in impressive grosses on Disney films in the past. It would not be until the 1980s that Theresa again got the opportunity to have the Disney name featured on her marquee.

A return engagement of *The Best Years of Our Lives* in September of 1948, and this time at regular prices, attracted almost as many filmgoers as it had the first time around, a year earlier. Allied Artists also gave her a first-run engagement of *The Babe Ruth Story* with William Bendix and its success only reinforced how much Concord loved and continues to love baseball.

On Nov. 21 the 1948 Olympic Games were shown in a special color documentary. Long before the Olympics became a staple on television, more than 4,500 people flocked to the Concord Theatre to see what they'd not been able to witness.

The second-run films the Concord played were a mixed bag leaning toward slightly better than average business. At least most of them were from the major studios including MGM, 20th Century Fox and a Deanna Durbin musical from Universal. As the 40s wound down, it seemed that the Concord Theatre was getting more of the quality second-runs that would once have automatically gone to the Star Theatre, a fact that did not go unnoticed by John J. Ford of the Maine-New Hampshire Theatres Company in Boston.

The Capitol Theatre continued to play most of the top-flight films while the Star sometimes repeated one of the Capitol's better titles and had some first-runs. A decade earlier the popular Tarzan films were being made by MGM as "A Pictures" and always played the Capitol. Once Tarzan moved over to RKO, however, the first-run was usually at the Star.

In 1949, the configuration for the Concord Theatre's split week was usually Sunday—Tuesday, Wednesday and Thursday and Friday and Saturday. Since each slot was filled by a double feature, that meant that on average, six movies each week were being displayed at the movie house. Monogram and Republic were happy to fill the bill and fortunately provided a plethora of titles of varying degrees of quality.

Eagle-Lion which was under the aegis of J. Arthur Rank was originally created in 1946 for the purpose of distributing British films in the United States. When they realized that would not sufficiently keep them going, they began distributing a number of "B Pictures" from some of the Hollywood majors. These titles usually cost under $500,000 to make. A January 1949 first-run film from Eagles Lion—*Million Dollar Weekend*—did well enough for the Concord but not anywhere near what prior first-run titles had done. In fact it didn't even measure up to a typical Bowery Boys crowd.

A Republic title in March, however, did great business. *The Wake of the Red Witch* starring John Wayne, turned out to be the theater's top moneymaking film in the first quarter of 1949. Wayne was always and would continue to be a big draw at the Concord, but some titles, and this was one of them, would reach the next level of popularity. A second-run of the Bob Hope-Jane Russell western comedy, *The Paleface,* did better than it had during its first local engagement. Theresa attributed that to the fact that everyone in town seemed to be humming the film's Oscar-winning song, *Buttons and Bows*.

The biggest flop of 1949 was a film called *The Lawton Story*, which was distributed by Hygienic Productions and Modern Film Distributors. Theresa told me that less than 100 people showed-up to see it during the short run and that the quality of the production was the worst she ever saw in her life. *Mourning Becomes Electra* was another picture that nobody cared to see.

During the summer of 1949, the Sky-Ray Outdoor Theater, as it advertised itself as being, attracted a lot of Concord curiosity seekers. With admission only 50 cents and children under 12 free, the Hooksett theater had an eight-month season that did well. Several years before Concord saw the Concord Drive-In become a local staple, two smaller drive-ins popped up in the general area. One was simply called Drive-In Theater and was located on Route 103 in Warner. The other was called Arnold's Drive-In Theatre and was located on Fowler Street in Penacook. Neither stayed around for very long. I have yet to find anyone who remembers them, although they both ran ads in the *Concord Monitor* touting their films at the time.

Whenever Theresa Cantin would reflect warmly on the changes that took place at the Concord Theatre in the wake of the Cantin family taking over in 1947, a title that would always be included would be *The Red Shoes*. In rare interviews in the 70s, 80s and 90s, *The Red Shoes* warranted special mention in the same breath as *The Best Years of Our Lives, Life with Father* and *The Tales of Hoffmann*.

The Red Shoes, which played at the Bijou Theatre in New York City for 110 weeks set a new standard for ballet and its acceptance as a film form by audiences. The movie, which opened in limited release in the fall of 1948, was nominated for an Academy Award as Best Picture and even those who didn't care for ballet beyond *The Nutcracker* found themselves dazzled by the brilliance of the filmmaking and charmed by the story.

With a great deal of fanfare, the Concord Theatre announced in early September of 1949 that *The Red Shoes* was to play for two days only (September 21 and 22) with a matinee and one evening performance scheduled for each day. All seats were to be reserved and tickets were available in advance at either the box office or by mail. There was a price increase due to the cost to the Concord Theatre to play the film exclusively within a certain territory.

Matinee prices ranged from 90 cents to $1.50, depending on the location of the seat. For evening performances, the price range was $1.20—2.40. Three days prior to the opening, every seat (1,996) had been sold.

The Red Shoes became an event film that everyone wanted to see. Theresa received dozens of telephone calls from those unable to purchase a ticket, offering to pay double or triple if she could somehow manage to secure them a ticket.

Nothing for the remainder of the year could hope to come close to generating the excitement that *The Red Shoes* had. Nevertheless, in addition to the Monogram and Republic titles that came and went, a couple of British films found a considerable audience.

Saraband (Saraband for Dead Lovers was the British title but sounded too depressing for American audiences) was a Stewart Granger historical film that did very nicely. The still popular Anna Neagle brought in a lot of area customers for *Spring in Park Lane*, reportedly the biggest moneymaking film released in England in 1948 and seen by some 20 million in that country alone. In her ad for *W. Somerset Maugham's Quartet* which opened on October 30, 1949, Theresa noted: "The Concord people are very fortunate to be able to attend the picture *Quartet,* for it will be shown at regular admission." Although J. Arthur Rank touted it as taking its place beside *The Red Shoes* and *Hamlet* as the third in a trio of great motion pictures, it didn't live up to expectations. In fact, the film that preceded it, *Far Frontier* with Roy Rogers, drew a larger crowd.

The year ended with a very popular first-run Disney animated film entitled, *The Adventures of Ichabod and Mr. Toad*, released by RKO. It told two stories—*The Wind in the Willows* and *The Legend of Sleepy Hollow*. With school vacation, almost every performance was filled.

As Theresa and her family said goodbye to the 1940s, she was content that during her first two years of "running the show," a great deal of progress had been made at the Concord Theatre.

The arrival of the Concord Drive-In Theatre in the 1950s radically changed the movie habits of local residents. A second drive-in, the Sky-Hi in neighboring Boscawen, was often referred to as "the passion pit."

Chapter Nine

THE WORLD, AS WELL AS THE MOVIES in Concord and elsewhere, began to change during the 1950s. The habit of regularly going out to a movie was no longer the choice of millions of Americans. The industry itself was undergoing reluctant changes, some of it predicated by legal issues that the business itself had created and was continuing to face and some of it by a new competition.

Theresa Cantin was enjoying her role in helping to shape and mold her theater and making decisions as to what her paying customers had the opportunity to see. While she was still limited in bringing all of the pictures she would have preferred to book, she could accept the necessity of playing some Monogram and Republic Pictures as long as she could also play titles from the major studios. Some of those titles she played were second-run after the Capitol or Star, but there were some that were also first-run in the Concord market.

When the telephone rang one day at the theater, Theresa answered as she always did, "Hello, this is the Concord Theatre," certain that it was someone asking what was playing or what time showtimes were. Theresa was always grateful for her powers of concentration and her ability to return to what she was doing after taking one of dozens of daily phone calls. This one was different.

A man on the telephone identified himself as "Mr. John J. Ford," from Maine-New Hampshire Theaters Company. Although they'd never met, Theresa was well aware as to who Mr. Ford was. While the theater chain was owned by Joseph P. Kennedy, Mr. Ford handled the day to day operations and had been Mr. Kennedy's friend since they roomed together in college. Mr. Ford was not prone to being as charming as Mr. Kennedy was known to be, if it suited him.

Mr. Ford informed Theresa that he and Mr. Kennedy had made an unplanned visit to Concord to check on the Capitol and Star and that Mr. Kennedy would like to see Theresa's theater. Without waiting for a response, Mr. Ford said they'd be out front in about ten minutes.

Theresa, when recalling this visit years later, remembered that her initial impression of Mr. Kennedy was that he was smaller than she'd expected. She'd been thinking of him as a bigger than life figure and he wasn't. Mr. Ford barely glanced at Theresa and didn't shake her hand when she put it out to him. As she walked them up the long lobby, she noticed Mr. Kennedy looking everything over as though "appraising it." She asked if they'd like to go upstairs to her office and Mr. Kennedy said they didn't have very long and needed to head back to Boston.

She walked them through the upper lobby and proudly pointed out her new concession area before taking them inside the auditorium. Kennedy scrutinized the theater and said, "It's not much."

When they returned to the upper lobby, Theresa offered to get Mr. Kennedy and Mr. Ford a seat but they declined instead suggesting she sit in her seat at the box-office counter. Mr. Kennedy pulled himself up and stood in front of her, appearing taller than her as he launched into his clearly rehearsed (Theresa's words) spiel.

"Miss Cantin, this is a tough business. Running a first-run movie theater takes a great deal of stamina, something most women lack."

He paced a little in the lobby as though collecting his thoughts before returning to her and resuming his talk but with what Theresa felt was a harsher tone.

"You women are fine selling tickets, sitting there and greeting the patrons. You're also fine selling your popcorn. In fact some of you are honest enough that you can probably keep the books, too. However, booking films, knowing what works, getting your hands dirty, now that's a man's job."

Theresa tried to interrupt him to explain a little bit about the kinds of movies she felt would work in her theater but he continued without catching a breath, it seemed to her.

"The Capitol and the Star are doing fine with the product that we get. I have no issue with your little house playing some of the second-runs after my houses have played them. There's usually still some business to be had, according to Ford here, so you'd have a little something for yourself and you'd get some good terms for playing second-run."

Theresa told me she finally stood up and used her strong voice to respond. "Mr. Kennedy, Mr. Ford, this is a family business and it reflects our name in this community. We don't mind playing a few second-run films after another house. However, we want our name to represent something of value and quality and that means playing as many first-run films as we can."

Theresa said that both Kennedy and Ford looked annoyed and angry. She felt they had expected her to cave in and agree with what they were saying. She didn't agree, however, and was not about to step quietly aside.

After a few more awkward moments, Joseph Kennedy put his hat on and indicated to Mr. Ford that they were finished. As Theresa walked them to the front door of the theater, Kennedy turned to her and said, "Rest assured, Miss Cantin, it's only a matter of time before we close you." Neither gentleman said goodbye as they walked out the door and got into the waiting car and drove away.

In discussing this years later, Theresa still had the determination in her voice that she had clearly displayed that day and it was obvious to me that she'd not even been intimidated in the least by her encounter.

The U.S. government brought an anti-trust case that accused the eight largest film companies of monopolizing film distribution and exhibition due to their owning first-run theaters. They were also accused of "collusive practices." Five of those studios owned approximately 65 percent of the first-run theaters in the United States. In a great many instances, they would offer one another favorable terms when handling distribution and exhibition, also favoring well-connected theaters who could rely on a steady stream of good films. This left many independent exhibitors, like the Concord Theatre, with a difficult time in getting a fair share of releases.

By no longer being able to engage in this practice, the studios lost a great deal of their revenue, forcing them to cut back their film production schedules and thus their releases. MGM had at one time released nearly 50 films per year and in the 1950s it was often only half of that. This also contributed toward the decline of the "Studio System" whereby studios had many stars under contract and provided regular films for them to appear in.

Even more deadly in reducing the regular attendance at movie theaters everywhere, was the growing importance of television. It is estimated that in 1950 there were almost 4 million households with television sets in the United States. Within five years, that number swelled to over 30 million households. The number continued to jump throughout the 1950s and beyond.

Weekly movie attendance that had peaked in 1946, right after the war had ended, had declined some 50 percent by 1956. The combination of less product due to the anti-trust case, the rise in television sales and the growing popularity of the drive-in movie resulted in hundreds and hundreds of indoor theaters closing their doors in the 1950s.

The drive-in was a new toy for millions of Americans who liked the notion of not having to get dressed-up to go to the movies and then search for a parking spot. With this new form of entertainment, they could load the family into the car, bring along their own snacks if they chose, and watch the double feature without the necessity of leaving their vehicle. In 1948 there were less than one thousand drive-in theaters in the country. By 1958 that number was more than 5,000.

The Concord Drive-In Theatre arrived in time for the summer of 1951. It touted it was located at the "First right over River Bridge." It was located on Black Hill Road, right off Manchester Street. Local residents packed the drive-in and on Sunday morning at church, it was a big topic for discussion. Nearby Hooksett already had the Sky-Ray Drive-In but now it was no longer necessary to drive 10 or 11 miles to take in an outdoor movie.

The impact upon the Capitol, Star and Concord Theatres was immediate and devastating. Theresa noted that attendance was down about 30 to 35 percent. In conversations with Mr. Eldredge, the Capitol's manager, he was shaken by a drop of more than 40 percent. He felt his drop was steeper since the Capitol regularly played family-style and Disney films and the families that frequented that type of movie, were now heading to the drive-in.

On December 1, 1951, in its ad in the *Concord Monitor*, the Star Theater announced: "Notice To All Our Patrons. At the completion of today's program the Star Theater will close its doors until further notice. To all of our loyal patrons, the management wishes to extend its thanks. A.M. Stretton, Manager"

The final double feature to play the Star Theater was Alfred Hitchcock's

Strangers on a Train and Johnny Mack Brown in *Trails End*, a sadly prophetic title for indeed the Star had reached the end of its trail.

Any thoughts or rumors about the Star reopening were eradicated when this news appeared in the January 12, 1952, issue of *Boxoffice Magazine*: "*The former Star Theatre building in Concord has been purchased by Nile E. Faust, a local automobile dealer, who plans to convert the ground floor into two stores and the second floor into business offices. When the Star was closed December 1, Concord was left with only two film houses. The Star property has an assessed valuation of $55,780.*"

For 36 years the Star had provided entertainment to local audiences. Fortunately the building still stands, more than one hundred years after being erected. A diminishing number of individuals still fondly recall sitting in the dark at the Star and enjoying movie magic.

At the end of 1952, the Concord Theatre's long association with Republic Pictures seemed to finally pay off. On Sunday, December 7, 1952, *The Quiet Man* opened a five-day engagement, longer than most films played at that time. The Technicolor film, shot in Ireland and starring John Wayne and Maureen O'Hara, would become a classic and may deserve the title as the most acclaimed film ever made by Republic. Nominated for seven Academy Awards including Best Picture, it won two including an Oscar for the film's director, the legendary John Ford, who was no relation to the John J. Ford who worked for Joseph P. Kennedy.

The Quiet Man played to more than 6,500 people during its run and Theresa would note, many years later, that not a single person had anything negative to say about it on their way out. In 2013 the film was selected for preservation by the National Film Registry by the Library of Congress. Seen today, it remains an exquisite masterpiece and one of Wayne's finest performances.

The popularity of the Concord Drive-In was such that in 1954 another drive-in, the Sky-Hi opened in the immediate area. The Sky-Hi was located on Route 3 in Boscawen, about eight miles from Concord and only a couple of miles from the Palace Theatre in Penacook, which felt the impact almost immediately.

Hollywood, in order to try to combat the rising popularity of television, tried all kinds of gimmicks in an effort to hold onto the public's interest.

3-D had a briefly successful run and films like *House of Wax* with Vincent Price did very well. Within the framework of a horror movie, 3-D seemed to add something that audiences found intriguing. However, it didn't work so well with other types of films. MGM filmed the screen version of the hit Broadway musical, *Kiss Me Kate* in the 3-D format but quickly found out it didn't increase business, and dropped the idea, releasing it in the regular format of the time.

Cinerama was introduced but theaters exhibiting films in this format had to be specially designed for maximum effect. There were several dozen including one in Boston that ran films made in Cinerama for a year or more. Without the special curved screen and needed equipment, the films didn't do well elsewhere. There would soon be introduced a new way of showing films that would eventually catch-on everywhere—Cinemascope.

*The Palace Theatre in Penacook was owned and oper-
ated by the Irwin family for many years.*

Chapter Ten

CINEMASCOPE OR WIDE-SCREEN as it was commonly known by many, was created by Spyros P. Skorous, the president of 20th Century Fox. The anamorphic lens that was developed created an image almost twice as wide as what audiences had been used to. Bausch and Lomb even won an Academy Award in 1954 for its development of the Cinemascope lens.

Showing a film in Cinemascope required a theater to install a new and wider screen and to have a lens that would properly display the image on that screen. This was a very expensive investment and some theaters went out of business because they lacked the finances necessary to convert their out-of-date systems.

To combat a severe drop in patronage, the Palace, although classified as more of a neighborhood theater, installed an expensive Cinemascope screen as well as a stereo sound system. Its admission prices increased for films presented in these formats. It now cost 65 cents for adults and 24 cents for children.

The Sky-Hi charged 50 cents for adults and children under 12 were free. In its advertisements it noted it had the "Largest Screen in New Hampshire." While no one disputed that claim, the eventual installation of Cinemascope screens at the Concord Theatre and Capitol Theatre made their claim more questionable.

The Concord Theatre unveiled its Cinemascope screen on Sunday, October 11, 1953. In an announcement in the previous day's newspaper, the theater's ad said:

SEE!!! SEE!!!
Our New Panoramic Wide Screen

The first-run Columbia release, *Cruisin' Down the River* starring singer Dick Haymes, that opened that day was not in Cinemascope. In fact it would be a long while before Concord got to see a film in the new wide-screen format. The picture that was on the new screen was larger and much sharper and clearer than anything that had been seen at the Concord Theatre previously. The Technicolor production looked like the first-class production it really wasn't, but people turned out and were duly impressed by what they saw. This is the screen that would continue to show audiences a wide array of films for the next 41 years until the theater closed. It would be the Palace Theatre in Penacook, however, that would first show the area the wonders of Cinemascope.

The Robe based on a popular book written by Lloyd C. Douglas and starring Richard Burton, Jean Simmons and Victor Mature, was the first film released by 20th Century Fox in the Cinemascope format. Released in September of 1953, it had proven to be a mammoth success even playing for months in larger cities throughout America. It finally arrived, exclusively for the Concord area, at the Palace in Penacook on April 22, 1954, playing to full houses throughout its run.

The Palace had paid a great deal of money for its new screen, stereophonic sound system and to secure the rights to play, ahead of any theater in Concord, a series of films made in the new Cinemascope format. *How to Marry a Millionaire* with Betty Grable, Marilyn Monroe and Lauren Bacall followed *The Robe*. An MGM film, *Knights of the Round Table,* also did very well but a number of other titles did less so. Films like *New Faces, Hell and High Water* and *Night People* had been costly for the Palace to book, but audiences from Concord didn't make the trek to Penacook for most of them. While they'd been initially awed by this new wonder, they quickly discovered that they also wanted a good story to be included in the deal. Reportedly, because of the apathy that quickly developed due to some of these films, the Palace lost a great deal of money in the long run. It soon returned to playing the second-run films that continued to draw respectable crowds and that came at a less hefty price tag.

While the Concord Theatre had its screen already installed, it had no opportunity to show anything in Cinemascope for most of 1954. It instead continued with typical programming of minor first-runs with a few exceptions. It also screened repeats of films that had previously played the Capitol. The two biggest successes in the first four months of 1954 were two

Disney animated classics, back for a revisit and released by RKO. *Pinocchio* which opened on February 21, 1954 was an enormous hit, both at matinees and evening performances. *Peter Pan*, which arrived in April did almost as well. RKO, however, insisted as a part of the deal that the Concord play a couple of lesser titles including a reissue of the 1936 Fred Astaire and Ginger Rogers musical, *Follow the Fleet*. The black and white film which had been a huge hit when originally release, turned out to be a bomb. There was a similar fate with titles like *The Golden Blade*, *The Juggler* and *Riot in Cell Block 11*. *Sea of Lost Ships* starring a young actor by the name of John Derek, didn't do any business, however Derek's last wife, Bo, starred in one of the biggest hits in the Concord Theatre's history—*10* in 1979.

On Friday, July 2, 1954, the Capitol Theatre finally relented to the constant insistence of its manager, Mr. Eldridge, and had a new Cinemascope screen installed, opening its first release in Cinemascope on Sunday, July 4, 1954. Doris Day in Warner Brothers *Lucky Me!* Was the inaugural film and from all reports, Concord audiences loved the new screen. Theresa even took in a matinee performance, wanting to see whether it indeed lived up to the title of "Largest Indoor Screen in New Hampshire!" She agreed that it did.

For several months, every film made in Cinemascope played the Capitol Theatre, even a few titles that had previously played the Palace in Penacook. The Capitol titles included, *Rose Marie*, *The Student Prince*, *River of No Return*, *The High and the Mighty* and *King Richard and the Crusaders*. The only title that the Palace secured, exclusively, was *3 Coins in the Fountain*.

The Concord kept going by alternating between first-runs like *Melba*, the story of singer Nellie Melba that was too heavy on the operatic portions of the story to find much appeal. A Disney film, *The Sword and the Rose* did okay but not as well as *The Bowery Boys Meet the Monsters* which only reinforced that the passing of time had not lessened the enthusiasm of their many fans. Whenever Theresa would ask a salesman about the possibility of her playing a film in Cinemascope, they'd suggest she be patient.

Finally on December 5, 1954, nearly 14 months after having the new screen installed, the Concord Theatre played its first release in Cinemascope. *Sitting Bull* was a new release from United Artists and starred Dale Robertson. It opened for a five-day engagement. It had been so long since Theresa had announced the installation of the screen that she felt it necessary to remind Concord audiences of that fact. In addition to her typical ad which included the wording "Panoramic W-I-D-E Screen under the name of the theater, she advised readers of the newspaper, "This theatre is now equipped to show Cinemascope Pictures." Theresa and her family were thrilled with how Cinemascope looked on their screen, and better than average business continued throughout the picture's engagement.

Years earlier when Technicolor had first arrived, the Technicolor Company would secure a licensing fee from any studio that decided to shoot a film in the more costly Technicolor process. This eventually resulted in other studios seeking to avoid paying such a licensing fee and developing their own color systems. Among the new systems were Ansco, Eastman Color, Warner Color, and Color by Deluxe. In much the same way, 20th Century Fox would license the use of Cinemascope to other studios wishing to film in that format. Columbia, Warner Brothers, Universal, Disney and MGM gladly paid the fee in order to enhance their various projects. Paramount, however, balked at doing this and developed their own system, which they dubbed VistaVision. Their first film to be released in VistaVision was its costly holiday film, *White Christmas* starring Bing Crosby, Danny Kaye and Rosemary Clooney. It arrived in Concord at the Capitol Theatre on Christmas Day of 1954.

Panavision would later be developed and by 1967, even 20th Century Fox was giving up Cinemascope for Panavision. Their last two films shot in Cinemascope were *In Like Flint* starring James Coburn and *Caprice* starring Doris Day. Both films have a connection to me and to Barry Steelman, former owner of Cinema 93.

In Like Flint the sequel to the popular *Our Man Flint* was the first film to play at Cinema 93 when it opened its doors in April of 1967. *Caprice* was the film that brought me to the Concord Theatre in June of 1967 and began my long association with Theresa and her theater.

The major motion picture companies often held what were known as "trade meetings" in Boston. These were designed to show-off the upcoming product that each studio would be releasing in the months ahead. It also served to help them tout their own importance. The salesmen for the various film companies would attend, as would some regional executives from the film studios. The most important attendees, however, were the theater managers, booking agents and executive personnel from the various movie chains. As a courtesy, Theresa was usually invited since her theater was a first-run theater. Theater owners and managers of theaters known as "neighborhood theaters" or who played mostly second-run releases, were usually not included on the guest list.

Theresa would occasionally drive to Boston with her sister to meet with some of the sales personnel with whom she was familiar from their having visited her theater or from regular chats over the phone. It was not unusual for Theresa and her sister to be the only women in attendance at these meetings in the capacity of a theater owner. Some of the executives brought along their secretaries or girlfriends in the hope of dazzling them with what many considered the highpoint of these meetings—clips from upcoming movies and, in some instances, screenings of the entire film. Occasionally there would be a celebrity guest—a star of one of the forthcoming films.

There was a lot of drinking that went on at the meetings and Theresa always felt out of place because she recognized it was a "Men's Club" for all intents and purposes. Some of the language and suggestive remarks that were made offended her at times and with the exception of a few people she knew from the Shea Circuit in Manchester, nobody bothered to make much of an effort to engage with her.

In an interview with Eithne Johnson which was also filmed for historic archives, in 1993, about a year before the closing of the Concord Theatre, Theresa referenced the trade meetings.

> I never bothered to mingle. I was a woman. A lot of people used to go to Boston to these meetings. They were mostly men that were running the movies, the exhibitors were mostly men and I never bothered. Not the meetings. I used to go for films.
>
> We used to go to Boston every two weeks or so. I used to go and see the branch managers. After a while I knew them all. I did some business and then we'd take in a ballet or take in a movie or opera.

Theresa eventually established a good working relationship with most of the branch managers. What had begun as a grudging respect developed into much more as time went by. They soon found out that Theresa knew her business and would fight to get pictures that would please her audience. She could quote grosses, remarks made by customers, and express her opinion in such a way that it was often difficult to argue with her logic. She could be a tough negotiator but was always fair and honest.

Although she continued going to Boston for meetings with the branch managers well into the 1970s, she stopped attending trade meetings after an especially unpleasant encounter with J.J. Ford from Maine-New Hampshire Theatres.

Always aware of her weight issues, Theresa usually dressed in such a way as to understate the pounds she carried, Theresa had no illusions about being a great beauty. Before going to a meeting or working at the theater, she'd always fix her hair nicely and put on make-up. As the face of the Concord Theatre, she felt it important to be more than presentable.

She was late in arriving at a trade meeting in Boston and entered the packed room by herself. Her sister was running an errand at Jordan Marsh, a popular downtown Boston department store.

As she walked into the room and glanced around to see if there was any-one she knew, John Ford's voice loudly announced to the gathered group, "Here comes the fat, French bitch!!"

There was some nervous laughter before Edward Fahey from the Manchester Shea Circuit rushed to her side and greeted her warmly. Theresa vowed to her sister on their way home later that day that she'd had her fill of these trade meetings and would no longer allow herself to be placed in an awkward situation.

When Theresa told me about this incident in the 1970s, it was obvious that it had been something she'd never forgotten. Even 20 years after it occurred, it had been a defining moment in her professional life.

Chapter Eleven

THE LATE 50S BROUGHT WITH IT a visit to the Concord Theatre from a couple of film stars, neither of whom was in Concord to tout their latest motion picture. Doris Day and David Niven, who would co-star as husband and wife a few years later in a popular MGM comedy entitled, *Please Don't Eat the Daisies,* dropped into the Concord Theatre while in town on separate dates. Interestingly, both found themselves staying at the same bed and breakfast establishment on South Main Street.

The Franklin Pierce Inn, named after the 14th president of the United States and the only president to hail from New Hampshire, had originally been built in 1852 at 52 South Main St. as a residence for Pierce and his wife Jane. Both would eventually die in the house. As a B & B, it was a popular stop, especially for parents of students at the exclusive St. Paul's School in Concord. Sadly, the historic building was destroyed by a fire in 1981.

Doris Day and her husband Martin Melcher were coming through Concord in June of 1958 on their way to location filming for the 1959 Columbia comedy, *It Happened to Jane* which co-starred Jack Lemmon and Ernie Kovacs. Day, prior to her years as a popular Big Band singer and going to Hollywood, in 1947 had performed on the radio with Betty Abbott. Betty, who had a professional career of her own, eventually moved to Concord and a lovely residence on Mountain Road. Betty was director of Recreation and Parks for the City of Concord and frequently could be heard performing in a local Concord Community Players production at the City Auditorium. She and Doris had remained in touch in the 15 years or more since they'd worked together. While this visit to Concord occurred before Doris and I had begun our correspondence, when we first met in the summer of 1973 at her home in Beverly Hills, Doris talked about her visit to Concord as though it had happened a day earlier.

The Melchers checked into the inn and decided to stroll around what they immediately perceived to be a charming New England town, a far cry from their residence on North Crescent Drive in Beverly Hills. Doris was especially delighted to find that Concord boasted three five-and-dime stores on its Main Street—J.J. Newberry, S.S. Kresge and F.W. Woolworth. She and Melcher visited all three and she loved the squeaky stools at Newberry's. When the desk clerk at the hotel told them about the Concord Dairy Bar, located a couple of miles from the downtown, on North State Street, the Melchers drove up and sampled several flavors.

After enjoying a dinner with Betty Abbott and Grace Pennington (Penny) Surber, Doris and Marty walked downtown again and decided to check out the movie playing at the Concord Theatre. When they asked for two tickets, Theresa immediately recognized Day and refused to accept their money.

"The people in Concord are crazy about your movies and I know that because they never let me play them first-run. I just played *Pajama Game* but only after the Capitol had taken most of the business. Someday they'll let me play one of your pictures first."

David Niven had worked steadily in films for some 20 years by the time he showed up at the Concord Theatre. He, more often than not, played supporting roles in Hollywood films although he co-starred in several well-known pictures and had a somewhat better career in British films. His first wife, by whom he had two sons, had died in an accident in the 1940s and he had remarried. He was with his second wife, Hjordis, when they came to Concord to see his son, James (Jamie) from his first marriage.

Jamie was a student at St. Paul's. After taking his son out for dinner in Concord, Niven and his wife decided to see the latest film playing at the Concord Theatre.

Niven's very distinctive voice gave him away as soon as he asked Theresa for two adult tickets.

"Mr. Niven, please be my guest. I'm honored to have you in my theater and have to tell you how much I've admired your talents for so many years."

David Niven smiled at Theresa, clearly pleased at the compliment and asked her, "Oh, do you get the chance to play many of my films?"

"Oh, no," responded Theresa, "You don't draw flies in Concord!"

Without hesitation Niven put down his money for his tickets and remarked, "Perhaps one day I'll make a good one!"

The Nivens did accept Theresa's offer for free popcorn and complimented her on the quality of the corn.

Niven's career would finally win him international acclaim and tremendous box-office success soon after, with the release of *Around the World in 80 Days*. Interestingly enough the film would play to large crowds at the Concord Theatre. Theresa asked her sister Laurie whether she should write a letter to Niven telling him that she could no longer say that he didn't draw flies. Laurie advised her to leave well enough alone.

David Niven finally was Oscar-nominated as Best Actor for his role in the 1958 film, *Separate Tables,* and took home the award. He was asked by a reporter, at the time, whether winning the coveted award would change him as a person and make him full of himself.

"Absolutely not," snapped Niven. "And that's thanks to a movie theater owner in Concord, New Hampshire!"

In a precursor for what would become a cause élèbre less than three years later, the state-wide newspaper, The *Manchester Union-Leader*, in the summer of 1957, wrote an editorial entitled, "Shame on Maine," The editorial blasted the Pine Tree State for welcoming the cast and crew of the 20th Century Fox film, *Peyton Place*, to its state for filming. Although set in New Hampshire and written by Grace Metalious of Gilmanton, New Hampshire, the book created such a controversy, it was decided to film in Maine.

The editorial stated, "Maine's desire to get down and wallow in the pigsty of what is modern-day Hollywood must seem very strange indeed to those who have labored hard in days gone by to make Maine a great and respected state."

Edmund Muskie was then the 64th governor of the State of Maine and the Union-Leader seemed to continue to have a contentious relationship with him. In 1972 when Muskie ran for president, the *Union-Leader* was relentless in its displeasure with the man and his politics.

When *Peyton Place* opened in Manchester, the *Union-Leader* would not allow the theater to advertise the film's title in its advertisements. It didn't deter the crowds from pouring into the theater. It arrived in Concord at the Capitol Theatre in early 1958 where it was held-over for a then unprecedented second week.

Both Monogram and Republic Pictures often provided a lifeline to the Concord Theatre and its ability to play first-run films. There were still devoted fans of the low-budget pictures turned out by each company, although the days of the serials were mostly gone by the 50s. Television was providing on-going stories that were captivating the younger viewers.

Despite being well into middle age, Huntz Hall and Leo Gorcey continued to headline the Monogram series of Bowery Boys films. In all there were 48 of them between 1946 and 1958, and the Concord Theatre, Theresa estimated, had played almost every one.

In talking about the films many years later she remembered that she could practically total up the receipts before the film even opened. "They were consistent. They never fell off. No matter how bad they were, the kids showed-up in almost the same numbers."

The Concord played some good titles in the 50s including *The King and Four Queens* with Clark Gable and *Friendly Persuasion* with Gary Cooper. Gary Cooper was well-liked by moviegoers in Concord. In the fall of 1952, the Concord Theatre had played the first-run of Cooper's classic western, *High Noon*. A double feature in April of 1957 of *Attack of the Crab Monsters* and *Not of This Earth* would have been better left for the Concord Drive-In which reopened for the season on April 24. The Capitol Theatre, in the meantime, was forced to play films like *Funny Face* day and date with the Concord Drive-In and the result was usually a sold-out drive-in while the Capitol played to several hundred at best.

In May of 1957, the Palace Theatre in Penacook pulled a real coup by booking the major re-release of the Disney animated classic, *Fantasia*, exclusively for the area. The theater's new stereophonic sound system was highly touted in the advertising and hundreds of people from Concord packed into the Palace to enjoy the film. Theresa had tried to book it previously but with RKO no longer releasing Disney films, the Disney studio seemed reluctant to let one of its pictures play her house.

The year 1958 would be a year of great highs and real lows. Pictures that had titles like *Mister Rock and Roll* and *The Story of Mankind* did not do anything for the Concord Theatre or its reputation. Monogram had morphed into Allied Artists, and Theresa continued to receive a few of its pictures, none of which were especially memorable. *Legend of the Lost* with John Wayne and Sophia Loren did fairly well and didn't create any furor with the ads that Theresa ran nor with the large poster displayed on the south facing side of her building. A couple of years later when it played a Manchester drive-in, the Manchester newspaper would refuse to allow the ad to run.

The Ten Commandments, which had been released in late 1956, finally made its Concord debut on March 25, 1958. Thousands of patient locals made the trip to the Concord Theatre to see the film and it was an enormous success for the theater. Similarly, the three-hour, all-star cast, *Around the World in 80 Days* which had premiered in October of 1956, didn't make its Concord entrance until November 13, 1958 when it too became one of the theater's biggest hits in the 1950s. Due to the long wait in getting the picture, Theresa did not raise the admission price as much as she had for *Commandments.* For *Around the World,* adults were 90 cents for matinees and $ 1.25 in the evening. Children's tickets were 50 cents at all performances.

The remainder of the year was very slow and a lack of available films kept the theater closed for several weeks in late November and throughout much of December. The theater reopened in time to show *The Big Country* for Christmas and *Another Time Another Place* with Lana Turner and a pre-Bond Sean Connery followed at year's end. The success Lana Turner had found earlier that year in *Peyton Place* was not replicated with what turned out to be more soap opera than anything else.

Chapter Twelve

IN EARLY 1960 THERESA NEGOTIATED to play a British-made film that was receiving an American release in February and March of 1960. The movie entitled, *Jack the Ripper*, had done good business after it was released in the United Kingdom in late spring of 1959. A U.S. distributor had picked-up the rights and the salesman had spoken with Theresa. While admitting that the story wasn't exactly what she herself would go to see, Theresa also recognized the potential box-office value of the film. In light of some of the films that had played the area drive-ins, she didn't feel anyone would necessarily carp about this film.

The movie was advertised as "based on an old English murder case which has never been solved." Critics overseas had noted that it was no more violent than the popular Hammer Film releases that were reinventing horror movies characters including Frankenstein and Dracula. The Hammer Films were shown at the Capitol Theatre and were especially appealing to teenage boys, who made up much of the audience.

Theresa was not prepared for the furor that raged after word got out that *Jack the Ripper* was scheduled to open at the Concord Theatre. More than a dozen people in Concord had protested the showing by contacting then Concord Mayor Johnson. While admitting he had not seen the movie, which reportedly contained "scenes of violence and horror," the mayor appealed to Theresa to drop the picture "in the public interest." The mayor had also been contacted by Bishop Charles F. Hall of New Hampshire, Msgr. Jeremiah S. Buckley, the pastor of St. John the Evangelist Catholic Church in Concord, Harley T. Grandin, secretary of the N.H. Council of Churches, Attorney Paul E. Rinden, an official of the Greater Concord Council of Churches, and John P.H. Chandler of Warner, a former executive councilor.

In addition, New Hampshire's then Gov. Wesley Powell had urged a boycott of the film if it was shown anywhere in New Hampshire.

Mayor Johnson recognized that there was no legal basis for any action by him or Concord's police chief, Walter H. Carlson, but he asked Chief Carlson to also speak with Theresa about cancelling the film's showing. Mayor Johnson noted that "impressionable youngsters" might be adversely affected by the film although he admitted that an "adults only" label on the film might achieve the same result. Johnson urged Hollywood to produce "more constructive films, rather than dwell on the degraded part of life."

The *Concord Monitor* on March 2, 1960, heralded on the front page the cancellation of the showing of *Jack the Ripper* in Concord. Mayor Johnson also remarked, "I want to thank Miss Cantin for her recognition of public opinion, and her cooperation."

While Theresa was under no obligation to cancel the movie or to cave-in to the pressure she was put under, she also understood that it seemed apparent that not showing the film, which had clearly been pre-judged since no one had seen it, would support her own long-held feelings that she was in business to attempt to listen to what her customers wanted. She closed the theater for the week during which the movie had been scheduled since it was impossible to find another title to fill the schedule. For Theresa, whose faith was so important, the most troubling aspect of this debacle was the accusations from Msgr. Buckley at St. John's in Concord, a church she regularly attended. In a phone call to her, Msgr. Buckley had told her that she was a "sinful woman" and "you will never find redemption if you offer this abomination to your customers, some of whom would unknowingly consume it. . . ."

It would not be the last time Theresa would face accusations from a member of the local clergy.

The entire State of New Hampshire was reeling in early 1960 from a segment of the populace that was angry at what it perceived as a moral decline in the quality of motion pictures. The *Portsmouth Herald*, however, criticized Governor Powell for his recent action in urging New Hampshire theaters to ban the showing of *Jack the Ripper*. In an editorial it called that move "an infringement on the rights of the individual."

Louis Martel, a member of the New Hampshire Legislature in a speech in Somersworth declared that "continued apathy and indifference about objectionable film and television programs and obscene magazines will bring about 'the demoralization of our youth, of our society."

In Keene, New Hampshire, an organization was created that called itself "Committee for Good Movies," and in Manchester, the *Manchester Union Leader* refused to mention the name of the movie, *Suddenly Last Summer* in an ad placed by the State Theatre, the Manchester movie house showing the film. Instead, the ad asked the public to call the theater to find out the title of the movie. Frequently in the years ahead, the *Manchester Union Leader* practiced this form of censorship for particular movie titles or subjects that it felt were of questionable moral quality.

The ultra-conservative *Manchester Union Leader*, the newspaper with the largest daily circulation in the State of New Hampshire, remained at the forefront of openly expressing disdain for the product coming out of Hollywood. The paper even directed its anger at Paul Hatch, the manager of the Memorial Hall Theatre in Wolfeboro. The paper noted it "once had great confidence" in him. That changed when Hatch sent an invitation to the *Union-Leader* management inviting them to a private screening of *Jack the Ripper*. Almost everyone who was protesting the film had never seen it and Hatch felt that in fairness they should see the movie prior to condemning it.

An editorial in the paper stated that Hatch "should remember for his own good that hundreds of New Hampshire people have protested *Jack the Ripper* and that some theater proprietors have been so forthright as to cancel the showing." The paper concluded by stating, "No one should thumb their nose at public opinion and public welfare".

After a letter appeared in the same paper, written by a Derry resident who suggested that the paper conduct a poll among people throughout the state on the question, "Do you favor laws in New Hampshire to curb obscenity in the movies shown in our state?" Theresa called Mr. Eldridge at the Capitol Theatre and suggested they have lunch and talk.

The Derry resident had suggested that groups should be organized to draw up a "viewers code" to determine what films were acceptable in the opinion of representatives, parents, lawyers and the clergy. This alarmed Theresa and Mr. Eldridge and over lunch at Concord's Puritan Restaurant, they talked at length about the state of affairs in Concord.

Theresa was vocal in discussing the *Jack the Ripper* situation which was recent, and while Mr. Eldridge hadn't faced a similar furor yet, he recognized that if the anger and voices of a relative few were to have their way, going to the movies in Concord might be forever changed.

Mr. Eldridge had seen *Jack the Ripper* at an exhibitor screening in Boston and didn't completely understand what all the fuss was about. He admitted it was a movie for mature audiences but didn't feel the violence was overly graphic. He told Theresa that perhaps it was what was not shown that allowed an audience to fill in with their own imagination what they perceived they'd seen.

Both theater managers left the luncheon with a wait-and-see attitude. They were also grateful that the *Concord Monitor*, had not refused to run ads for more mature film fare.

Despite any concerns he might have felt about *Jack the Ripper*, Gov. Wesley Powell issued a proclamation designating April 4, 1960, as Academy Awards Motion Picture Theatre Day. The governor also paid tribute to the motion picture industry.

The outrage from some factions continued well into 1960 with the PTA in Hooksett launching a crusade against indecent movies. The Board of Selectmen in that community even considered putting through a new town ordinance that would force theaters to be licensed. The license would be revoked if, in the words of Mrs. Boubeau, chairman of the PTA, "a theater showed a movie which conflicted with the moral code of the community."

The Rev. Fay L. Gemmell of Grace Methodist Church in Keene went so far as to implore President Eisenhower to begin a nationwide investigation of the obscene-movie problem. This was a follow-up to a recent sermon she had given entitled, *The House that Jack (The Ripper) Built*.

Even "The Duke" (John Wayne) was not safe from the censors at the *Manchester Union Leader*. When Manchester's Pine Island Drive-In played *Legend of the Lost* co-starring Wayne and Sophia Loren, the paper refused to run an ad noting the film's name and once again told readers to contact the theater for the name of the feature. The same film had played the Concord

Theatre in January of 1958 and nobody had batted an eye even at the ads which showed Wayne and Loren posed together with Loren garbed in a cleavage-revealing peasant dress. Alfred Hitchcock's classic *Psycho* would suffer the same fate when it played the Strand Theatre in Manchester in the summer of 1960.

In June of 1960 the *Union Leader* ran yet another editorial, this time signed by the paper's publisher William Loeb. The editorial praised the *Cincinnati Enquirer* which Loeb pointed out "is as disturbed as we are about the amount of filthy motion picture and theater advertising constantly being offered nowadays to U.S. newspapers." In conclusion Loeb noted, "We not only congratulate the *Cincinnati Enquirer* but are going to give it the highest praise we possibly can—by adopting this code for this newspaper also. We will try our hardest to follow this code to the best of our ability. No one is infallible and we may have an occasional lapse, but with our advertisers' and readers' help we will try to live up to these high principals so boldly set forth by the *Cincinnati Enquirer*." It became a not uncommon sight for many years thereafter to see film advertisements in the Manchester paper that offered a phone number for readers interested in finding out what a local film attraction might be.

Theresa and Frank Eldridge followed the situation carefully for any hint that the outcry might become more localized. The *Monitor* continued publishing ads without hesitation and by late summer the entire movement seemed to be losing a great deal of its steam.

Times were difficult for both the Concord and Capitol Theatres as more and more people stayed home to watch television or to take in a movie at the drive-in. The Concord and even the Capitol were often reduced to playing double-features that might better have worked at one of the "ozoners," as drive-ins were referred to in the movie business. The Concord had a pair of first-run hits in April. Both *Heller in Pink Tights* and *On The Beach* had received critical acclaim and brought good audiences to the theater. Once the Concord Drive-In opened on April 22 for the season and the Sky-Hi soon after, May 13, business dipped at the Concord, even the Capitol saw a drop.

The Capitol found itself playing the same feature as the Concord Drive-In with audiences seeming to prefer the drive-in where you got a second feature and paid less for a carful. Disney films in particular seemed to follow this pattern, and Mr. Eldridge confided to Theresa that Disney films were selling-out on the weekend at the Concord Drive-In but his business was off about 35 percent from a few years earlier. Where once the Capitol Theatre had averaged more than $100,000 a year in gross revenue, representing more than 300,000 admissions, even with higher ticket prices, they were averaging less than $65,000 annually.

During much of the summer of 1960, Theresa was only open five days each week (Wednesday through Sunday) because of a paucity of strong film product. Monday and Tuesday had always been the slowest days of the week for indoor movies and the city, in general, seemed to slow down on those days, especially in the summer. Most of the pictures the Concord Theatre played that summer were obscure titles, often double-billed.

Web of Evidence coupled with *War of the Satellite* was an example, as was the pairings of *Jayhawkers* and *The Whole Truth*, *Vice Raid* and *The Pushers* and *Purple Gang* and *Johnny Rocco*. All would have played better at the Boscawen outdoor theater and were not the type of film that enhanced a theater's reputation. As evidenced by the lack of business, most prospective moviegoers took one look at the titles and decided to skip the Concord. Theresa made the decision to close the theater for the Fourth of July week.

Facing a long bleak summer of bad pictures, Theresa reached out to someone she hoped would be able to help her even though their two prior meetings had been less than warm. It had been nearly a decade since her encounters with Joseph P. Kennedy and she was hopeful that age might have mellowed him a little. She sent a telegram on July 16, 1960, hoping for an opportunity to discuss the situation in Concord with regard to the allocation of films.

The response she received was in the form of a letter from John J. Ford, dated July 25, 1960.

It read:

Dear Madam:
Mr. Kennedy's secretary has referred to me your telegram of July 16. Frankly, I don't know what it's all about.
The entire country knows there is a shortage of pictures and, since we do

not make pictures, or sell pictures, I don't see how we are involved. I don't know of a theatre in the country that is not crying for pictures.

You have had an opportunity to bid for pictures and since we have nothing to do or say about that, then it looks to me as if the proposition is yours and yours only.

Very truly yours,

Concord Operating Company

By J.J. Ford, Treas.

The Concord Operating Company was a division of Maine and New Hampshire Theatres Company.

In 1960, Maine and New Hampshire Theatres Company found itself selling some of its indoor theater properties. The combination of the public's support of drive-ins coupled with television's increased popularity, had vastly reduced the profits the company was used to. The Capitol Theatre no longer boasted the large staff that had once set it apart from other theaters. Maine and New Hampshire Theatres Company while never a huge chain was powerful thanks to the influence of Joseph Kennedy. In the 1940s it boasted nearly 30 theaters in Maine, New Hampshire, Vermont and Massachusetts. By the early 1960s there were only nine open. Five in Maine, two in Vermont and two in New Hampshire. The two New Hampshire sites were the Colonial in Portsmouth and the Capitol Theatre in Concord.

Although a repeat of one of her most popular attractions, *Around the World in 80 Days*, this time at popular prices, did well enough, the rest of the summer and early fall descended into another barrage of bad movies. *Guns of the Timberland, Queen of Outer Space* and *Blond Blackmailer, Macumba Love* and *3 Came to Kill* were all embarrassing.

After the drive-ins concluded their season, business picked-up a little and *Last Days of Pompeii* did okay and two first-run hits, *The Apartment* and *Elmer Gantry,* saw a lot of people who'd not been in the theater all year, return. Theresa raised admission prices to 85 cents. Despite having a big hit with *The Magnificent Seven*, by December things had gotten bad and even the Capitol Theatre was playing something entitled, *Legions of the Nile,* and doing something they'd never been forced to do before—close because nobody showed up for two performances.

While *The Snow Queen* was gracing the Capitol's screen for Christmas, the Concord had no product available and simply took out a newspaper ad wishing the readers a Merry Christmas and a Happy New Year.

In January of 1961, the Capitol Theatre had three especially big pictures play to large crowds. *Butterfield 8* which would win Elizabeth Taylor her first Academy Award a few months later, was followed by *Sunrise at Campobello,* and the Doris Day-Rex Harrison suspense thriller, *Midnight Lace.* The Concord Theatre, unable to secure films to play, kept its doors closed January, February, March and most of April in 1961. It was the longest closing in the theater's history.

Chapter Thirteen

WITH MORE TIME ON HER HANDS, Theresa decided to send another letter to Joseph P. Kennedy, in the hope that this time the letter would reach him. She wanted to convey to him, in her two-page typed letter, the frustrations she was experiencing due to the inability to get any kind of quality film for the theater. The lack of films and the need to close the theater for periods of time was greatly affecting Theresa's physical health. While financially the family was doing okay, thanks to investments and rental income, Theresa also recognized that the current situation could not continue for an indeterminate period of time.

On January 6, 1961, two weeks before his son John would be sworn in as the 35th president of the United States, Joseph Kennedy dictated a letter to Theresa from his Park Avenue residence in New York City. The letter, which he signed, stated:

> My dear Miss Cantin
>
> I have your letter and I am taking this mat ter up with Mr. Ford. I have suggested that he look into it at once and I am sure he will do that. Thanking you for bringing it to my attention.
>
> I remain sincerely yours,
>
> Joseph P. Kennedy

Theresa responded in a two-page typed letter to Kennedy's on Feb. 13, 1961, outlining some of her concerns and noting that her theater was closed at the time due to the lack of appropriate films to show. In one sentence she stated, "After being restricted to the worst pictures that can be found in the cans of the motion picture industry . . ." she expressed how much the theater meant to her and to her family for over 27 years.

From their residence on North Ocean Boulevard in Palm Beach,

Florida, Rose Kennedy dictated a note, which she signed on March 13, 1961, regarding receipt of the Feb. 13 letter from Theresa. It read:

Dear Miss Cantin:

I opened your letter to Mr. Kennedy, as it was sent air mail special delivery.

Unfortunately, Mr. Kennedy will not be here until the end of the week, so I do not think it is possible for you to receive an answer until a later date.

Sincerely,

(Mrs. Joseph P. Kennedy)

A March 20, 1961, letter from James A. Payne of The Joseph P. Kennedy Jr. Foundation in New York, said that ". . . under present circumstances he cannot inject himself into any controversy . . ."

Theresa talked with her family about what, if any steps, should be taken. Months of seeing the theater closed had taken a toll on her spirit. It had been a seemingly endless winter and she decided it was time to reopen the doors and hope that the movies she could get would be an improvement over what she'd been showing throughout much of 1960.

The Concord Theatre reopened on April 20, 1961, with a double feature of *White Warrior* and *The Heist*, two titles that might have been more at home at the Concord Drive-In Theatre which also opened for the season that same night. Fortunately, the next attraction, *The Facts of Life* with Bob Hope and Lucille Ball was a distinct improvement both in quality and in local response at the box-office. The Capitol was opening the long-awaited *Ben Hur* and it played for two weeks, unusual for that theater, however, even though the film was over a year and a half old, there was great interest in its first local engagement.

The following months were a mix of misfires and several good films for the Concord. *The Misfits*, the last film made by Clark Gable and Marilyn Monroe, did better than expected. Theresa found that a lot of those who came were disappointed that the movie was in black and white but otherwise liked it. *Hell to Eternity, Herod the Great, Fast and Sexy* and *Underworld USA* were part of a string of "clinkers" as Theresa often referred to a film that did poorly. The theater resumed closing on Monday and Tuesday and running the titles for only 5 days. A return of two of the theater's biggest hits, *The Apartment* and *Elmer Gantry* still found an audience and *The Alamo* which opened in June, drew lots of John Wayne fans. Theresa raised the admission price for adults to 90 cents, with children remaining at 35 cents. This price stayed in effect for the well-received *The Hoodlum Priest*, although a local member of the clergy expressed concerns about the subject matter and title.

In late summer and early fall, Theresa met with several lawyers to talk about what options might be available in court for the Concord Theatre. She was concerned about the possibility of having to close the doors for another extended period of time at the end of the year and throughout the winter. She knew that was likely if the quality of the films she played didn't regularly stay at a better level than they often sunk to.

Titles like *Carthage in Flames* and *Hand in Hand* barely kept the lights on and only played Friday—Sunday but Gary Cooper's final film, *The Naked Edge,* attracted some better than usual business. The Capitol had several films that would be warmly remembered by moviegoers years later and they included *Breakfast at Tiffany's* and *Splendor in the Grass.*

A couple of films with similar titles—*The Mark* and *The Mask* enabled Theresa and the family to have a few nights off because nobody bothered to venture downtown to the theater. *The Mark,* released by Continental Distribution, had an unseemly storyline involving molestation, while *The Mask,* a horror film with numerous 3-D sequences, was such a disaster that when the theater closed more than 30 years later, there were still boxes filled with unused 3-D glasses from that engagement.

Fortunately John Wayne once again rode to the rescue, this time with *The Commancheros,* which played at Christmas and did very well. *The Second Time Around* with Debbie Reynolds rang in 1962 and proved to be very popular with the family trade. In the meantime, Theresa and the family had pretty much resolved the need to file some kind of action in court with respect to their inability to secure a more regular stream of quality films and not ever again find the need to close the theater for months at a time.

During the first half of 1962, the Concord's most popular attractions included, surprisingly, William Wyler's screen version of Lillian Hellman's controversial work, *The Children's Hour.* The film starred Audrey Hepburn, Shirley MacLaine and James Garner and did well enough to warrant a holdover week. Not as surprising was the success of the family comedy, *Mr. Hobb's Takes a Vacation* with James Stewart. Theresa told me that Concord audiences had always taken to Stewart's "aw shucks" type of charm, no matter whether the film was a comedy, western or Alfred Hitchcock thriller.

The Concord also got to play a pair of films featuring hugely popular stars from the 30s and 40s, stars whose pictures were never allowed to play the Concord Theatre at that time except as a possible second or third run. This time the Concord played them first-run and did well enough. The titles—*The Notorious Landlady* with Jack Lemmon, Kim Novak and the legendary Fred Astaire. There were also enough interested people to make the seventh and final "Road" film, T*he Road to Hong Kong* a hit. Bing and Bob as well as Dorothy Lamour were in the cast along with Joan Collins. Theresa had met Miss Lamour when she visited Concord during World War II on a bond tour. Theresa had joined the theater managers from both the Capitol and Star Theatres for a short "meet and greet." Much to the chagrin of the two gentlemen managers from the Capitol and Star, Miss Lamour was more eager and interested in talking with Theresa, the female member of the contingent.

A couple of fantasy films, aimed at the kids in town, did great during the matinee showings but hardly anyone showed-up in the evening. *Jack the Giant Killer* was the first and *The Magic Sword* was the second, with this author being one of several hundred in attendance on Saturday, Sept. 29, 1962, to both watch the movie and oogle what we thought was the sword from the film, on display in the lobby. It was also the first time I was permitted to go, unescorted, to a downtown movie, and therefore I felt an overinflated sense of self-importance and of being trusted. In actuality a few months earlier I had said I was going to the Concord Public Library and instead headed down to the Capitol Theatre where *That Touch of Mink* starring Doris Day and Cary Grant was playing. I stood outside in a line that barely seemed to crawl along for more than a half hour, making it to within five feet of the doors leading into the lobby where the box-office was located. Suddenly Mr. Eldridge appeared and announced to the several hundred still outside waiting that the theater was full with over 1,400 people. Very dejected, I did actually head over to the library.

Considerably less popular was *Two Weeks in Another Town* which played in September but was far overshadowed by another event involving the Concord Theatre.

The most important milestone for the Concord Theatre during 1962 occurred on Sept. 10. In the United States District Court for the State of New Hampshire, the Concord Theatre, Co., Inc. as plaintiff filed an anti-trust suit. Theresa and her family had reached a point where they felt the only option available to them was in a court.

"Concord Theatre Sues for Damages" was the headline in the Sept. 24, 1962, issue of the trade publication, *Boxoffice*. The story detailed the action filed:

> Concord, NH—Concord Theatres Co., represented by attorney Jean Campoliano of Lawrence, Mass. Has filed an antitrust suit against a group of exhibitors and major Distributors. Triple damages totaling $5,500,000 are asked.
>
> Named defendants are the Concord Drive-In Co., Maine & New Hampshire Theatre Co., which owns the Capitol Theatre here through its subsidiary Concord Amusement Co., Lockwood & Gordon Theatres, which operates the Concord and Sky High (sic) drive-ins in this area, and the following producer-distributors: Loew's (MGM), RKO, 20th-Fox, Paramount, Warner Bros., Republic and Universal.
>
> The Concord Theatres complaint charges the defendants seek to control the Distribution and exhibition of films. Specific allegations are asked on the allegation that first run prices were set at unreasonable levels: that the defendants fixed admission Prices: that Concord Theatre had to boost prices and playing time on occasions, and Had to book pictures it didn't want, including productions "offensive to the taste and Moral standards of its patrons."

The immediate response that Theresa heard came from several salesmen that Theresa had a good working relationship with. They warned her that this suit could backfire and the result could be the closing of the theater or the film companies refusing to even provide her with Grade B films to play.

Fortunately that did not prove to be the case. Although there were times in which the quality of the films was not, and even weeks when a feature would only run Wednesday through Sunday and the theater would close on Monday and Tuesday, for the next 32 years, the Concord Theatre never again had to close for an extended period of time. Salesmen who had treated Theresa with an air of indifference suddenly were taking her calls and willing to discuss terms with her. One salesman from 20th Century Fox even confided to her that "you have guts, lady, I gotta hand it to you!"

In actuality, during the months following the filing of the suit in court, the Concord Theatre actually found itself almost thriving. Some of the films that played were not big hits—*No Man is An Island, I Thank a Fool* and a double feature of *Tower of London* and *Vampire Ballerinas* but some of the others did very well and a few were even destined to be looked upon as classics in their genre, in the years ahead.

West Side Story having won the Best Picture Oscar, was enthusiastically received although when it was brought back more than six years later as part of a national reissue, it did even better. *Judgment at Nuremberg, The Miracle Worker* and *The Manchurian Candidate* even had my parents noting that "all the good movies seem to be playing the Concord lately."

Although there would be years in the future in which the Concord Theatre brought in more revenue, due to increased ticket prices, and played what seemed like an amazing streak of good films, Theresa would often use the year of 1963 as an example of a year in which the good films far unnumbered the bad. She didn't waver in her belief that in the aftermath of the filing of her lawsuit, the film companies had—in her own words, "come a' courtin!" It was a year in which "we had a wealth of critically praised films, box office hits and often a combination of the two."

Chapter Fourteen

IN 1963 THERESA FOUND THAT SALESMEN for the various companies would usually take her call. If she had to leave a message, her calls were more often returned within an hour or two. After sharing a greeting, the next words out of their mouth were now, "Theresa, have I got a film for your house!"

The Capitol had a huge success with *Whatever Happened to Baby Jane* in January, and both *Gypsy* and *To Kill a Mockingbird* had lines forming. Not surprisingly a couple of Disney release (*In Search of the Castaways* and *Son of Flubber*) also did very well but in-between there were a lot of duds, unusual for the Capitol. They even found themselves repeating *The Robe* as well as a pairing of two Hitchcock films from the mid 1950s.

The Concord, on the other hand, had a string of hits including *Billy Rose's Jumbo*, a big MGM musical with Doris Day, Jimmy Durante, Stephen Boyd and Martha Raye, that played in January of 1963 to sell-out crowds at every performance. It still stands as one of the five top ticket sellers in the theater's history in the category of musicals. Theresa said the MGM salesman told her that it did far better, per-capita in Concord, than in many other cities nationwide.

Taras Bulba, Period of Adjustment, The Lion, Follow the Boys and *A Child is Waiting* were also popular during the first months of the year. The year was filled with a slew of titles from United Artists, Paramount, Fox, MGM, Universal and Embassy. For the first time since the drive-in theater had come on the local scene, the period between May and September was not a wasteland but instead was filled with good films and large audiences to appreciate them.

While titles like *Sword of the Conqueror, Wonderful to Be Young* and *Five Miles to Midnight* were reminiscent of the lean years, there were lots of romantic comedies that made the building on South Main Street rock with laughter. *Love is a Ball, My Six Loves, Papa's Delicate Condition* which introduced the popular song, *Call Me Irresponsible,* and the Elvis Presley film, *It Happened at the World's Fair* all clicked. In what might have been a first, the Capitol Theatre repeated the Presley film some months after its Concord Theatre run had concluded.

Foreign and art films retained a special spot on the schedule. *Boccaccio 70* was very popular with its all-star Italian cast and *Divorce Italian Style* was a close second. The three-hour screen version of Eugene O'Neill's *A Long Day's Journey into Night* starring Katharine Hepburn, did better than a lot of popular, lightweight Hollywood pictures did, reinforcing Theresa's belief that there was a large market in Concord for something serious if it was well done. Luchino Visconti's *The Leopard* starring Burt Lancaster was also a big success.

The first of the James Bond series that continues to this day introduced Concord audiences to Bond in the personage of Sean Connery. *Dr. No* arrived on June 12, 1963, scheduled for a four-day run but held over for three additional days. While it drew almost sold-out performances during the run, it was a far cry from the three- to five-week runs demanded for Bond films that played the Concord Theatre in the late 70s and early 80s.

American International's *Beach Party* made a splash at the Sky-Hi Drive-In when it opened on Aug. 21, 1963. The teenage audience in Concord instantly took to the Frankie Avalon and Annette Funicello series, which mostly played the local drive-ins over the course of the next several years.

While mature fare like *Toys in the Attic* and *The Caretakers* were playing the Concord Theatre, the Capitol, surprisingly, found itself stuck with titles such as *Shock Corridor, The Castilian* and *The Man with the X-Ray Eyes.*

Bob Hope scored a win with *Call Me Bwana,* while Frank Sinatra brought in the crowds at the Concord for *Come Blow Your Horn.* The all-star epic, *The Longest Day,* was held over by popular demand. While not a success in some places, Paul Newman and Joanne Woodward seemed to satisfy a goodly segment of the Concord population with their comedy, *A New Kind of Love. The Wonderful World of the Brothers Grimm,* direct from its long roadshow engagement in select cities, was the Christmas attraction with matinees filling more than evening performances.

John Wayne was definitely the star of the year where the Concord Theatre was concerned. Not counting his guest role in *The Longest Day*, "The Duke" starred in three very popular releases that helped fill Theresa's coffers. *Hatari* and *Donovan's Reef* from Paramount, and the film that wrapped up the year—*McLintock*, a reteaming with Maureen O' Hara, and proving as popular as their pairing, more than a decade earlier, in *The Quiet Man*.

In a letter dated April 23, 1963 and addressed to the United States District Court in Concord, John J. Ford attempted to deflect the focus of the lawsuit Theresa had filed, away from Maine and New Hampshire Theatres Company. Because of the pace at which the case was moving, the clerk of court did not even respond to the letter until Jan. 20, 1966, at which time Mr. Ford was urged to have "legal assistance for the proper drafting of your pleadings." Mr. Ford would pass away before the matter ever made it to court.

On Friday, Nov. 22, 1963, the world was shocked by the assassination of President John F. Kennedy in Dallas. For the next four days the world seemed to come to a virtual halt as the shocking news sunk in, and television viewers were riveted to their sets as they watched the story unfold. The Concord Theatre was playing a dramatic tearjerker called *Stolen Hours* starring Susan Hayward. It was a remake of the classic 1939 Bette Davis film, *Dark Victory*. Nobody showed up on Friday or Saturday evening and only a handful came on Sunday. Out of respect, Theresa did not open on Monday, the day of the funeral.

The Capitol Theatre was screening a Warner Brothers lark designed for the teenage audience called *Palm Springs Weekend*. While it remained open over the weekend, Mr. Eldridge later told Theresa that the audience that did come were clearly not having the time of their lives as Warners had intended the film to be. All theaters in the Maine and New Hampshire circuit were closed on Monday out of respect for the owner of the chain's son.

Much as had been the case in 1963, in 1964 there were still enough pictures to go around for both the Capitol Theatre and the Concord Theatre to thrive. Even with the spring opening of the drive-in theaters, the Concord had more good titles than bad. The Concord Drive-In continued to play a number of features day and date with the Capitol, which continued affecting the Capitol's attendance adversely, especially for Disney or more family-oriented titles. Although offered the opportunity to play day and date, Theresa declined. The drive-in would occasionally play five features on a program, advertising it as "From Dusk till Dawn." They found a willing audience who would arrive at 7:30 in the evening and remain until 6:30 the following morning.

While 1964 started with an innocuous Dean Martin comedy entitled, *Who's Been Sleeping in My Bed*, the real gem opened on Jan. 15. *Lilies of the Field* was receiving acclaim from critics and the film-loving public. Sidney Poitier would win an Academy Award as Best Actor for his performance, and during the picture's run, there wasn't an empty seat to be found. Theresa even scheduled a special Saturday morning screening for all of the priests and nuns in Concord and Penacook. These special screenings were scheduled several times each year, whenever Theresa felt a film might appeal to the religious.

Following a week of Joan Crawford scaring up a good crowd in *Strait-Jacket*, *Lawrence of Arabia* arrived on Jan. 29, replete with a massive poster on the outside of the theater. The long-awaited film was held-over during its engagement. Some of the Capitol's counterprogramming included Disney's *The Sword in the Stone*, *Charade* and *Mary, Mary* as well as Otto Preminger's *The Cardinal*. The Beach Party gang returned in *Muscle Beach Party* at the drive-in and proved to be one of their biggest draws of the entire season.

The Incredible Mr. Limpet, an animated film starring Don Knotts, wasn't expected to make very much at the Concord but was very popular with the family crowd. Theresa renamed, *Paris When It Sizzles* as *Paris When It Fizzles* after the Audrey Hepburn romantic comedy flopped. This was a rare occurrence since Hepburn was very popular in Concord. A visit from *Tom Jones* did very well and the film would return several months later. The first in the popular Inspector Clousseau series, *The Pink Panther*, was also very popular. Later that year the second in the series—*A Shot in the Dark*, also provided a lot of guffaws for large audiences.

It wouldn't be a year without a handful or more of films that hit the skids and there were plenty including *Flight from Ashiya, Advance to the Rear, Psyche 59 and Wild and Wonderful*. Fellini's *8 ½* was very much appreciated as was *The Best Man, The Conjugal Bed*, and even *Cleopatra* despite the naysayers who had condemned Elizabeth Taylor and Richard Burton for their on-the-set romance. Stanley Kubrick's *Dr. Strangelove* proved to be the Capitol Theatre's surprise hit of the year. Not expecting it to do any business, they had to open the balcony to handle the crowds on two instances, something that rarely happened except when a Disney feature was playing.

When Theresa played *How the West Was Won*, she raised her admission prices to a dollar for adults and 35 cents for children. At the time the Capitol was getting 75 cents for adults and 25 cents for children, except for Disney releases at which time children's admission was 35 cents.

The Carpetbaggers, because of Harold Robbins' fans, was popular while *633 Squadron, Honeymoon Hotel* and *The Visit* didn't interest very many. Clearly everyone was at the Capitol Theatre watching *The Unsinkable Molly Brown* when Theresa played *Kisses for My President*, the story of the first female president of the United States. Polly Bergen played the president and Fred MacMurray was the first man.

With no court date set by the beginning of 1965 and having been informed by her lawyers that it might be another year or more, Theresa called upon her inner fortitude and faith to help keep her going. For the third year in a row, it seemed as though the films she was able to secure, leaned more toward good than bad. When you start the year by playing Richard Burton and Peter O' Toole in one of the most acclaimed costume dramas, *Becket*, you can grin and bear it when titles like *Joy House, The Pleasure Seekers* and *Kiss Me Stupid* also find their way into your movie house. Whatever you could say about some of the titles, they were a decided improvement over some of the schlock that had come and gone in past years.

Goldfinger, the most successful Bond adventure up to that time, arrived on Feb. 24 and was held-over as crowds braved the cold temperatures and sometimes adverse weather to escape to the world of Bond, his beautiful women and an increased emphasis on gadgetry. Concord audiences also took to a new face—Rita Tushingham—when she starred in *The Girl with Green Eyes. Hush Hush Sweet Charlotte* with Bette Davis and Olivia de Havilland scared a large segment of the population with the two venerable stars from Hollywood's Golden Age. However, when the Capitol played two other legends who had once packed their house in the 30s and 40s, Robert Taylor and Barbara Stanwyck in *The Night Walker*, hardly anyone showed-up.

The Fall of the Roman Empire, another in those epic stories that Hollywood was still making in the aftermath of *The Ten Commandments* and *Ben Hur*, made an appearance. It did a lot better than *John Goldfarb Won't You Please Come Home*, an infamous dud that didn't do much for Shirley MacLaine's career at the time. *Cheyenne Autumn* proved popular as did, surprisingly, *Die Die My Darling* which had Tallulah Bankhead chewing up every available bit of scenery.

The late Jean Harlow, who had died in 1937, was all the vogue in 1965 after a best-selling biography had been read by millions. Hollywood, not one to miss out on an opportunity, made two biographies about Harlow that year, one starring Carroll Baker and the other starring Carol Lynley. The Baker version had more publicity attached to it and played the Capitol Theatre where it did okay. The "other version" played the Concord, and Theresa reported catcalls and more walk-outs than she could recall ever having had.

That spring the Capitol started playing Beach Party movies day and date with the drive-in, starting with *Beach Blanket Bingo* and later that year, *How To Stuff a Wild Bikini*. While packin' them in at the drive-in, the Capitol was almost deserted for these titles that were more clearly designed for the ozoner trade.

When Theresa tried to negotiate with Disney for *Mary Poppins*, they wouldn't even talk about the possibility and the screen classic opened at the Capitol Theatre on July 28, 1965, almost a year after opening in large cities throughout the country. *What's New Pussycat* was the clear winner at the Concord Theatre during the summer of 1965. Playing for three weeks and featuring Peter O' Toole, it found itself competing with another O'Toole film playing the Capitol—*Lord Jim. Pussycat* was clearly the bigger hit as far as local audiences were concerned. More serious fare that did well for

Theresa included *The Collector* with Terence Stamp, *Contempt* and *The Pawnbroker* starring Rod Steiger.

With the drive-ins closed for the season, the Capitol picked-up some fare that would have been best served outdoors. *Beach Ball* and *Doctor Goldfoot and the Bikini Machine* were both major flops. The Concord's biggest success was a held-over run of *Ship of Fools* as well as with both Joan Crawford and Bette Davis making appearances in, respectively, *I Saw What You Did* and *The Nanny*. Their success proved there were still fans willing to come out and see them. On the negative side, *Once a Thief*, *Red Line 7000* and Sean Connery's *The Hill* were quickly forgotten and did nothing for the ledger sheet.

Theresa and her sister Laurie utilized the free time they had during 1965 by preparing detailed charts for the court case. These charts were broken down by film company name and indicated how many films the company had released and to whom they were allocated. The Concord Theatre found that typically, during a 10-year period, the Concord received less than 20 percent of films from the major film companies named in their suit.

The Cantin family remained hopeful that in 1966 they would finally see their case go to court.

Chapter Fifteen

IN 1966 THE WAR IN VIET NAM was creating conflicting feelings throughout the country and while Concord remained somewhat isolated from the
protests that were happening, a number of young men were enlisting or
being drafted into the service. The United States had more than half a million troops stationed in Viet Nam. The mini skirt was growing in popularity
and could even be found in a few clothing stores in Concord. Emmons in
the Capitol Shopping Center had them for sale, but they were discretely
not "front and center" in the popular store. Both *Batman* and *Star Trek* were
rabidly watched on television by a large number of fans. The Monkees' *I'm
a Believer* was one of the big song hits.

The Concord Theatre would mark its 33rd anniversary during 1966 and
the Capitol Theatre would quietly mark 39 years since its gala opening.
The drive-ins were still popular but more for teens and young adults than
the family trade that had distinguished their first decade and a half of local
existence.

Concord's Main Street was still bustling with local shoppers and the
dreaded collapse of Main Street when the Capitol Shopping Center had
arrived several years earlier didn't materialize to the extent feared. The
downtown businesses, many of which had been present for generations,
were family-run in many instances and there was a loyalty to supporting the
business we knew. Friday night continued to be a hubbub of activity with
many shoppers finishing their buying and taking in the evening's second
show at the Concord or the Capitol.

There had been a couple of recent developments in Manchester that
had sometimes lured the curious from Concord down to the "Queen City"
area. The Bedford Mall had opened a couple of years earlier and adjacent
to it, Jordan Marsh, the beloved New England department store whose

flagship in downtown Boston was a must on most visitor lists. Within the Bedford Mall was a two-screen General Cinema, the first of its kind in the area. While the Shea Circuit which operated the downtown movie houses in Manchester tried to dismiss the new cinemas as unimportant, Mr. Hickey the manager confided in Theresa his concerns about even a slight drop in business. It wouldn't be long until the downtown State Theatre would be split into two cinemas and renamed the Queen Cinema and eventually Cine 1 and 2.

During the first half of 1966, the Capitol Theatre played a trio of Disney films that did better than most recent Disney titles had performed. *Those Callaways, That Darn Cat* and *The Ugly Dachshund* all did well enough to warrant the opening of the balcony, something which had become increasingly rare. *My Fair Lady* which had opened in the Boston area in the fall of 1964, finally arrived at the Capitol Theatre on March 29, 1966, where it enjoyed a run of several weeks. In the meantime, the Strand Theatre on Hanover Street in Manchester was heavily promoting its roadshow engagement of the year-old *The Sound of Music*. It would be another 15 months before that film opened in Concord.

Zorba the Greek was January's biggest hit at the Concord Theatre, and Theresa tried to get an additional week but was told the print was needed elsewhere. Nothing compared that year to the business generated by yet another Bond thriller. *Thunderball* came into town like a whirling dervish on Feb. 16 and stayed for a then unheard of three weeks. It brought in more customers than the combined numbers for *Dr. No* and *Goldfinger*. Connery's drawing power as Bond did not carry over later that year to his starring role opposite Joanne Woodward in *A Fine Madness*. Even putting on the marquee—Sean Bond Connery—didn't create even a little interest.

There were a lot of titles that promised a lot and had good name stars attached to them but didn't deliver. *Billie* with Oscar-winning actress Patty Duke, Natalie Wood's *Inside Daisy Clover* and Warren Beatty and Leslie Caron in *Promise Her Anything* are examples. On the other hand, smaller films like *The Knack* and a teaming of Brigitte Bardot and Jeanne Moreau in *Viva Maria* brought in big crowds. *Darling* for which Julie Christie had just won a Best Actress Oscar was very well liked and during the summer months, there were three big epic films with religious overtones.

The Greatest Story Ever Told opened in May and was a hit as was *The Agony and the Ecstasy* with Charlton Heston. *The 10 Commandments* had not yet shown up on television so there was a very appreciable audience for the De Mille classic when it returned for a week.

Theresa was invited to play, day and date with the Concord Drive-In, *The Ghost in the Invisible Bikini* but having watched the Capitol do poorly on these American International titles, decided to sit that one out.

Who's Afraid of Virginia Wolff was the biggest hit to play the Capitol Theatre that summer, in fact all year. The Concord also found itself doing well with a little foreign (*Marriage Italian Style*), a little from Broadway (*A Thousand Clowns*) and a big costly chase film that audiences loved (*Those Magnificent Men in Their Flying Machines*). The best received film, from audience response and ticket revenue, was *How To Steal a Million* with Audrey Hepburn and Peter O' Toole.

The Academy Award-winning Best Foreign Film, *The Shop on Main Street*, was warmly received and Theresa was pleased to find an ever-growing appreciation in Concord for foreign language movies. In the years ahead she would always try to diversify her programming selections to include a nod to foreign films whenever possible. If they made money, that was fine but even if they didn't, her decisions would not be based on monetary gain but on making choices available for the interested local movie lovers.

The first on-screen teaming of Jack Lemmon and Walter Matthau, this time under the direction of Billy Wilder, was popular later in 1966 in *The Fortune Cookie*. While not nearly as successful as some of their later pairings, the theater rocked with laughter from an appreciative throng. The Capitol actually closed one day during the run of *Dr. Goldfoot and the Girl Bombs*, another in the seemingly endless American International series that were clearly running out of steam. A beach film hardly seemed like the kind of film that would draw audiences in the weeks before Christmas and Theresa was grateful to have once again said "no" to the American International salesman.

The Blue Max which had been shown as a road show attraction for some months, was the Christmas attraction and was very popular with both the men and women who lined up to see it. The weeks immediately preceding it had been slow, which was typical of December. Holiday parties and the need to buy "one more gift" seemed to negate a trip to the local movie. In the meantime, Theresa's attorneys were telling her that there might be a court date in 1967 but they could not guarantee it. The various defendant's in the case were seeming to try to delay it as long as possible, perhaps, one of them told Theresa, in the hope that "you'll give up or throw in the towel or decide it's not worth the expense . . ." They clearly didn't know Theresa.

As 1966 rolled over into 1967, the lobby of the Concord Theatre was filled with posters for upcoming pictures. Theresa told me later that year after I'd come to work there, it was rare to know that you have three or four pictures booked ahead. "There are times," she would laugh, "when we're booking something on a Monday to start on Friday and barely have time for National Screen to get the Press Book and print materials to us in time. . . ."

While the cast of the year's first picture was impressive—Alec Guinness, Gina Lollobrigida and Robert Morley—the audience that attended the film, *Hotel Paradiso*, during its short stay, thought it very "stagey"(it had been a stage success for Guinness in 1956) and not American enough for their taste. *Dead Heat on a Merry Go Round* with James Coburn did better and even an unfunny comedy like *Not With My Wife You Don't* passed muster.

The Capitol had an extended run with the mammoth *Doctor Zhivago*, which had been released in late 1965 but didn't make it to Concord until Jan. 18, 1967. The haunting theme song was going through everyone's head as they dabbed their eyes with tissues on the way out. I will admit the enormous Capitol Theatre screen did full justice to David Lean's beautifully made film.

In February the Concord got to play one of those films that mesmerized Theresa for both days of its limited run. The Royal Ballet's production of *Romeo and Juliet* starring Rudolf Nureyev and Margot Fonteyn just about filled the house. For many it was their first opportunity to see the mastery that was Nureyev. For both nights, Theresa kept the curtain leading into the auditorium wide open and sat in her seat at the box-office counter entranced. She also remarked that she probably didn't sell 20 popcorns to the more than 900 who attended. "Maybe I should have opened a wine concession with cheese and crackers," she opined.

After The Fox had the first screenplay written by Neil Simon. It starred

Peter Sellers and was amusing at best. *Any Wednesday* attracted more people but the three biggest hits of the late winter/spring season were not made in Hollywood. All three had catchy theme songs that were on the charts and the films themselves resulted in some SRO business.

Georgy Girl with Lynn Redgrave charmed everyone and really created a new star in the process. *Alfie* also solidified Michael Caine's rising star. Seventeen years later he would appear on the Concord Theatre screen in a little gem entitled, *Educating Rita*. Theresa declared *Rita* her favorite Caine performance but she considered *Alfie* to be a very close second.

A Man and a Woman, the French love story which won the Academy Award as Best Foreign Language Film was an instant hit in Concord. The score, including the title song written by Francis Lai, was a haunting piece of music that stayed with everyone long after they had seen the movie. Claude Lelouch directed the story and won an Oscar for his writing, although he did not win an Oscar as Best Director although nominated.

A great many people returned to see that several times, and it remained one of Theresa's favorite French films, one she would reference frequently in the years to come. *A Man and a Woman* would return to the Concord a couple of months later "due to popular demand." That expression, sometimes used in an ad, meant that at least 50 people had requested the film, either while attending another movie at the theater or by phoning or sending a letter. Fifty was the threshold for Theresa to consider bringing a film back. She'd found, in the past, that fifty represented about 5 percent the number of people she could expect to attend if she brought the film back.

After the string of *Georgy Girl, Alfie* and *A Man and a Woman, The Quiller Memorandum* was somewhat of a letdown despite good work, on-screen, from George Segal, Alec Guinness and Max Von Sydow. Harold Pinter wrote the screenplay and the mostly male audience that attended during the one-week engagement, seemed to like it.

Jane Fonda's future husband, Roger Vadim, would direct her in the French-language *The Game is Over* which did well overseas but not so well in this country. Despite advertising it for "mature audiences," Theresa received a great many phone calls that accused her of running a porno-graphic motion picture. Few if any of these outraged concerned citizens had even seen the movie. As was her wont, Theresa thanked them for their concerns and went back to her work, not knowing that in 1968 two films will create something of a controversy of somewhat greater magnitude.

The Night of the Generals reunited the stars of *Lawrence of Arabia*—Peter O' Toole and Omar Sharif. It didn't come close to duplicating the business and didn't last long. *The 25th Hour* with Anthony Quinn didn't cause a ripple either and at the Capitol Theatre there were plenty of empty seats. Frankie and Annette had forsaken the beach for racing cars and their latest American International film, *Fireball 500* didn't please their fans. In fact, it would be their last on-screen teaming for more than twenty years until they reunited in a late 80s satire, *Back To The Beach*.

One place that didn't have empty seats was Concord's first new indoor movie theater in 34 years. Cinema 93 on Loudon Road opened its doors on April 28, 1967. Concord immediately took a liking to what they found in the King's shopping center. In its ad it boasted of "Ample Free Parking—Air Conditioning—Arm Chair Seats—Modern Concession Stand—New Projection" and for no charge, you could make advance phone reservations. The first feature was the 20th Century Fox sequel, *In Like Flint* starring James Coburn. Cinema 93 kept the customers showing up with an impressive line-up of films including Michaelangelo Antonioni's controversial, *Blow-Up, Casino Royale* and *War Wagon*, to name just a few. Cinema 93 quickly took its place beside the Capitol and Concord Theatres as a place to go for quality motion pictures.

The Capitol Theatre, however, seemed more and more to only be able to attract large crowds whenever a Disney film played. Its other fare, often targeting the teen audience, rarely achieved that goal. With titles like *The Wild Angels* or *Hot Rods to Hell*, the Concord was usually the chosen downtown theater for quality film fare.

Michael Caine's *Funeral in Berlin* was successful because the spy film craze was still going strong and everyone had loved Caine's performance in *Alfie. Fahrenheit 451* directed by Francois Truffaut and starring Julie Christie had real fans in the Concord area, although the film, nationally, was not successful. The curiosity factor brought a surprising number of people to see Charlie Chaplin's return to directing in *A Countess from Hong Kong*. Marlon Brando and Sophia Loren headed the cast.

A trio of duds—*Tobruk, Triple Cross* and a Jules Dassin directed film entitled, *10:30 PM Summer* starring his wife Melina Mercouri made Theresa start wondering whether the summer of 1967 was going to be a return to the kind of pictures and business that she'd had prior to filing the lawsuit. The summer would, however, bring an unexpected new addition to her family.

Chapter Sixteen

THE CONCORD, NEW HAMPSHIRE of the early summer of 1967 was not a great deal different than it had been 34 years earlier when the Concord Theatre had first opened its doors. The population had been about 26,000 in 1933 and in 1967 was just under 30,000. The lovely and historic downtown area was where the majority of people did their shopping. While a shopping plaza had opened about 5 years earlier, just a block or so east of Main Street, replacing the beautiful railroad station, Main Street remained a mecca for finding just about anything you might need.

A couple of years earlier, the Giant Store had opened in nearby Penacook and it was still considered quite a trek to shop there if you were a Concord resident. Just across the Merrimack River, the shopping center that held Cinema 93, also had an IGA grocery store as well as King's Department Store. To this day, there are still some who refer to the shopping plaza as the "King's Shopping Plaza."

In downtown Concord you could find everything you needed at one of scores of beloved stores. From Thorne Shoe Co. to Tonkin and Fraser, French's Music Annex, Carroll's at 9 North Main Street as well as Merrimack Wayside Furniture. The people who owned the businesses were friends you valued. Ozzie Waite, Edward Fine, the Makris family, the Silvermans and Levensalers had been a part of our community seemingly forever. Harry's Steak House, across from the Capitol Theatre, provided an amazing assortment of delicious food. You could buy jewelry at Scott's, clothing at Rosen's or David Heller and appliances at Cole's.

Some of the store names were nationally known and included the A & P, Grants, Penney's, S.S. Kresge, F.W. Woolworth, J.J. Newberry and Sears.

A few days after I started my job, an important part of our local history ceased to be. On June 30, 1967, the last passenger train to Concord pulled into the local station at 7:12 p.m. Concord had once been a hub for the Boston and Maine Railroad as well as other lines that came through the area. The end of that era was barely noticed but more than 50 years later, there remains hope among some that the railroad will once again be a part of Concord.

"I'm going downstreet" was the phrase that you typically said when you went to Main Street or the immediate surrounding streets to do some shopping. You could get just about anything you needed from one of these merchants, and the thought of going to Manchester or Boston to make a purchase was considered the height of extravagance by many. Our little city near the banks of the Merrimack River was a perfect place in which to grow up.

Most evenings I walked to my job at the Concord Theatre. It took about 15 minutes to make the trip from home, which was located near White Park. The only reason it might take longer would be my tendency to stop and look in the windows of the various stores. Each merchant seemed to understand the value and importance of attractive window displays to catch the eye and they certainly caught mine.

Friday evenings I allowed additional time to get to work because it was shopping night in Concord and all of the stores and businesses remained open until 9. Traffic was usually bumper to bumper and thousands thronged the sidewalks creating the illusion of a far larger community than we were.

When I started at the Concord Theatre, evening shows were at 6:30 and 8:30 with the doors opening for ticket sales promptly at 6 and not one minute earlier. I would try to get there for 5:45 in order to go inside and make sure everything was swept and clean and neat for the anticipated throng.

I was incredibly naïve when I started at the theater. I knew little if anything about the method in which movies were chosen and why certain theaters seemed to always play a particular type of movie. As far as I was concerned, everyone reached into a large bin and pulled out a film title and voila—that was the movie that would play. Over the weeks and years of working there, I was privy to the various machinations that went into securing a film to be shown.

My job, which didn't really have a title in the beginning, was to try to make sure nobody snuck in, which was a lot harder than it sounds. Because the men's room was located in the lower lobby, I had to mentally remember each person who went to the men's room, who'd already bought a ticket, in order to allow them to return to the theater and see the film they had paid for. Because of this set-up it was not unusual to have outside individuals who'd not purchased a ticket, walk in and use the men's room and then attempt to enter the theater without paying for a ticket. Theresa did not give an actual ticket to the person purchasing it. Instead, the ticket was thrown, intact, into the antique ticket chopper located next to the box-office counter where Theresa sat. In the days when there were ushers, their job included tearing the ticket in half, retaining one half and giving the other to the customer. With a lack of ushers, that previous method was no longer used. Theresa had also found out that providing the customer with a ticket stub more often than not necessitated picking hundreds of them off the floor nightly while cleaning the theater.

At the start of each evening, Theresa came downstairs carrying her trusty cardboard box which had the tickets in it as well as the necessary cash for the evening. She would dutifully write down her opening ticket numbers—adult and children. As she sold her tickets, she was always care-ful about putting a ticket for each sale into the chopper. At the end of the evening, she would write down her final ticket numbers and when cashing out would make sure that tickets sales equaled the revenue generated. I don't ever recall her being off when she cashed out.

Once the film started, I would sweep and clean the lower and upper lobby, restock candy in the concession stand and talk with Theresa about movies. Her two sisters Rena and Laurie helped out on especially busy evenings when needed. In the early years Laurie was also the spare projec-tionist, having learned the ropes from her older brother Maurice who was a union projectionist of long-standing.

Theresa patiently explained to my very inquisitive mind the process of bidding for films and the necessary time that had to be spent in analyzing upcoming releases and determining what would work best for "my people." Her customers were her people and she took the responsibility of playing a real cross-section of films that would appeal to every taste and not just a few.

"When we took over in 1947, I vowed that I would at least try to play movies that would leave the audience satisfied. I'd rather have 100 people come and each of them be happy with what they'd seen than have 500 come and half of them hate the picture I played. I cannot just let every film we book be something I want to see. I need to listen to what the people say when they come out or when they call me or when they holler at me about some selection I chose."

Over the course of many years, we had thousands of conversations about the theater, movies, Theresa and her family. Between the start of the first show and the arrival of the audience for the second show there was a good 90 minutes of time for us to talk. It was quickly apparent to me that Theresa enjoyed sharing her stories as much as I enjoyed listening to them.

Part of my Friday routine was to pop into one of my favorite downtown stores—Bookland—and pick up a copy of the weekly show business "trade paper," *Variety*.

Since 1905, *Variety* had been published and was considered to be "The Show Business Bible." *Variety* did seem to cover all aspects of show business in depth and in detail. Stage, screen, radio and television, nightclubs, recordings and reviews that were eagerly read by motion picture exhibitors. A *Variety* review was honest and direct and usually right on target. The box-office grosses of movies in about 20 major US cities were also reported and I would be absorbed as I read and memorized each weekly edition that I'd buy from the Paulson's store.

Theresa also subscribed to *Boxoffice Magazine* and the *Motion Picture Exhibitor* and would allow me to read them while I tended the theater, after the second show of the evening began.

At least in the beginning, the second show would begin about 8:30 and Theresa would leave the box-office open for about 15 minutes for any latecomers. There were always a few, especially on Friday evening when finding a parking spot could be a momentous task. The concession stand, too, would stay open until 9 at which time she'd cash-out and take the money and go upstairs to her office to reconcile the day's receipts. I would then sit in her seat charged with making sure no mayhem broke out and to watch the film to make sure that the sound and picture quality remained consistent. There was a buzzer that I would press—once for sound problem (either too high or too low) and twice for a picture problem (out of frame, focus, etc.).

Five minutes before the second show concluded, I would open the red velvet curtains at the back of the theater for the exiting audience. After they'd left, I would make sure nobody was still inside, asleep or otherwise occupied. Next, I would check the men's and women's rooms to make sure they were empty and to refill any supplies needed, finally locking the front doors.

The clean-up procedure varied little from what it had been in the 1930s and was a routine that worked very well. I'd walk through the theater lifting up each and every seat that was down from having been sat in. Next, I'd walk through and collect all the empty or mostly empty popcorn bags. In the early days they were bags but were changed to cups several years later. What remained consistent whether in a bag or cup was the quality of the popcorn popped at the Concord Theatre. The popper, which Theresa had purchased in 1948, made the most delicious popcorn I had ever consumed.

I would then collect all of the candy wrappers and soda bottles that had been snuck in from the lobby's drink vending machine. Most customers seemed to heed the sign that asked them not to take bottles inside. However, especially in the winter when it was easy to conceal a bottle in a parka or heavy coat, there were inevitably a dozen or more bottles that made their way inside.

Theresa deliberately had a vending machine that dispensed glass bottles of Coke products. She felt that in a glass bottle the drink was much colder, and it was. A bottle of soda when I started at the Concord was 20 cents and worth every cent.

To break things up, I'd next vacuum the carpet in the upper lobby, making sure that not a speck of dirt, dust or discarded popcorn was visible. It was a thick carpet rich red in color and I took genuine pride in making it look as good as I could. A complete sweeping, in between each and every seat that had been occupied, was followed by a wet mopping in between each and every seat. With hot water, it guaranteed that any stickiness from a wayward bottle of soda or a crushed piece of candy, would be vanquished.

If you attended the first evening showing of a film at the Concord Theatre, I could guarantee that you would not find any stickiness on the wooden floor. Unfortunately, due to the fact that the second show of the evening would start within 15-20 minutes of the conclusion of the first, there was not the necessary hour available to do the same cleaning routine in anticipation of those attending the second show of the evening. In those more innocent times, it was common practice to let someone stay to see the movie a second time if they wished and therefore scheduling was done differently than it is today. Today there is often a half hour to 45 minutes between showings, allowing time for ushers to go inside and clean up.

I'd usually wrap up my chores, turn out the lights, call upstairs to Theresa and leave, tired but satisfied, about 11:45 p.m. Fortunately I'd have done any homework before leaving home for the theater. Getting home a little after midnight meant I could go right to bed. There never seemed to be a problem waking up at 6:45 a.m. alert and being ready to head off to Bishop Brady High School by 7:45.

On Tuesday or on Thursday night, depending upon whether the new feature started on Wednesday or Friday, the marquee had to be changed after the second show began. I letters for the marquee were stored in the now unused lower box office and I would prepare the lettering as to what was to be displayed on both sides of the marquee.

I climbed the ladder to attempt to change the letters once and only once. Swaying over Main Street with the greatest unease was not my idea of a good time. The ladder, which in the 1940s might have been a work of art, had long since lost its reliability as far as I was concerned. I crossed my arms and refused to climb up there again. Fortunately for me, Theresa understood and stated that she'd not climb up there either.

From then on, I held the ladder and passed the letters up to the unfortunate soul who was paid $10 to change the marquee on the appropriate evening.

After the second show Tuesday or Thursday evening, I would wait for the projectionist to prepare the film reels for their return and then bring the large film canisters from the projection booth to the lower lobby. A driver from National Screen would usually arrive in the middle of the night to pick-up the old film and leave the film scheduled to start on the next day, together with any additional items that had been shipped. These would include trailers, posters for upcoming releases and a press book or two.

The Press Book was important since it provided materials to be used in the creation of the ads that would run in the newspaper. A good ad in the paper could go a long way toward selling a picture that might not be the best.

Word of mouth was, in Theresa's opinion, the best way in which to sell a picture. She often told me that the largest ad in the world couldn't sustain business for a film if those who had seen it bad mouthed it.

One of her longtime business tenants was United Shoe Repair. A family-run business for many years, the owner at the time was Joe Annicchiarico. Joe was also a talented musician and had played professionally. Because his business was open late on Friday evenings, Joe and Tony Sorrentino who worked with him would alternately drop into the Concord Theatre to check out the latest movie. Theresa always looked forward to their visit and would ask me to make sure to give them each a bag of the freshly popped corn she had made that evening. She enjoyed their assessment of what they'd seen on the screen and long before Siskel and Ebert rated movies on television, Joe and Tony would share their personal opinions of what was playing with Theresa.

Chapter Seventeen

UNTIL THE SPRING OF 1967, the Concord Theatre had been able to get a fairly healthy selection of films that were both commercial and critical successes. The top moneymaker that spring had, in fact, been *A Man and a Woman*, the Academy Award-winning Best Foreign Language Film. With its haunting theme song, it had drawn thousands of paying customers, a remarkable feat for a foreign film at that time.

The Concord Theatre and the Capitol Theatre seemed to co-exist well with the Capitol continuing to grab the Disney titles and a fair share of big Hollywood productions. The arrival in April of 1967 of Cinema 93 had made the ability to negotiate a deal in a relatively easy fashion, much more difficult. This was clearly evidenced by the titles of the films that followed *Caprice* at the Concord Theatre.

Welcome to Hard Times, which would aptly describe the week of non-business that particular western generated despite the presence of Henry Fonda, *The Caper of the Golden Bulls, Woman Times Seven, Made in Italy*. There were evenings in which there were not even a total of 20 people in attendance, between the two evening showings. The one bright spot was *Two for the Road*, a Stanley Donen directed comedy/drama starring Audrey Hepburn and Albert Finney. It held for a second week and most of the comments from the customers were positive. We wanted to hold it for a third week, but the film print was promised elsewhere.

As the result of my regular talks with Theresa, I began putting together a weekly report. On the report I would provide an outline of upcoming film releases. I based my information on what I'd read in the various trade magazines including Variety. The salesman from Columbia Pictures had verbally promised Theresa a playdate for *The Taming of the Shre*, one of their major 1967 releases. It starred Elizabeth Taylor and Richard Burton.

When he reneged on that agreement, Theresa realized that she would need to educate herself even further about forthcoming releases if she was going to not only survive but to thrive as a viable and competitive theater. Theresa and I did make our first visit to Cinema 93 that summer to see *The Taming of the Shrew*. Barry Steelman, then the manager, could not have been more friendly and welcoming to us.

"I had a call from the salesman at Fox today," she told me one evening that summer. "They have a title that won't be ready to play Concord until after the first of the year, but they want a commitment now—nearly six months ahead." When I asked her what the title of the film was, she replied, *Valley of the Dolls*.

"You'll break records with that one," I enthusiastically responded before telling her a little about the story's premise.

Valley of the Dolls had become an enormous best-seller despite receiving reviews that were barely civil in tone. Jacqueline Susann, the author, had proudly boasted that her book had ". . . sold more copies than the Bible . . ." and that in itself probably offended a great many people.

In reality it did sell approximately 17 million copies, which was no small feat.

I hesitated to tell Theresa that I had read the book. Like *Peyton Place* written a decade before by a New Hampshire woman, *Valley of the Dolls* was one of those books you didn't discuss in most polite circles. It was explicit for the time with its depiction of the underbelly of Hollywood and the entertainment industry. It didn't hold back in talking about the use of drugs, sex and promiscuity. There were rumors that the characters were based on real-life celebrities, all of which made it must reading.

At Bishop Brady High School where I was a student, you would never dare to mention the name of the book except in a whisper. If word got out that someone had or was reading it, they were branded a sinner. *Variety* had breathlessly reported the casting of the major roles in the film. There were expectations that it would probably surpass *Peyton Place* as a box office sensation when it was released in the major cities in time for the Christmas holidays in 1967.

I urged Theresa to do whatever she had to do in order to secure the film. I did everything but swear on the Bible that it would make the theater a fortune and she actually listened to my sales spiel. I probably sounded as though I owned a piece of the production. I told her who the various characters in the book were reportedly based on and why the public, that had kept the book on the best-seller list for months, would be eagerly awaiting the film version. I told her that it wouldn't matter whether it was good or bad. "People will want to see this!" I concluded.

The next day she called the salesman from 20th Century Fox and offered one of the most lucrative deals she had ever offered up to that time, for a movie title. She told me she was going out on a limb solely based upon my sales pitch.

As a teenager, there is something extremely gratifying about having your employer, who was nearly 40 years older than me, listen to your rationalizations and thoughts and in return show you a level of respect for having an opinion. Theresa valued what I had to say. Where movies were concerned, there was no divide between us. It was as though we were contemporaries, both of us wanting to make the best choices for films to play the Concord Theatre.

When she was awarded *Valley of the Dolls*, more than five months before it was scheduled to open, it freed me up to express my own concerns about the string of less than successful films that had seemed to be the summer's norm that year. While I recognized that the drive-ins were busily drawing large crowds and there was the competition of two other indoor theaters, I was hopeful that we could start playing more successful titles. There had been a great many films released in the 1965-66 period that were roadshow attractions. I told Theresa that many of them would soon be available in the Concord market. In many cases, there was a certain prestige attached to these films which would benefit the Concord Theatre's reputation.

The salesman from 20th Century Fox had urged Theresa to play *The Sound of Music* during that summer of 1967. The film, which opened in about 25 major U.S. cities in March and April of 1965, played record-breaking runs of more than a year as a roadshow. It would finally be available in the summer of 1967 for showing in Concord, 27 months after it had originally opened.

There had been rumors that the film might be playing Cinema 93, in the months leading up to its opening. Ultimately it was not booked there.

Theresa had gone to see it during its extended Manchester roadshow engagement in 1966, as part of the films second wave of release. While she enjoyed it, she felt the terms and the suggested running time for an engagement in Concord, were excessive, especially for a film that was more than two years old. She declined to play it and it ended up playing at the Capitol Theatre, where it did okay. However, so many local Concord residents had rushed to see it in Boston or Manchester during its first flush of success, there were not enough left to warrant the month it was forced to play. Its run, however, set a record of a different kind for the Capitol Theatre. The Capitol, which had marked its 40th anniversary in January of 1967, had never played a film for the length of time that "Music" played.

Theresa did heed my suggestion about pursuing some of the other former roadshow opportunities as they became available. During the following five months, we would play four of those for runs of three to five days with a better than average degree of success. In each case our ads touted, "Direct from their roadshow engagement. First time at popular prices!"

Hawaii from the James Michener novel arrived on Aug. 10 to much hoopla. For the first time in several years, Theresa splurged on an enormous poster to cover the south side of the building. She also ran a radio ad on local station WKXL and printed and handed out flyers at various locations throughout the city. All of this paid off with sold-out performances the first three evenings and for one of the weekend matinees.

Because of its length, which was 189 minutes including intermission with music, *Hawaii* could only be shown once each evening. Concession sales were way down since it seemed as though the crowd that supported this type of film had arrived at the movie after enjoying a dinner out and wasn't in need of snacks. Theresa, nevertheless, popped fresh corn each evening and the smell wafted throughout the auditorium, enticing a few to venture out into the lobby.

The next title we played that had headed into general release was *A Man For All Seasons*. It was the Oscar-winning Best Picture from 1966 and one of the most popular roadshow releases across the country throughout the early months of 1967. The print we were sent of the film was a shambles when we screened it on the first night. It had not arrived until about two hours before the scheduled first show, so there was no opportunity to preview it. The film had been spliced and re-spliced so many times that there were jumps on every reel due to major sprocket damage. A great many of the first-night attendees were extremely disappointed. The response to their feelings provided me insight into how Theresa placed the needs of her customers first and foremost.

She offered refunds to anyone wishing one and also offered to provide them with a free pass to return another evening. Finally, she gave free popcorn to the disgruntled mass as they exited the theater. First thing in the morning she was on the phone with the salesman and with National Screen demanding that a good print of the film be sent immediately and it was. It arrived at 5:30 that day and the projectionist had it ready when the evening's performance began. It appeared to be a new print of the film. The quality, sound and picture were exceptional.

When working at the ticket counter, Theresa wore a comfortable black jumper. Aware of her weight, she felt the black was more flattering and provided her with pockets for storing important items that she never liked to be without, in particular, a Rosary and a change purse that was filled with coins at all times.

It didn't take me long to release the importance of the Rosary, since she would often pull out the beads and say a Rosary on an especially slow night, while sitting at the box-office. She told me it brought her peace and helped her to keep her priorities straight and not focus on the sometimes meager turnout for a particular film.

Barely a night went by without her pulling the change purse out. On a busy evening, it was not unusual that someone would show up to purchase a ticket, pulling money out of their pocket and realizing they were short a nickel, dime or quarter. Rather than send them home to get more money and possibly risk their missing out on the film, Theresa would pull out the change purse and make up the difference for them. Over the decades that I knew her, I saw her do this hundreds of times, to the delight of customers and further strengthening the bonds she had built with "her people!"

The film version of Richard McKenna's *The Sand Pebbles* with Steve McQueen continued our trend of former roadshow epics and it helped to continue the steady business that was becoming the norm. McQueen was very popular with Concord audiences and would become even more popular during the next few years. *The Sand Pebbles* was another film with a running time of 180-plus minutes. With a starting time of 8 p.m., the film didn't break until after 11 and by the time I'd cleaned-up and started home, it was nearly midnight. I don't know how I managed to continue to rebound in the morning and head off to school, but I think the adrenaline from seeing the theater seeming to prosper after a meager summer, had something to do with it.

Theresa received a lot of flak for the Thanksgiving offering—*Reflections in a Golden Eye*, from a Tennessee Williams story and starring Elizabeth Taylor and Marlon Brando. In keeping with much of Williams' work, it was frank, sexual and not for every taste. Theresa received a slew of letters from angry local residents objecting to the film and continuing to object to Elizabeth Taylor being allowed to ". . . occupy the movie screens in our community . . ."

The film lasted for three weeks and the next picture compensated some for the mature nature of the previous film. John Huston's *The Bible* was the Christmas attraction. Its full title was *The Bible: In the Beginning* and at 174 minutes it almost seemed short in comparison to some of the more recent titles that had played. Huston had also directed *Reflections in a Golden Eye* and *The Bible* was about as far removed from that film as a movie could be. It would not, however, be without some controversy.

The first two weeks brought big business, during the Christmas and New Year holidays. By the third week, however, business dropped to a trickle and several letters objecting to the simulated nudity of Adam and Eve during that sequence of the film, suggested we find a way to block out those scenes. Theresa explained to one angry caller that in the Bible, that's the way the story is told. She noted that there is nothing offensive about the way it is presented in the movie. One person told Theresa she was ". . . going to Hell for playing the film . . ."

The minor upheavals associated with *Reflections in a Golden Eye* and *The Bible* would be nothing compared to the maelstrom waiting on the horizon with the January opening of *Valley of the Dolls*.

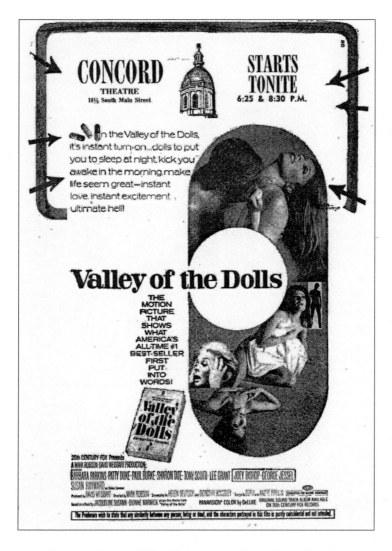

"Valley of the Dolls" sold the most tickets of any film that played the Concord Theatre during its 61-year history. More than 15,000 tickets were sold during the film's run.

Chapter Eighteen

THE VALLEY OF THE DOLLS was scheduled to open on Wednesday, Jan. 17, 1968. We began displaying the posters for the film in the lobby shortly before Christmas, soon after the movie had premiered in major cities on Dec. 15, 1967. Almost immediately there was a backlash from members of the audience for *The Bible* and *Fitzwilly*, the Dick Van Dyke comedy film that followed *The Bible* for a one-week run.

The National Catholic Office for Motion Pictures (NCOMP), formerly the National Legion of Decency which had been established in 1933, had given the film a Condemned (C) rating. It was one of four films that received that rating in 1967. Another, *Reflections in a Golden Eye*, which we had played months before, didn't raise many eyebrows for the C rating but only because of the presence of star Elizabeth Taylor.

In the years before the Motion Picture Association of America film rating system that is still in use to this day began, the Legion of Decency and NCOMP held a great deal of power in controlling what the public saw. Producers would edit their films, if necessary, in order to not get a dreaded C rating.

Theresa declined to run a trailer for *Valley* during the run of *The Bible* and *Fitzwilly*, feeling that the mature content in the trailer would not be appropriate for audiences attending the more family-friendly films. She also planned to note in her advertisements in the newspaper that *Valley* was "recommended for mature audiences."

For the last time in the theater's history, a huge poster was placed on the south side of the building to promote the film. She ceased this practice because of the problems inherent with getting the poster placed correctly. The poster for *Valley* had nothing really offensive on it and, in fact, was quite eye-catching.

Finding someone who was able to go up on a ladder and appropriately piece together the several components that made the final poster was not an easy thing. Pasting it to the side of the building correctly was often difficult. In addition, the January temperatures made it more difficult to get the paste to adhere.

Charlie, a longtime acquaintance of Theresa, who had regularly been a patron of the theater since his youth in the 1930s, offered to do the honors. The drinks he had enjoyed at the Legion prior to taking to the ladder resulted in two pieces of the poster being reversed and the final result looking somewhat indecipherable. After plying him with coffee and carefully going over what needed to be done, Charlie again ascended the ladder and this time it all worked out, thanks to Theresa standing outside bundled up and offering Charlie encouragement. Because *Valley* played for a number of weeks during periods of extreme cold, snow and wind, by the third week of the run the costly poster was in shreds.

Valley of the Dolls was breaking records in many cities across the country so the buzz about its upcoming run at the Concord Theatre was considerable. Theresa was not prepared, however, for a phone call on the Monday before the film opened from the pastor at St. John the Evangelist Church in Concord. Located down South Main Street from the theater, Theresa frequently attended mass at St. John's.

Father told Theresa that he wanted to talk with her in person and invited her to stop by the rectory later that day. She happily obliged, curious as to what he wanted to talk with her about.

While she was greeted warmly, the priest quickly got down to the business.

"Miss Cantin, I'm going to share a story with you. I hope you can appreciate it. I am sure since you're a very Catholic woman, you know the story of Adam and Eve and the Garden of Eden."

Theresa now thinking her being summoned was with regard to the recently shown *The Bible* was prepared to defend the taste in which the scenes depicting the Garden of Eden had been portrayed. However, father had something else in mind.

"You know how Eve offered Adam the forbidden fruit and thus began the beginning of sin. Well, you are Eve in my story and you are offering the people of this good community sin in the form of the abomination, *Valley of the Dolls*, that you dare to open this week at your movie house."

It had been almost eight years since Theresa had pulled *Jack the Ripper* after pressure from local, state and church officials. She was not going to do the same thing this time and with as much poise and tact as she could muster, told the priest so.

"I'm afraid then, that you can no longer attend services at St. John's. You are not welcome in our church!"

Theresa found a glimmer of humor in the situation when she told me about her visit when I arrived at work that evening.

"When he told me that, I almost expected a clap of thunder and a bolt of lightning to strike me!"

All humor aside, for someone whose faith had been a mainstay in her 54 years of living, this was a devastating blow. Still she never set foot in St. John's Church again and began to attend services at nearby Sacred Heart Church on Pleasant Street.

At Brady, I was told to meet with a priest who was on staff about "a situation that has been brought to our attention".

I had no idea what that meant as I walked into his office and sat in front of him.

"Paul, I understand you work at the Concord Theatre evenings," to which I replied in the affirmative.

"It's also been brought to our attention that the Concord Theatre is about to open a film that has been rated Condemned." He continued, barely pausing for a breath or my reaction. "I hope you realize that there is occasion for a Mortal Sin each and every time you are in the presence of this film. If you should die before you have the opportunity to confess your sins—namely being in the presence of this film—you will be damned to hell."

As politely as I could, I explained that I had a job working at the theater and I could not afford to take weeks off after making a commitment to do my job. As though disembodied, I found myself saying, "I'll go to Confession each Saturday afternoon and hope and pray that nothing happens to me in-between".

I kept my word and each Saturday afternoon I showed up at St. Peter's

Church and confessed to having "seen *Valley of the Dolls* 14 times since my last confession." You can't make this stuff up!

One Saturday when I arrived at the church, the priest who was hearing confession was Father Goodwin, who was also a teacher at Bishop Brady High School. It made me just a little bit nervous but I went into the confessional, knelt down and said the obligatory, "Bless me Father for I have sinned."

As I had done for several previous weeks, I stated that I'd been in the presence of *Valley of the Dolls* a total of 14 times, adding, "Twice each evening for seven days."

After what seemed like a momentous silence, Father Goodwin asked, "Were there no matinees?"

Late 1967 and early 1968 was proving to be a box office bonanza for local theaters. The Capitol did great business with the thriller *Wait Until Dark*, starring local favorite Audrey Hepburn. They also had a highly successful engagement of *Guess Who's Coming to Dinner,* the final on-screen pairing of Spencer Tracy and Katharine Hepburn. In the meantime, Cinema 93 was flourishing with the widely acclaimed *Bonnie and Clyde* and a film destined to become a classic, *The Graduate.*

On opening night for *Valley of the Dolls*, I arrived earlier than usual. The film was scheduled to show at 6:25 and 8:30. Theresa's two sisters were manning the concession stand while popping fresh corn for the anticipated crowds. The concession stand was packed with fresh candy and the soda machine was filled. We were not disappointed.

When I had arrived at 5:40, there was already a long line assembled outside the theater waiting for the doors to open. There was almost a party-like atmosphere as people huddled in their heavy coats staving off the cold, dark evening. More than 500 attended the first two showings which is remarkable for a Wednesday evening. Theresa, with her amazing agility in selling tickets, managed to get everyone in with only a five-minute delay for the start of the second showing.

I was unprepared for the "wreckage" I encountered after the second showing ended when I went inside to survey what I had to clean-up. Despite doing good business on a number of recent films, the attendees did not purchase concession items with the same frenzy and fury that the crowd for *Valley of the Dolls* seemed to. It was well after midnight when I left that evening.

Each successive night only brought more crowds and, on the weekend, the "sold-out" sign went up a number of times. While I didn't hear too many positive remarks about the film, it seemed as though it was a "must see" for the thousands who made the pilgrimage to the Concord Theater that January and February. Theresa began to privately refer to the film as "Valley of the Dollars."

Word got out about the crowds and some nights there were already 200 to 300 hundred in line well before 5:30. The lines would go up Main Street from the theater to Pleasant and then head up Pleasant to South State and continue on South State.

Star Hot Dog, a popular eating spot on Pleasant Street, was ecstatic with the business they found themselves doing in the evening from the waiting hordes. People would take turns running inside to buy a coffee or get something to eat while waiting. It was also a break from the cold which was biting some evenings with wind chills hovering around zero.

It wasn't until the fourth week of the run that business started to taper off and we realized we had to start discussing other films to play. Suddenly it seemed as if salesmen from the various movie companies were looking at the Concord Theatre in a very respectful way. Word had gotten out about the business for *Valley of the Dolls* and it seemed as if everyone had another *Valley of the Dolls* they wanted to sell.

One evening toward the end of the run, I walked in to find Theresa grinning like a Cheshire Cat. She told me how grateful she was that I'd urged her to play *Valley of the Dolls* and also how much she appreciated the background information I provided about other movie titles.

She presented me with fourth row tickets to a performance in Boston of the Metropolitan Opera during their annual spring tour. Each year they would come to Boston and perform at what was known as the War Memorial Auditorium. Several productions starring some of their most illustrious stars were presented during this tour. Theresa loved opera and knew that I had an appreciation for it also and wanted me to experience it with her. It would become an annual tradition for several years, until the Met ceased its yearly tours. The opera was always preceded by lunch at Anthony's Pier 4.

Theresa had a beautiful voice and a rich background and understanding of opera. During a particular aria she would often mouth the words to the aria and was able to sing, fluently, in Italian, French and German. In church, her rich and full voice would soar while singing hymns, often making those seated around her stop singing and listen to her lovely vocal instrument.

During the run of *Valley of the Dolls*, I learned a new meaning for a word I thought I knew—checkers. I thought checkers was just a game that I played rather badly. However, in the lexicon of movies, it has another meaning.

A checker is someone a movie company sends to the theater to make sure you're reporting accurately on the number of tickets being sold. With so much at stake, especially with a popular draw like *Valley*, the company wants to make sure they are getting every cent due to them.

The studio that released *Valley of the Dolls* (20th Century Fox) was to receive more than 60 percent of all receipts generated at the box office. When Theresa would open the box-office in the evening, she would check her tickets and mark down the first ticket number to be sold. At the end of the evening, when closing out, she'd mark down the number of the last ticket she'd sold, subtract the opening number from the closing and know how many tickets had been sold. She would then multiply that by the admission price, doing the same thing with any children's tickets, and then be able to determine what monies should be reflected in sales. She'd then be able to know how much of those receipts would be returned to the film company as well as how much she would be keeping for the theater. In rare instances, some film releasing companies actually wanted their share sent on a daily basis.

Although I am not aware of it ever happening at any theater in Concord, there were instances in other places of tickets being re-sold. A theater could write down the opening number and closing number but by not providing patrons with actual tickets, could state they sold 200 tickets when in actuality they sold closer to 300, thereby providing themselves with additional revenue generated by the 100 un-reported sales.

The checker would count the number of individuals purchasing tickets to make sure what the checker clicked on their clicker was comparable to the numbers on the report for the evening. Sometimes the checker did this from outside the theater without notifying the manager. They would then show up at the box office after the conclusion of the show and ask to see the numbers on the report. More often than not, they arrived a few minutes before the box office opened and introduced themselves and then stood by the box office, clicking, as tickets were sold.

I was always introduced as Theresa's associate and someone who worked in various capacities at the theater. Because I was still a teen, they'd often look at me with a look of incredulity as though I were just a kid deserving to be ignored by them.

In my opinion, checkers were among the most humorless people I have ever met. Maybe the importance of their job removed any vestiges of courtesy or humor, but they seemed to take to their role as though they were hoping to announce loudly, "Gotcha!" We would sometimes offer them a bag of freshly popped corn as they went about their clicking, but they always declined. It might have something to do with their job structure. Theresa's meticulous attention to detail made the reports always balance perfectly.

Late in February of 1968, Theresa brought another new word into my vocabulary when she asked me if I would like to attend a trade screening for an upcoming film from Metro-Goldwyn-Mayer. When she further told me that the film starred Doris Day, I eagerly accepted. On several levels it would be a first for me.

The screening for *Where Were You When the Lights Went Out?* would be held outside Boston in a new two-screen cinema in Braintree. Since I was far from being able to drive, I coerced my mother into driving us, suggesting it be an early birthday gift—eight months early. She convinced Dorothy Levensaler, a good friend and the wife of Concord Camera Store owner Whitman Levensaler, to come along too.

Trade screenings were often held in suburban theaters for many films that were not due to be released for several months. The screenings were packed with studio executives, press, sales personnel, exhibitors and some of the general public. Rating cards were given out to be completed by audience members after the screening. From these cards, edits or changes would be made in the film, if appropriate. These screenings often helped a studio plan their marketing strategies for the film.

It was the first time I had been to a two- cinema theater and the gleaming new facility was indeed a wonder to behold. The seats were also comfortable. We arrived with my invitation from MGM about a half hour early. We sat and watched the conclusion of the film currently playing in that particular cinema, which was the roadshow engagement of the Universal musical, *Thoroughly Modern Millie.*

I loved the Doris Day movie and rated it highly on the card. The laughter throughout the screening from the full house necessitated the sound being turned up in order for some of the lines to be heard. I felt the movie would be a good summer performer for the Concord Theatre, since the movie was not scheduled to be released until summer. The next evening, Theresa made a note to talk with the sales person from MGM when the time came to talk about upcoming product.

For a few days after *Valley of the Dolls* departed, it was almost blissful to have the theater return to something resembling quiet. We were, however, already mapping out a strategy for the months ahead.

Chapter Nineteen

THERESA WAS VERY FIRM IN HER FEELINGS about what was shown in her theater. In some ways she felt that she was inviting people into her home and thus had a responsibility to provide them with a nice and often memorable evening. It was not necessary that every film shown be a *Valley of the Dolls*. She would just as soon balance a moneymaker like that title with a smaller film that satisfied a more select group of discerning film lovers.

Through the spring we played titles like *Half a Sixpence*, an English musical that didn't draw a lot of fans but was tuneful. Theresa loved hearing music in the theater and we would often select a musical just because it was available. *The Scalphunters* was a popular western with Burt Lancaster and *Far From the Madding Crowd* was a beautifully photographed but overly long story, well-acted by Julie Christie, Alan Bates and Terence Stamp.

The terms for *Madding* had been so high that Theresa suggested we go to Manchester, where it was playing prior to being available for showing in Concord. We saw it at the beautiful State Theatre located on Elm Street.

Edward Bernard Hickey was the manager at the time and the State Theatre was clearly his pride and joy. Although she had known him for many years, Theresa always called him "Mr. Hickey" and he called her "Miss Cantin". He was delighted that we'd driven down from Concord to check out the movie and joined us, briefly, as we watched the story unfold on the State Theatre's huge cinemascope screen. The projectionist that day, Merton Tolman, was also a longtime acquaintance of Theresa and the two friends had a joyous reunion in the projection booth. Mert, as he was known, had once lived two houses from my family in Concord and I'd been friends with his son, Tom.

After the film concluded, we all chatted in Mr. Hickey's office and he was very frank in telling us that the business the film was doing in Manchester was not especially good. "It's definitely not what Manchester audiences enjoy and some people write it off simply because the characters speak with an English accent."

Theresa and I had enjoyed the film and even taking into account the possibility of it not being a big hit at the box-office, she talked with the MGM salesman and offered terms that were slightly below what he had been asking. We were awarded the film and it played for two weeks to modest but appreciative audiences.

Some of the titles we played that spring don't even seem to turn up on television years later on the Late, Late Show they were so bad. *Here We Go Round the Mulberry Bush* was a dud. *The Anniversary* starring Bette Davis, with a patch over one eye, generated little business and was rated Condemned. Why it received that rating escaped us since there didn't appear to be anything either excessively violent or that could be construed as obscene in the film when we watched it.

Berserk starring Joan Crawford did surprisingly well and brought a lot of Crawford's fans out to see it. The suspense story, set in a circus and featuring some grisly murders, could probably have held over beyond the one week we had it scheduled for. Theresa had always enjoyed Joan Crawford as an actress because of the strong women she often portrayed on the screen. On more than one occasion Theresa told me that of the stars of the Golden Era, Crawford, Katharine Hepburn and Garbo were the three she would most have liked to meet.

In April, lines once again formed up Main Street when *Planet of the Apes* opened for an extended engagement. The complexity of the make-up, the expensive budget, and the presence of well-known actors, all contributed toward making it something truly unique in its time. It continued its run into May when we once again hit that lull that seemed to be inevitable. The last weeks of the school year, proms, a desire to work outside and the lengthening days, all made attendance at a movie low on the list of "must-dos."

Controversy again reared its head in the summer of 1968 when we booked a film that we knew, in advance, would be for mature audiences. Although not rated as Condemned, *The Fox*, based on a novella by D.H.

Lawrence, and starring Sandy Dennis, Anne Heywood and Keir Dullea, was raising the hackles on many individuals, ever since its release in limited engagements at the end of 1967.

The implied lesbianism between the two female characters was frank for its time but the film received very good reviews. Roger Ebert called the film ". . . a quiet, powerful masterpiece . . ."

This time Theresa did not hear from any members of the clergy, but there was an outcry from some of the public. Letters poured in to the theater, asking her to cancel this "sin-fest". Letters to various media outlets called it a "dirty movie" and reprimanded the theater for not noting that in its ads.

The Fox opened in late June and was held over for many weeks. The overall response from audiences was closer to what Roger Ebert had noted. Theresa received many comments thanking her for her bravery in showing an adult film that told an adult story. On the face of it, it would seem that we made a complete turnaround with the next scheduled attraction.

Thoroughly Modern Millie had been released as a roadshow musical about 15 months earlier and had proven successful thanks to the drawing power of star Julie Andrews, in the title role. It also marked her return to musicals after a pair of more dramatic roles. I had, of course, seen part of it earlier that year while attending the trade screening of the Doris Day film in Massachusetts. According to Mr. Hickey, in Manchester *Millie* had drawn very good business. The Concord was able to secure a playdate for July of 1968.

The public flocked to see the film once it opened and there was not so much as one negative word about the story or the content. Theresa and I had a lot of laughs about that over the years.

In reality, the story of *Thoroughly Modern Millie* is just as risqué as anything found in *The Fox* and possibly even franker.

The story of "Millie" involves a boarding house in New York City run by a Mrs. Meers. She takes in young ladies, many of whom do not have anyone else in their lives. Mrs. Meers is able to have the girls drugged, tossed into a laundry basket and sold as prostitutes for a white slave ring. Opium is used in the film, although it's all tied up so neatly with music, dance, Andrews, Mary Tyler Moore and Carol Channing, and clothes by

Jean Louis. Apparently the seamier aspects of the story could therefore be overlooked amidst the fun and frivolity?

Walter, the salesman for Universal Pictures, was an enthusiastic cheerleader for everything Universal. His disarming good humor was sometimes hard to resist and he truly believed that each and every film made by or released by Universal, was destined to become a classic.

Boom was the latest title he was trying to interest Theresa in. The film was the screen version of a not very successful Tennessee Williams play entitled, *The Milk Train Doesn't Stop Here Anymore.* Tallulah Bankhead had starred in the stage production and the critics had been merciless in tearing it apart. Now it seemed Universal had given the project a hefty budget and a director named Joseph Losey who was briefly the talk of Hollywood. To further enhance the package, there were two huge stars—Elizabeth Taylor and Richard Burton. Walter swore it would be bigger than *Virginia Wolff* and *The Taming of the Shrew.*

In order to view the film and make an informed decision, Theresa, her sister Laurie and I made a trip to Burlington, Massachusetts where the film was showing. For two hours we took in the stunning cinematography. The film had been shot on the island of Sardinia and from a scenic perspective, it was indeed a knockout. While we sat chatting after the movie, we weren't sure what to think.

Theresa felt that "the thinkers" might appreciate its message and meaning. Laurie felt it would appeal to even fewer customers than had attended *Reflections in a Golden Eye,* also written by Williams and starring Taylor. I was just a teenager and didn't want to appear unsophisticated, so I went along with Theresa's reasoning, feeling that there would be a segment of the population that might find it interesting. Had we made a bet, Laurie would have won hands down.

By the third day of its playdate, we were privately referring to *Boom* as "Bomb" and with great finesse, Theresa was able to talk Walter out of our two week obligation and cancel the film after one week. Audience members exiting the theater after watching it, seemed to be averting their eyes and not wanting to talk to Theresa or myself. It wasn't unusual to have more than half the audience walkout during the film. To make matters worse, Theresa had asked Walter to send an "appropriate short subject" to accompany the feature and he had sent a Woody Woodpecker cartoon that we'd been sent no less than 3 or 4 times during the previous year. One person did stop and tell Theresa that the cartoon was the best part of the evening.

Prudence and the Pill a comedy from 20th Century Fox and starring David Niven and Deborah Kerr, did much better. It fact it held for a few weeks and brought large crowds that chuckled at the comedy built around birth control pills. I half-jokingly told Theresa two weeks into the run that she owed David Niven a letter of apology since in this film he was clearly drawing more than flies.

Theresa finagled special tickets for me, my mom and Dot Levensaler in August to attend the world premiere of Doris Day's new film *With Six You Get Eggroll* at Boston's Orpheum Theatre. Doris had written and told me she was very pleased with the film but would not be attending the opening due to the recent passing of her husband of 17 years, Marty Melcher, who produced the film. I urged Theresa to try to secure the film but she found it had already been booked at the Capitol Theatre for early October.

September and early October brought with it the usual meager pickings and low attendance figures although some of the films we were forced to play didn't exactly excite our patrons.

Hagbard and Signe, If He Hollers Let Him Go (another Condemned rating), and *Great Catherine* a film better known at the Concord Theatre for the number of daily walk-outs. In fact on one particular evening, less than a half hour into the film, every paying customer had departed. When I informed Theresa, she called upstairs to Mr. Bunker, who was running the projector, and told him to "stop the show!" Fortunately the salesman from MGM urged us to play three titles they had available, and two of them helped to turn the tide.

Finally, four months after its release, *Where Were You When the Lights Went Out?* with Doris, played the Concord in late October. Arriving as it did, two weeks after *Eggroll* had concluded a successful run at the Capitol, Theresa didn't have high expectations for *Lights*. In addition, the film had played most of its dates during the summer months. We were all pleasantly surprised when it did exceptional business during its week run, including two near sell-out shows on Saturday night. *Hot Millions*, also from MGM and starring a young Maggie Smith with Peter Ustinov, did better than expected. The third MGM title and another Condemned film, *The Legend of Lylah Clare,* was an embarrassment. *Paper Lion* starring Alan Alda in his days prior to *Mash*, attracted a larger than anticipated largely male audience and *Shalako* a Sean Connery western did okay.

I found myself with a nickname bestowed on me that fall—"Big Paul." Theresa's nephew, Paul Constant, who lived with his family in the apartment over the lobby portion of the theater, was dubbed "Little Paul" at the same time. There were so many instances in which Theresa, Rena or Laurie had called out for Paul to do something, with both of us responding. Because I was older by several years, I was "Big Paul" and he was "Little Paul," a sobriquet he didn't especially care for as he got older and I can perfectly understand why.

When I had first started at the theater I always called Theresa Miss Cantin. Within a week or so she told me to please call her Theresa. By the end of my first month she told me to use the nickname that family and close friends used—TT.

Theresa marked her 55th birthday on Dec. 15 and I gifted her with a film book featuring many portraits of the stars from Hollywood's Golden Age. She loved it and said that what she'd love for her birthday would to be able to continue her work until she was at least 80. There was no reason to doubt that she wouldn't get that wish since she seemed to continue to be delighted by what she did and with the films she saw.

Arthur and Vaulien Dame would regularly drive in from Pittsfield each time we had a new attraction on the screen. Their friendship stretched back nearly 30 years and Arthur loved talking movies with Theresa. He also appreciated the input she provided him when he would book a title for his Scenic Theatre. Assessing the response a film generated at the Concord would also enable him to ignore titles that might not work for his audience and to focus instead on those that might bring in revenue and satisfied customers. Listening to Theresa and Arthur talk was an education in itself.

Arthur regularly contributed his feelings and comments about the movies that played the Scenic in *Boxoffice Magazine*. There was a column entitled, "The Exhibitor Has His Say About Pictures," in which theater owners from across the country made their feelings known about the product that had played their theaters. Arthur never minced words in calling out a film that he felt he'd been lied to about regarding its merits. He was just as forthright, however, when praising a film's value. Each year Arthur and Theresa made a special point of completing the annual *Boxoffice Magazine* poll to determine the top-ranked male and female box-office attractions in the country. They also voted in the Quigley Poll conducted by the *Motion Picture Herald* to determine the top box-office draws.

The Christmas attraction, I had learned, was always something you tried to carefully book for wide appeal. There were always a great many visitors in Concord, spending holidays with family and friends. Having a good movie to go out and see in the evening was a popular pastime. *Camelot,* which had been released as a roadshow attraction in October of 1967, was finally ready to make its Concord debut in December of 1968. The Capitol Theatre had also booked a musical for its Christmas picture—*Doctor Doolittle* with Rex Harrison. Cinema 93 had the highly anticipated *Bullitt* with Steve McQueen and one of the most exciting car chase sequences I have ever seen on the screen.

Bullitt was clearly the winner in the box office sweepstakes and *Doctor Doolittle* the loser. I attended a matinee of *Doolittle*, expecting the Capitol Theatre to be filled. Alas there were only four of us sitting in the cavernous theater which seated about 1,400. I dozed off for a while, waking up in time to see the Lunar Moth. I was probably exhausted from cleaning up from the crowds that came for *Camelot.*

The year 1968 had definitely been one for the history books. The tragic assassinations of Dr. Martin Luther King Jr. and Senator Robert Kennedy as well as the demonstrations and unrest on campuses all across the country over the unpopular Viet Nam War. It had also been a year in which Lyndon Johnson declined to run for a second term and America elected Richard Nixon as our next president. Movies, too, had begun changing and evolving due to a new generation of filmmakers who wanted to tell their stories in their own unique ways.

Camelot, however, was a perfect way to end 1968 at the Concord Theatre. It was romantic, tuneful, lushly produced and thoroughly enjoyed by the thousands who ventured downtown to 18 1/2 South Main Street. For me, watching it night after night for weeks, a line from the title song would haunt me. "Don't' let it be forgot, that once there was a spot . . ."

In the years to come I would often think of those words, even more so after the 1994 closing of the Concord Theatre. They became a mantra for me in making sure the spot that was the Concord Theatre was never forgotten.

Chapter Twenty

THE LAST YEAR OF THE 1960S dawned with continued good business for *Camelot*. It played a total of four weeks and would probably have been able to stay a fifth if we were not booked for the national re-release of the Oscar-winning *West Side Story*. The film had played the Concord Theatre when it originally was released some years earlier.

We'd book *West Side Story* for one-week feeling that a re-release didn't warrant a longer run but after the first two days of tremendous business, we were able to hold it for a second week. Remarkably the film did better business on this reissue than it had during its original run. The Beatles' *Yellow Submarine* followed, and Theresa noted that it was the first time in the theater's history that three musicals had played in a row.

There was something for everyone in the films that followed, although Otto Preminger's *Skidoo* was a disaster and a film that many in the cast disowned in years to come. When Carol Channing came to Concord in 2007, I told her about the run of *Skidoo* and she rolled her eyes and said, "Oh that thing!" in that unmistakable voice of hers. *100 Rifles* was a well-received western starring Burt Reynolds, Jim Brown and Raquel Welch and *Where Eagles Dare* with Clint Eastwood and Richard Burton brought out action fans in large numbers. John Wayne scored really big in *Hellfighters*.

The Wayne film was from Universal, and Walter's enthusiasm for it was so great that Theresa couldn't say no. "Besides," she noted, "Concord loves John Wayne and they love Doris Day. If those two would team up on the screen, we'd probably outgross *Valley of the Dolls*." Theresa would often talk about the stars who were held in a special affection by local audiences.

Stanley Kubrick's *2001: A Space Odyssey* would open on April 30, 1969, after playing lengthy roadshow engagements around the country and generating a great deal of talk—pro and con. The terms that MGM wanted for the film were steep but after studying the reviews and audience comments from other cities, Theresa decided that it was worth the risk.

As it had nationally, *2001* was both loved and reviled by Concord audiences, who started lining up on the first night more than an hour before the doors were scheduled to open. Some exited the theater calling it one of the greatest films ever made. Others were more muted in their response and still another faction referred to it as awful or an oft-heard remark, "I don't understand what all the fuss is about!"

Theresa, not one to normally sit through an entire sci-fi film, sat down and watched it from beginning to end. She respected what Kubrick had created on-screen and liked his style of filmmaking. Because of that, she would book two more Kubrick titles in the years ahead—*Barry Lyndon* and *The Shining.*

One title that did not play the Concord was *Candy.* Based on a very popular 1958 book written by Terry Southern, *Candy* was being released by a relatively new company, Cinerama Releasing. The salesman was likeable enough but he seemed to be trying too hard in telling Theresa she would make more money than she had with *Valley of the Dolls* if she would book his film. On a Friday afternoon he called her just before five and told her he needed to know on Monday morning whether she would agree to the terms of the contract.

Sunday morning after attending the 11 a.m. mass, Theresa called me at home and invited me to attend the afternoon showing of *Candy* in Manchester at the Rex Theatre. Because of the book's reputation as well as the reviews for the film, I didn't tell my parents what we were going to see only noting that Theresa needed my help with something.

The Rex Theatre was a small but unique movie house located on Amherst Street, a few buildings down from the office of the *Manchester Union Leader,* the state's largest newspaper. William Loeb, who had made no secret of his disdain for the kind of film Hollywood was producing, had, if anything, grown even more angry since the days of *Jack the Ripper* earlier in the decade. I was surprised that "Candy" was playing so close to the paper's office and expected thunderbolts to come hurtling down Amherst and strike the Rex.

I had never been to the Rex Theatre and was surprised and delighted with the stadium seating the theater had. Today it is commonplace, but when the Rex opened and still, in the late 60s, it was innovative. As we entered I was delighted at the reality of there not being a single bad seat in the theater. A quick look around seemed to indicate that I was the youngest person in the theater.

The Motion Picture Association of America rating system had only recently begun in November of 1968. *Candy* was one of the first films to receive an X rating. This was especially surprising at the time since the movie boasted a cast that included Richard Burton, Marlon Brando and Ringo Starr. As we sat there waiting for the film to start, I self-consciously pulled my knit cap down further over my head and pulled up my turtle-neck sweater.

Candy was and is a debacle and an embarrassment to all involved in its production. As confused as I might have been at a film like *Boom*, the summer before, *Candy* just left me feeling very uncomfortable and grateful that we'd not had to pay to see it. The salesman from Cinerama Releasing had arranged for us to see it for free.

I didn't dare turn to see Theresa's response to what we were witnessing, but about 15 minutes into the film I noticed some activity out of the corner of my eye and turned to see what was happening. Theresa had reached into her pocket and taken out her rosary beads. She was beginning to silently say her rosary. At that instant I knew that *Candy* would never play the Concord Theatre.

Over lunch at Angelo's, a restaurant on Hanover Street, we talked about everything but the movie and afterwards stopped briefly at her home to retrieve some items. She no longer spent extended periods of time at the house since her theater duties required her presence into the wee hours. The upper two floors of the triple decker in Manchester were rented and the first floor, which was her home, was regularly cleaned and maintained.

Monday morning, shortly after 9, Theresa placed a call to the salesman at Cinerama Releasing and told him, "Your film isn't fit to occupy the dumpster outside my theater!"

Theresa spent much of the first half of the year preparing for the long-awaited court date for the anti-trust suit that had been filed nearly seven years earlier. Because she kept meticulous records dating back to the time she had officially taken over the theater more than twenty year earlier, the needed and extensive records were relatively easy to compile for her lawyers. The emotional toll, however, was unexpected to the normally healthy Theresa.

The Concord Theatre made the wire services in June of 1969 and not for anything related to the court case but because of a deliberate marketing effort for a picture we played as a last-minute fill-in.

The Southern Star was not a major film release although it boasted several names among its cast. George Segal, Ursula Andress and Orson Welles lead the cast of this adaptation of a Jules Verne story entitled, *The Vanished Diamond*. The salesman for Columbia Pictures, the company releasing the film, offered it to Theresa for next to nothing, so eager was he to get a playdate. Theresa jumped at it because she had some space to fill on the schedule while we awaited our next major film, Warner Brothers musical, *Finian's Rainbow* starring Fred Astaire and Petula Clark. *Rainbow* was also an early directing effort by Francis Ford Coppola.

The press book we received for *The Southern Star* didn't contain a great deal of material that we felt we could work with as we pieced together the newspaper ads that would run. Our consensus was that it would be a lean week, comparable to some of the lesser titles that were typically sprinkled in between those movies you hoped would stir some local interest.

I took a chance and asked Theresa if she'd mind me coming up with something clever to put on the marquee and she gave me permission to do "... anything that'll help us to recoup our expenses ..."

As was my custom, Thursday evening I carefully laid out all the letters in the proper order on the floor in order to have them put on the marquee once we had taken down the current attraction. I would then hold the ladder and pass the letters to the "lucky" individual who would be changing the marquee that week, while balancing precariously above South Main Street. We had three lines to fill and I felt almost giddy as to what I'd come up with.

After we changed it the marquee read:

SEE URSULA UNDRESS

IN

THE SOUTHERN STAR

On June 23, 1969, both the AP and UPI wire services featured The Concord Theatre's new feature in stories across the country.

Ursula Andress is Overpublicized (CONCORD, N.H. (AP)—The sign on the theater marquee read "See Ursula Undress in Southern Star." *The movie playing Friday night was* Southern Star, *but the featured players were Orson Wells and Ursula Andress.*

Ursula's Billing May Be Chilling CONCORD, N.H. (UPI) -The Concord Theatre is showing the film Southern Star *with Orson Welles, George Segal and Ursula Andress. The marquee reads,* "See Ursula Undress in Southern Star."

The business the film did during its one-week run was even better than we had hoped for. The Columbia salesman told us we took in far more than other cities two or three times the size of Concord. "Maybe you guys should be heading our marketing department," he said with a laugh.

Unfortunately the long-awaited court case did not have such an amusing or financially successful conclusion. After the jury reached its decision, the judge confided to one of Theresa's counsel that there was a possibility he might have erred in what he allowed shared and felt the defendants should make a settlement. Theresa's sister, Rena, who could be very blunt and direct when she chose to be, would henceforth refer to Attorney Chretien, one of two attorneys representing Theresa, as "Attorney Secretion"!

Theresa was married to her theater in the best possible way. In her life, three things mattered—her faith, her family and her theater. The Concord Theatre was not a job, because that didn't sum up what it was. It was a way of life for Theresa. She sold the tickets, made the popcorn, ordered the concession items, did the bookkeeping, studied and booked the films, paid the bills, designed the ads. She did everything except run the film and she probably could have done that too since she'd watched others do it for decades. She was also the landlady, for her business tenants (United Shoe Repair and a popular pet and aquarium shop in Concord), and those who rented from her at her Manchester residence.

The loss in court did not make her faith waver in the least, nor did it change the connections she kept with her family members. It did, briefly, rock those portions of her life that were built around the theater. For 36 years she had been in that building for the sole goal of providing entertainment and pleasure to those who walked through the front door. It was not all about making money since a dwindling number of pictures actually turned the kind of profit that you could live on. She had income from tenants and investments and that took some pressure off living on pins and needles and hoping the latest movie would do well. Far more important was being able to select titles that would arouse enough interest in someone so that they would choose to leave their home and come downtown to take in a movie.

In the four months after the court case was concluded, Theresa's health failed and she lost more than 100 pounds. She was hospitalized for several weeks and then bedridden for some months after returning home. She still roused enough energy, even from her room at Concord Hospital, to speak with film salesmen, book movies, and keep close tabs on ticket sales. Her brother Maurice and his wife Lucille worked the box office and concession in her absence with Maurice, a licensed projectionist, handling those duties. Rena and Laurie did more than their share. Theresa and I spoke on the phone almost daily.

One thing that Theresa was emphatic about doing was paying her bills. The grudging respect she had earned through the years from the sales people at the various movie companies had been partly due to the fact that she paid her bills quickly. When a movie concluded its run, a check needed to be written to the film company for the percentage to which it was entitled from the gross income the film had brought in. There were instances in some theaters of taking weeks and sometimes longer to forward the appropriate reports and paperwork along with a check. Occasionally, if a film didn't do well, a theater would try to withhold those monies for an indeterminate period of time.

With films more typically concluding their run on Thursday evening. Theresa would try to "close out" the paperwork over the weekend and have a check in the mail to the appropriate company on Monday morning.

During her recovery Theresa found great spiritual strength that helped her accept what had happened in court and to not become bitter or angry.

When she finally returned to her place at the box office she looked strikingly different due to the weight-loss and what she'd been through. She did not discuss the cancer or the colitis that she had developed while ill. When one of her regular customers, clearly thrilled to see her back at the helm, would comment about all of the weight she had, lost she would thank them and tell them that she'd found a wonderful diet secret and had decided that at 56, she'd carried around all that extra weight far too long.

The most popular movie to play during the fall of 1969 at the Concord, was the Paramount comedy-drama, *The Sterile Cuckoo* starring Liza Minnelli. It didn't hurt that a song from the film, *Come Saturday Morning*, became a big success. We had an unusually large number of people return to see the film two or three times and even had to put up the "Sold-Out" sign more than once.

Battle of Britain didn't have a chance, not with the Capitol Theatre playing *Midnight Cowboy* and Cinema 93 doing even better with *Butch Cassidy and the Sundance Kid*. That last one had virtually every customer walking out the door, after seeing the film, humming *Raindrops Keep Fallin' on My head*, the show's hit tune. *Flareup,* one of Raquel Welch's lesser efforts, started the month of December and it only went downhill from there with *Journey to the Far Side of the Sun.*

For her birthday that December, I didn't get the usual heavily frosted but delicious cake from a local bakery, Polly Susan. Instead I purchased a couple of their legendary eclairs and Theresa and I feasted on them while mapping out strategy for the right film to welcome in a new decade— the 1970s. Unfortunately the Christmas/New Year attraction was not well-received.

The Gypsy Moths certainly had talent attached to it. The MGM production was directed by John Frankenheimer and starred Burt Lancaster, Deborah Kerr and Gene Hackman. Lancaster and Kerr had co-starred twice previously including the classic 1953 film, *From Here to Eternity.* The studio promoted this movie by letting everyone know that the 48-year-old Kerr would be doing her first nude scene on screen. Nobody seemed to want to see it.

On New Year's Eve, not a single person showed up to purchase a ticket and so we closed early, putting a sign on the door that read "Happy 1970— See you at the Movies!" The crowds would be back but the new decade that was dawning would forever change the way that Concord residents went to the movies.

Chapter Twenty-one

IN THE 1970S ONE OF MANY CHANGES that took place in the motion picture business and in the perception the public had of the movies, involved the "Star System." Almost since the advent of the moving picture, there had been stars. From the earliest days, the public took to certain individuals they saw on the screen and designated them as movie stars. Some lasted for many years and others shone briefly and then faded into obscurity. Where once a particular name like Gable or Garbo or Astaire and Rogers, could almost guarantee success that was not always the case in the 1970s. The producer and director became much more prominent players than they'd been in the past, and movies were becoming more about the subject matter and whether that appealed to an audience. Big hits like *Bonnie and Clyde, Easy Rider* and *The Graduate* were not wildly popular because of the names attached to them but rather because of the story and general appeal to a public that was seeking edgier and more mature filmmaking.

Quigley Publications had been annually publishing a list, since the early 30s, of the top moneymaking stars—those whose name alone brought in the crowds to a movie. Each year when Quigley sent out the annual ballot to Theresa, she completed it and mailed it in. Often, after having sent the ballot, Theresa would chat with Arthur Dame about the polling and its importance. Arthur was adamant about doing it since he felt strongly about movie exhibitors having a place at the table and being heard.

In 1970 Quigley also published a list of the top drawing male and female star of the decade of the 1960s. The top male was John Wayne and the top female was Doris Day. Interestingly these were also the most popular local stars. In fact Arthur Dame told Theresa one evening, while visiting the theater, that "I wish I could play Doris Day or John Wayne every weekend out in Pittsfield. They both sell-out and Vaulien and I wouldn't have a care in the world if we could alternate between those two stars."

Wayne had been making movies for more than 40 years and Day had been a star for more than two decades. Wayne would only make a few more films, wrapping his legendary career with a well-received 1976 film entitled, *The Shootist* which played Cinema 93. Several years later he would succumb to a long battle with cancer.

Doris Day had already moved on to television where her CBS comedy series had a long and successful run well into the 70s. Despite dozens of offers to return to the screen, she would not. Wayne and Day, however, remained fixed in audience minds for several more years as well-loved film stars. *Family Weekly*, in a 1972 polling of their readers found that Wayne and Day were still the "Favorite Movie Stars" of their many readers!

While there were still some name stars from the mid-50s who commanded audience loyalty, especially in Concord, including Paul Newman, Robert Redford and Steve McQueen, Elizabeth Taylor barely caused a ripple.

At the Concord in early 1970, we played her latest film, *The Only Game in Town*, co-starring Warren Beatty, fresh off "Bonnie and Clyde." We didn't draw 500 people during a two-week run. The terms from 20th Century Fox were so high that they would have seemed to indicate a major hit. The film, however, didn't generate sales anywhere, posting an enormous loss in the millions.

Clint Eastwood was well-liked by Concord audiences. The former television star had really begun making a ripple on the big screen in the mid-60s and throughout the 70s and 80s, he would become extremely popular. Barbra Streisand, on the other hand, never connected in a big way with Concord audiences. If she happened to be in the right role and the story appealed to an audience, it would do well but simply putting her name on the marquee, did not guarantee a good return.

The Concord Theatre played a couple of movies in which she starred. *On a Clear Day You Can See Forever* was a big-budget Paramount musical about reincarnation, directed by Vincente Minnelli. It played in late summer of 1970 for two weeks and we could barely give away tickets. *Up The Sandbox* was a comedy that disappeared with barely a trace when it played.

I recall several people walking out and noting as they passed the box office that it seemed like it was a comedy without any laughs. On the other hand, a comedy like *What's Up Doc* went over very well, and when Cinema 93 played *The Way We Were*, there were lines.

Other stars who sparkled on the silver screen in the 70s included Jane Fonda, who had been building a steady career in the 60s but won two Oscars as Best Actress in the 1970s. Jill Clayburgh and Marsha Mason both earned Academy Award nominations for their work in the 70s, and names like Stephen Spielberg, Woody Allen, Neil Simon, Martin Scorsese, George Lucas and Peter Bogdanovich were among the prominent names creating the magic behind the camera.

The 1970s proved to be especially difficult for the smaller, second-run theaters like the Palace in Penacook and the Scenic in Pittsfield. With more and more families having two cars, people were less willing to wait to see a movie when it would finally reach their local theater. The Manchester theaters began advertising in the Concord paper, promoting titles that would not play Concord for some weeks and, in many cases, months.

The State Theatre in Manchester was divided into two with an escalator taking patrons from the first floor up to what had been the balcony. That area had been converted into a second cinema. It was rechristened Cine 1 and Cine 2. The Rex on Amherst Street was renamed The King Cinema, and these theaters along with the two-screen General Cinema located in the Bedford Mall, lured many Concord residents to Manchester.

By the mid-70s, the entire releasing pattern for movies began to evolve, due to the arrival of what became known as "The Summer Blockbuster!"

Theresa also commented how some patterns of viewing had greatly changed during the 60s, leading into the 1970s. For decades, attendance would drop radically during Lent. It seemed as though, during that six-week period, Catholics stopped going to the movies. Theresa wondered whether they'd made abstinence from moviegoing their Lenten vow. By the 70s, that seemed to no longer be the case. If you had a film people wanted to see, they definitely turned out to see it.

During the summer of 1970, the Concord Theatre played a musical film that would rank as the most attended musical film in the Concord Theatre's history.

Woodstock the documentary about the 1969 concert, was three hours in length, which limited the number of daily screenings we could have, but virtually every performance during the first week was a sell-out. It continued doing strong box office for several more weeks. It seemed as though the vast majority of the attendees had never been to the Concord Theatre before, based upon the inquiries as to where the rest rooms were.

Elsie Campbell, the house mother at the Friendly Club next door, was extremely concerned about the crowds showing up at the Concord to see this particular film. It was a completely different element than she was used to seeing hanging around outside the theater.

Elsie was by no means overly stuffy and I knew her from the Concord Community Players. She also had three extraordinarily talented daughters who could sing, dance and act and even Elsie had taken to the stage at the Concord City Auditorium on several occasions.

The Friendly Club had been a mainstay in Concord for many years. Their message had been:

"The Friendly Club of Concord, New Hampshire, is a club for girls and women. Its object is to form a social center for mutual service and education of women, which shall provide for self-improvement,' recreation and friendly intercourse. Its sphere of interest and action is unlimited. It is non-sectarian. It embraces all classes."

Now suddenly the driveway between the theater and the Friendly Club was filled with what Elsie referred to as "those hippie types" and there was a smell of smoke filling the air that was unlike what anyone had smelled before. "Those definitely aren't Winstons," she exclaimed more than once. She took her responsibility to her girls with a great deal of seriousness although she was not domineering, demanding, or lacking in a great deal of warmth. She was in actuality a very engaging and funny person and frequently visited the theater to chat with Theresa.

Concord Police Chief Walter Carlson would often stop at the theater during the run of *Woodstock* to make sure the audience wasn't getting out of control. On a regular basis, Chief Carlson had the officer who had the "downtown beat" drop by the theater to be a presence. These officers including Bill Barnard, who became a fixture with his evening visits, reminding us of how fortunate we were to live in a community where you felt a genuine connection and concern between people. Officer Barnard would stop in each evening when he was on duty, promptly at 7:45. He would come in, greet Theresa and then go inside the auditorium and look around to make sure nothing of concern was going on. Theresa enjoyed the reassurance his visits brought.

We quickly discovered during the engagement of *Woodstock* that the audience wanted the music cranked up to the maximum. They wanted to feel as though they were attending the concert and you could practically feel the building vibrating from the throbbing beat of the music.

Less successful that summer was a Julie Andrews musical from Paramount. *Darling Lili*, co-starring Rock Hudson and directed by Julie's soon-to-be husband, Blake Edwards, was long and not especially memorable. In the two years since *Thoroughly Modern Millie* had scored big at the Concord, Julie's star had dimmed considerably. In-between had been *Star*, a costly 20th Century Fox film that we pulled after one week of dismal business. Fortunately the next time we played a film featuring Julie Andrews in 1979, the crowds would come out in force. That 1979 film—*10*—had people more focused on the antics of Dudley Moore or the alluring presence of Bo Derek, than on Miss Andrews.

The last time we had played a movie adaptation of a D.H. Lawrence story, *The Fox*, we had run into all kinds of flack locally. Nobody complained at all when we played Ken Russell's movie version of Lawrence's *Women in Love*. The film won an Oscar as Best Actress for Glenda Jackson, who would win a second Oscar several years later. It co-starred Alan Bates and Oliver Reed and did tremendous business despite the nudity and other explicit scenes that it contained.

Theresa liked Glenda Jackson's style of acting and un-movie star look. Glenda had made an impact on PBS when she played Queen Elizabeth I. As a movie actress Jackson became a regular fixture at the Concord during the next few years, starring in *Mary Queen of Scots, A Bequest to the Nation* which was released in the United States with the title, *The Nelson Affair* and the hugely popular comedy, *House Calls* co-starring Walter Matthau. Jackson's cameo appearance in Ken Russell's musical, *The Boy Friend* starring Twiggy, went a long way toward convincing Theresa to book that particular film.

The Boy Friend was another of the many musicals to grace the Concord Theatre's screen during the 1970s. In Theresa's way of thinking, it was never about making a fortune by playing a musical. It was about providing an option for movie fans who liked musicals, the chance to enjoy one. If the planets were aligned and the film musical also proved to be a success at the box office, all the better. Theresa was firm, however, in her belief that you should not always take the safest route possible.

Of the musicals that played in the 70s, the two most popular were clearly *Saturday Night Fever* and *Grease*. Nothing else even came close. During *Grease* in the summer of 1978, some attendees proudly boasted that it was their 30th, 40th or even 50th time seeing the film. Both films generated an enormous energy in the theater. It was also not unusual to have members of the audience break into spontaneous applause after an especially spirited musical number.

Grease opened on June 21, 1978, and the evening before Theresa and I had talked about our expectations around the film's possible success. The deal with Paramount, the releasing company, was stiff but not as bad as for some titles that had played. I was working days at Blue Cross and Blue Shield on Pillsbury Street in Concord. I worked in the personnel department when it was called that and not human resources.

Throughout the day I'd heard and overheard dozens of conversations about how excited people were that *Grease* was opening in Concord. The excitement reached such a crescendo by 3 p.m. that I called Theresa at the theater and suggested we open the doors earlier than the scheduled 6:30. She reluctantly agreed after I told her what I'd been hearing.

When I arrived at the theater at 6:05, there was already a line outside stretching beyond nearby Endicott Furniture and so we opened the doors a bit after 6:10. The first showing was scheduled for 7 and by 6:55, every one of the 499 seats in the theater was filled.

Also musically successful was *Tom Sawyer* (1973) with music by the Sherman Brothers of Disney fame and starring Johnny Whitaker and Jodie Foster. It didn't just appeal to the kiddies at matinee showings, but a good number of adults decided to check out the new musical take on a beloved story. *New York, New York* (1977), a Martin Scorsese musical with Robert De Niro and Liza Minnelli and introducing a great title song, disappointed a few customers who were expecting a lighthearted musical romp. Instead they got a more gritty and tough drama with music. *That's Entertainment* (1974) the MGM anthology film was welcomed enthusiastically while the 1976 follow-up did not do well. When the salesman tried to talk Theresa into playing the third in the series, she politely declined.

Musicals hitting a sour note at the box office in the 70s included *Goodbye Mr. Chips, 1776, Lost Horizon, Man of La Mancha* and several others not even worth mentioning.

Without a doubt the worst musical that ever played the Concord Theatre and certainly one of the worse movies bar none was a 1976 film called *The Blue Bird*. It was a joint U.S.-Soviet production directed by the legendary George Cukor. Cukor was an Oscar winner and had directed some of the finest films of the 1930s through the 1960s. *The Blue Bird* starred Elizabeth Taylor, Jane Fonda, Cicely Tyson, Ava Gardner and Robert Morley. Based on a fantasy that had been filmed most notably starring Shirley Temple in 1940, there was no magic about this film and the music, such as it was, was tuneless.

It was not uncommon for parents to drop their children off at the Concord Theatre if there was a matinee performance for something even mildly acceptable for a child to see. Theresa sometimes referred to herself as a glorified babysitter, keeping an eye on the children while the parents shopped on Main Street or grabbed a bite to eat somewhere. During the brief run of *The Blue Bird,* a woman came in with two screaming children, paid for their tickets, got them settled inside and left, asking what time the film would let out.

I said to Theresa, "These kids are screaming before even seeing this thing. Imagine how they'll be after sitting through it!"

The Concord Theatre probably had the unenviable task of having played the five or six biggest bombs of Elizabeth Taylor's long career. Certainly *The Blue Bird* qualifies as the worse. However, *The Only Game in Town, Hammersmith is Out, Ash Wednesday* and *X Y and ZEE* also known as "Zee and Company" are almost equally bad.

At times when we had movies like *The Blue Bird* on the screen, Theresa would shake her head and note, "I'm glad I'm not relying on the income from a dud like this to put food on the table."

One evening in 1972, Richard O. Blanchard, an English teacher at Concord High School and fondly known as "Doc Blanchard," stopped in to chat with Theresa. He was a regular attendee at the movies. I knew him slightly from my mother having directed him in a Concord Community Players production of *A Man For All Seasons*, several years earlier.

"Miss Cantin, there is a movie in release that I feel has real value and it's called *The Trojan Women* from the Euripides story." Watching Theresa, it was obvious that she was taking in what he was saying with seriousness.

They chatted for about ten minutes and Theresa promised that she would investigate the availability of the film the next morning. She did indeed place a call to the salesman for Cinerama Releasing, the company distributing the film. This was the same company that had distributed the infamous *Candy* a few years earlier.

Theresa was able to buy a one-week run of *The Trojan Women* to play in September of 1972. She paid a flat rate for the film since it was not a title that many theater owners were eager to bid on or book due to its subject matter. On the plus side, it boasted a cast headed by Katharine Hepburn, Vanessa Redgrave, Genevieve Bujold and Irene Papas. Theresa acknowledged to me and her sisters that she didn't expect to make much money on the film but respected Mr. Blanchard and his opinion.

The Trojan Women played for a week and attracted about 150 paying customers. It was a crowd that barely bought concession and after paying for advertising, electricity, and other normal expenses, took a loss of about $650. That did not faze Theresa because she noted that almost every person who had attended stopped as they were exiting the theater to thank her for bringing the movie to Concord.

Later that same year the Concord Theatre played a movie that would be brought back for return engagements more than any other motion picture in the theater's history. It became a kind of "go to" film whenever there was either a lapse in the schedule or when another movie played and did not do the anticipated business.

Butterflies are Free was a Columbia release and starred Goldie Hawn, Edward Albert and Eileen Heckart. Miss Heckart would win an Academy Award as Best Supporting Actress for her role in the film. Prior to being filmed, *Butterflies* had been a successful stage play.

The summer of 1972 had been a rather dismal one at the theater. While you may aim high and try to get pictures that will draw large crowds, there is no guarantee that your efforts will yield the best results. Many of the films that played the Concord that summer are long forgotten. The titles included *Hannie Caulder, The War Between Men and Women, The Last of the Red Hot Lovers, The Burglars, Nightcomers,* and *Red Sun.*

While there were several films that were critically acclaimed including Roman Polanski's *Macbeth, Mary Queen of Scots,* the Oscar-winning Best Foreign Film, *The Garden of the Finzi Continis* and Robert Redford's *The Candidate,* none of them drew as well as some of the pictures that played the Capitol Theatre and Cinema 93. The Capitol had an especially big success with Alfred Hitchcock's *Frenzy* while Cinema 93 was packing them in with *Clockwork Orange, What's Up Doc* and *Cabaret.*

On August 3, 1972, the Jerry Lewis Cinemas opened in Hooksett, about a dozen miles south of Concord. This twin cinema attracted a great deal of attention in the greater Concord community and drew many customers that traveled from Concord, to this modern facility. Within a few years it would become The Movie Center. For many it also became the place known for having the stickiest floors of any theater they'd ever been to. One woman swore to Theresa that her flip-flops had stuck to the floor and she'd walked right out of them.

When Columbia awarded *Butterflies are Free* to Theresa they assured her it would be a nice film to play for the contracted two weeks and that she'd do nicely. Based upon those remarks, we were not expecting it to be an overwhelming smash hit. We did rationalize that Goldie Hawn was well-liked and the story sounded promising.

Butterflies are Free opened on Wednesday, October 25, 1972, for a two-week engagement. The first two days were slow but suddenly on Friday the business swelled. It continued over the weekend and didn't let up on weekdays as was often the case. Monday and Tuesday could be deadly, businesswise, which was one of the reasons that the Concord Theatre often found itself closing on those evenings in the early 1960s. *Butterflies,* however, remained strong and the second week surpassed the first in business. It was one of those instances when word of mouth did more to propel a film to success than anything else.

Naturally Theresa wanted to keep it a third week but was informed that the print of the film had been booked elsewhere. Our next attraction, *Cancel My Reservation,* should have been cancelled. The Bob Hope comedy had no laughs and no customers. Again Theresa called Columbia in the hope that *Butterflies* might be available and was again told that no prints were available for "some weeks." She asked to be placed on the list of those eager to bring it back should a print become available.

The films we did have scheduled were a somewhat sad lot. *Stigmas, You'll Like My Mother and Portnoy's Complaint,* based on a widely popular book that didn't translate to the screen with equal success. The Christmas attraction, *Ulzana's Raid* was probably the least successful film to play during the holidays in all the years that I was associated with the Concord. *Play it as it Lays* was so bad it was pulled out in favor of a British comedy, *Carry on Doctor,* which was several years old.

Finally on January 10, 1973, *Butterflies are Free* returned for one week. The business during that one-week was more than the film had made during its two previous weeks combined.

We could only keep it that one week having committed to playing *Travels with My Aunt* on the 17th. No one seemed to want to travel with this particular aunt, although Maggie Smith, in the title role, was outstanding. Every phone call the theater received only wanted to know if and when *Butterflies are Free* was going to return.

On Jan. 24 it did return for another week and the business was almost equal to the prior one-week run. We tried to extend it again but were told we'd have to wait as it was booked elsewhere. We proceeded with our scheduled film, *Hammersmith is Out*, probably the nadir of Elizabeth Taylor and Richard Burton's careers. If we thought *Boom* had been bad in 1968, it was a work of art compared to this dark comedy that cast Taylor as a waitress slinging hash.

Butterflies returned on Feb. 7 and on the first night Arthur Dame showed-up, too. He couldn't imagine why his friend Theresa was showing the same movie for a fourthh time and thought something might be going wrong. He was met by a wildly enthusiastic audience and left the theater that evening determined to book the film in Pittsfield as soon as possible.

He was hopeful of playing it before the drive-ins opened for the season and might book it.

This last engagement of *Butterflies* did very well, although it was finally clear that the film had been seen by most of those wanting to see it. There had been many repeat viewers and for some reason it hit a chord for the Concord audience that was completely unexpected. The movie was a box-office success nationally but not a blockbuster or anything approximating that. Columbia told Theresa that her engagement of the film had brought in more than the picture had taken in at any other New Hampshire theater.

Chapter Twenty-two

AMONG THE MANY WAYS that Hollywood attempted to attract audiences in the 1970s was by filming a series of disaster films. In some cases these motion pictures turned out to be disastrous. For a while, however, the genre produced enormous revenue for the studios and more than a few thrills for the audiences that flocked to see them.

Appropriately enough this type of film got off to a huge start in early 1970 with the release of *Airport*, based on the best-selling book of the same title. The fact that it was produced by Ross Hunter, who had an amazing track record of success, only further enhanced interest. The all-star cast was headed by Dean Martin and Burt Lancaster and the movie won Helen Hayes an Oscar as Best Supporting Actress. Universal released the title, and Walter was doing hand springs over the film's success. It did not play the Concord Theatre but found a home for its lengthy run at Cinema 93.

The series of *Airport* sequels that followed throughout the 70s, eventually helped to obliterate the disaster film genre. Before that happened, there were a few notable successes. Finally the tide turned and the public grew tired, resulting in diminishing box office results and an almost camp-like quality taking over the films in place of storytelling.

The first sequel, *Airport 75*, played to good audiences at the Capitol Theatre during its 1974 engagement. The third and fourth (*Airport 77* and *The Concorde—Airport 79*) ended up at the Concord Theatre. Walter promised Theresa that they would be bigger than the first! His effusiveness, at times, was impossible to resist. The 1980 comedy hit *Airplane* forever obliterated any chance that an audience would take one of the "Airport like" films seriously.

Irwin Allen, who had already been making films for years, helped to truly define the 1970s disaster film with his 1972 smash hit, *The Poseidon*

Adventure. Even Theresa and I ventured over to Cinema 93 to see what all the fuss was about and joined the crowd who audibly enjoyed every moment of the film. Theresa decided, after seeing the movie that she wanted to play the next similar themed film. Knowing Hollywood filmmakers after years of working in the business, she was certain that Hollywood would be eager to try to repeat a success.

Universal, and Producer Jennings Lang were eager to make what they decided would be the ultimate disaster movie—a film in which the audience would feel as though they were a part of the movie. *Earthquake* was the title they came up with, and they set about finding a way in which they could make the audience feel as though they were experiencing the same quake that stars such as Charlton Heston, Lorne Greene and Ava Gardner were feeling on-screen.

The sound engineers at Universal developed something they called "Sensurround." It consisted of a series of large speakers powered by amplifiers that would pump sound waves at 120 decibels. They tested the system at the world-famous Grauman's Chinese Theatre in Hollywood and it cracked plaster in the historic theater's ceiling. While the film did eventually play the Chinese, the theater, as a precaution, installed a net over the audience for the purpose of collecting any debris that might fall.

Walter, Universal's salesman for the region, arranged for Theresa and me to attend a screening of the film for the purpose of seeing and feeling for ourselves how dramatic the new effect was. Indeed it worked, keeping us awake, although the film itself, when the quake wasn't going on and the storyline was dragging, lacked the impact and power of *The Poseidon Adventure*. We found ourselves not especially caring about the characters in *Earthquake* or their eventual fates.

Theresa had genuine concerns about damage that might occur at the Concord Theatre if the large speakers were installed and played at the level required by the contract for a run of the film. She had the small chandeliers that hung in the auditorium replaced by fluorescent lighting at the juncture where the ceiling met the wall. While this lighting proved more efficient on several levels, it eliminated the nice touch of slowly dimming the theater lights as the red footlights against the curtain provided a lovely allure prior to the curtains opening and the start of a film.

The terms to play *Earthquake* ultimately led to our deciding against showing the movie. We also decided to not try to negotiate to play *Airport 75* and to instead go after, aggressively, the upcoming Irwin Allen film, *The Towering Inferno*. *Earthquake* eventually played the Capitol Theatre but without the Sensurround effects, which were really the only thing that made the film stand out. Without it, it was a rather tedious and unexciting drama. Universal used Sensurround for two subsequent film releases, *Midway* in 1976 and *Rollercoaster* in 1977. Neither film turned out to be overwhelmingly successful and the gimmick of Sensurround was discarded.

The Towering Inferno was a co-production between 20th Century Fox and Warner Brothers. From what the salesman said and from what we read, it seemed to have hit written all over it. With a cast that was headed by Paul Newman, Steve McQueen and Faye Dunaway, Theresa was confident that the response from her customers would be very good.

Although it opened in many major cities prior to Christmas of 1974, it was not available for Concord until Jan. 29, 1975. Even though the Manchester theaters continued to advertise in the Concord paper and we would lose some customers to Manchester, Theresa felt that as a film *Inferno* would be vastly superior to the two recent Universal disaster epics. She was right.

January had been a slow month, picture wise, with such titles as *The Odessa File* (Jon Voight), *The Destructors* (Anthony Quinn) and *The Klansman* (Richard Burton and Lee Marvin)

On Jan, the lines once again stretched down the street and continued to form daily during its five-week run.

The Towering Inferno would be nominated for eight Academy Awards including Best Picture. Many critics felt that it was by far the best of the disaster films churned out in the 1970s. Theresa was happy that she'd declined to negotiate for the two Universal films and had instead worked toward obtaining this film.

Sometimes a theater is fortunate and has two box office winners in a row. Having three in a row, however, is a genuine rarity but it does happen. In the time period between the opening of *The Towering Inferno* and the latter part of April, the Concord Theatre had three successive films that were both critical and box office powerhouses, to use a phrase often bandied about in *Variety* to describe a hit.

Young Frankenstein followed the five-week run of *Inferno* and did almost as well. Dozens of people came back to laugh it up a second or third time. On many evenings the sound at the theater had to be cranked up to the maximum in order to hear the onscreen dialogue over the loud and raucous laughter. Theresa had been concerned that someone might complain about the movie being filmed in black and white but not a word was said.

The third title in this triumvirate, *Lenny,* turned out to be the film that brought the theater the largest box-office profit of the three films.

While *The Towering Inferno* and *Young Frankenstein* had brought more than 12,000 attendees apiece, the terms for the films were stiff, with the majority of the box-office revenue being returned to the film company. Fortunately both titles generated great sales at the concession stand where many theaters actually make enough revenue to keep going. Arthur Dame often said that without strong concession sales, he wasn't sure if his Scenic Theatre could keep going.

Lenny was made by United Artists and was the story of comedian Lenny Bruce, as portrayed by Dustin Hoffman. Bob Fosse directed and the film was critically acclaimed, including being nominated for six Academy Awards. Despite that, the consensus was that the film was not going to be a great popular success outside of major cities. The salesman for United Artists, the film's distributor, told Theresa, when she called him that, "Theresa, this won't draw 500 people in Concord. Don't waste a booking."

Theresa had been doing her research as had I. We also knew that Hoffman was well-liked in Concord. He had recently co-starred in *Papillion* which was a big success for Cinema 93, and so Theresa continued badgering the salesman. He finally gave in and told her she could have the film for a flat rate of $2,500. In other words, every cent over that amount would be profit for the theater.

We designed some appealing ads and hoped that our instincts were right.

While concession was virtually non-existent during the picture's run of several weeks, the box office was very, very strong and the comments from audience members were almost unanimously raves. Theresa's profit, after paying the $2,500, was just under $10,000.

By the mid-1970s, the Capitol Theatre was falling on hard times. Mr. Eldridge, who had managed it as if it were his own, had retired and projectionist Brad Callahan was the new manager. The expenses associated with the enormous space were considerable. Heating, air conditioning and general cleaning and maintenance ran into the thousands each week. For years the Capitol Theatre had advertised their films not only in the newspaper but with scores of placards that were in windows of businesses throughout Concord. It was always eye-catching and with the theater usually doing split-weeks well into the 1960s, this allowed you the opportunity to prepare in advance for what you wanted to see. By the 70s the Capitol was playing a title for a full week and that often meant on a Monday or Tuesday having an audience of less than 100. In fact on Monday and Tuesday, in the hopes of drawing a few people, the Capitol Theatre would often only charge half price for tickets.

The days of the 1,400-seat movie palace were fast coming to a close. In December 1971, I decided to take in the latest Disney film playing the Capitol Theatre. *Million Dollar Duck* does not rank anywhere near the top of the list of Disney classics or the films made during Disney's life. It was a mildly amusing slapstick comedy with Sandy Duncan and Dean Jones.

There were probably less than 150 of us at the matinee I attended. As a child being taken to the Capitol Theatre for a Disney matinee, it was not unusual to see the place filled. There were even a few instances when we were turned away because no seats were available.

About 20 minutes into the film, a woman let out a loud scream. She continued screaming until the manager, Brad Callahan, had rushed to her seat. She explained she had been bitten by something running between the seats. There was blood visible on her ankle and Brad stopped the film, turned on the lights and arranged to have monies refunded to those in the audience. My parents knew the woman who had been bitten and her husband was a prominent businessman in the Concord community. A few weeks later she told my parents that Callahan had promised her and her family a lifetime pass to the theater if she did not involve code enforcement officials, health officials or Police Chief Walter Carlson.

She reluctantly agreed, not wanting it to go further but she did visit Concord Hospital and received treatment for what they determined to be a rat bite. Former Manager Frank Eldridge would have been appalled at how far his beloved theater had fallen.

The Alosa family, a name everyone in Concord knew and respected, took over the Capitol in the 1970s, continuing a policy of showing films and also bringing concert acts to the community. The concert acts did very well for a while. The Alosa family also continued the long tradition of presenting the free Gile Concerts at the Capitol. The Gile Concerts were the result of an endowment, the interest of which was utilized to bring a number of celebrated performing artists, orchestras and ballet to the city at no cost to those who attended. The ebullient John "Pudgy" Alosa ran the theater and because of Theresa's personal affection for him, she provided counseling to him on how to secure films. She also introduced him to several of the salesmen from the various companies.

For several years in the 1970s, Concord had the distinction of having three independently owned first-run movie theaters. The only theaters that were part of a chain during that time period were the two drive-ins owned by Lockwood and Gordon. Still later in the 1980s the Capitol Theatre once again tried showing films, often double features at bargain basement prices. It didn't work and by the late 1980s the place sat quiet.

The Exorcist had created quite a stir when it opened in late 1973. While critics hailed the film, various church groups had vehemently spoken out against it and a number of editorials had condemned the film for its frankness. Some accused it of being exploitive. Others called it an instant classic. It took over a year before The Exorcist finally arrived at the Concord Theatre and it made its landing in the fall of 1974 without so much as a whimper. Although hundreds if not thousands had gone to Manchester to see it when it played a lengthy engagement prior to the Concord booking, there were still large crowds that took it in at the Concord.

In 1969 John Wayne had etched a fine and memorable portrayal as Rooster Cogburn, earning himself an Oscar in the process, in the hit western, True Grit. It was one of Cinema 93's great hits at the time and when Walter giddily told Theresa that Universal was making the sequel to the Paramount classic, she decided it was a film worth pursuing. Theresa, her sister Laurie, my friend Mark Boback and I drove to Manchester to see the new film which was titled, *Rooster Cogburn*, at the Bedford Mall Cinema. The sold-out theater audience was clearly having the time of their lives that November day, and it convinced Theresa to agree to the somewhat steep terms of the contract to bring it to Concord. Our Christmas attraction for 1975 was the weakest in many years—a second-run showing of Universal's *Jaws*, a film everyone had seen the summer before. Walter, however, wanted us to play it and put pressure on securing the booking. Not wanting to upset Walter, Theresa agreed to play *Jaws*, anticipating a quick run and the opening in January of *Rooster Cogburn*.

Rooster Cogburn was a huge hit. The movie, which co-starred another legend, Katharine Hepburn, had received mixed reviews, and business had ranged from okay to very good across the country, according to Variety. Concord audiences responded in a way that would indicate "exceptional" being the appropriate description to use. As with any John Wayne movie, people came who'd not been in the Concord Theatre in years. One man noted that the last time he was there was in 1972 when he saw John Wayne in *The Cowboys*.

On the opening night an incident occurred that was so typical of Theresa. It was something I'd seen her do many times before and would many more times in the future. What made it different was the fact that it had never happened before with an audience exceeding 300.

About 15 minutes before the scheduled start of the first showing, Theresa received a telephone call from a man who lived in Henniker, a 20-minute drive from Concord.

The gentleman identified himself and Theresa knew instantly who he was. He was a longtime customer who had frequented the theater since the 1940s when he was a young child. He was one of those loyal customers of longstanding that she especially valued.

"Theresa," he began, "I am running a bit late and just now leaving the house. I probably won't be there for 20 minutes or so. Are there previews or a short subject first, before the feature? I don't want to miss the beginning of the movie."

National Screen, per orders of Walter, had indeed sent a short subject. However, after checking it the evening before when the feature was delivered, Theresa refused to run the short. It was a short subject that had been sent almost as often as that Woody Woodpecker cartoon that seemed to have taken up a permanent residence at the Concord.

The short, clearly filmed in the late 30s or early 40s judging by the quality of the photography, the clothes the children were wearing and the shabbiness of the production values in general, seemed to serve no purpose. Theresa had no intention of running it to a "Wayne audience" as she put it.

She assured the caller that she would hold the film until he got there but to please hurry along, adding, "But don't speed. A speeding ticket will cost you more than a movie ticket!"

Theresa asked me to sit in her seat at the box office for a few minutes while she went to the back of the theater to address the waiting crowd.

Her voice was clearly heard by everyone. "Excuse me, ladies and gentlemen. The movie is going to be delayed starting by about 5 or 10 minutes. One of our longtime customers is driving in from Henniker and will be a few minutes late. I realize this may inconvenience some of you and if it does, please come back to the box office. I'll gladly refund your ticket price and give you a complimentary pass for a future movie. While you're waiting, if anyone would like a free small popcorn, it's on the house!"

Almost every person inside came out for the free popcorn but not a soul asked for a refund. It took me and Theresa's two sisters, Rena and Laurie, to pass out the more than 200 free popcorns requested but the goodwill in the air was palpable. They'd come to enjoy "The Duke" and they did responding with applause at his first on-screen appearance and at the end. Almost, to a person, they thanked Theresa as they exited.

After the negative publicity surrounding the aborted showing of *Jack the Ripper* in 1960, Theresa had declined a number of requests to be interviewed about the theater and her long role in running it. In 1973, the theater's 40th anniversary, there had been a new spate of requests, all of which she declined.

In the fall of 1974, however, she agreed to talk with Judith Vachon for a story to appear in the Nov. 9, 1974 edition of the *Concord Monitor*. She refused to pose for a picture to accompany the article. She didn't like having her picture taken and was self-conscious as to how she appeared in a photo. She did agree to let a picture of the theater's marquee be taken to accompany the article.

The story noted the unusual relationship that Theresa held with her paying customers relating that they ". . . seem to feel free to discuss the pictures with her. They tell her when they aren't pleased . . ."

In the article Theresa stated, "In most places, people don't comment to the cashier or employees. But here it's more friendly. If someone comes up to me and says, 'Do you think I'll like this picture?' and I know they won't, then I tell them the truth."

Telling the truth was a key component in Theresa's long success just as it was with Barry Steelman and Cinema 93.

Chapter Twenty-three

THE TERM "FOUR WALL" would mean little to most members of the movie-going public. It would, however, mean something to anyone associated with booking films or running a theater in the 1970s. For a while "four wall deals" seemed to be the coming wave of movie distribution.

Sunn Classic Pictures, a Utah-based entity, was one of the biggest forces behind this method of film distribution. It met with phenomenal success for several years.

Four wall refers to the four walls of your theater. A "four wall deal" means the studio or distributor rents your theater for the length of time the film is scheduled to play, and takes all of the box-office revenue. You get to keep all of the concession monies and there are usually a lot of those. It also brings in a lot of individuals to your theater who do not regularly attend movies. Sunn International and the other studios/distributors that used this method for releasing films, heavily promoted their films on television, thereby increasing the public interest in what was to be shown.

The theater showing the film did receive mostly free print advertising, paid for by the company. It also received a weekly "nut"—terminology for your weekly expenses to keep the theater open. These expenses included salaries, insurance, electricity, taxes or rent, etc. At the Concord this totaled about $1,000 per week. Sunn or a similar releasing company would make out very well using this type of strategy, since these films would generally draw 4,000 to 6,000 customers in a week. It was not uncommon for it to see a profit exceeding $10,000 for some of the better titles. Of course it also sent a checker to every performance, just to make sure it didn't miss out on a penny.

Among the better-known titles that were distributed in this fashion were *In Search of Noah's Ark, In Search of Historic Jesus, Chariots of the Gods* and *The Life and Times of Grizzly Adams*, which later became a television series. Other titles included *The Wilderness Family, Beyond and Back, The Bermuda Triangle* and *The Lincoln Conspiracy*. Tom Laughlin also used the four-wall method to distribute his movie, *Billy Jack*. The Concord first went this route in 1974 with the Sunn International release of *Brother of the Wind*. While negotiating the deal, Theresa found the people associated with Sunn International to be rather difficult, demanding and, at times, disrespectful. During one conversation, the salesperson even insisted Theresa put on the phone, ". . . the man who runs your theater . . ."

Brother of the Wind opened a one-week engagement on Wednesday, Feb. 13, 1974. Sunn International dictated the number of showings it wanted during the week's run. There would be two evening shows Wednesday through Friday as well as Monday and Tuesday. On Saturday and Sunday, however, there would be five daily showings. The film ran 88 minutes and in consultation with Sunn International, Theresa scheduled the weekend showings for 2, 3:30, 5, 7 and 9. I urged her to reconsider the times, suggesting she allow more time in-between showings.

"What if you have 250 for the first show at 2 and the same number for the next showing at 3:30? You'll never be able to get everyone out and the new group in within that time frame." Sunn International was insistent on the times that had been set, and we accepted the demands.

Needless to say, the crowds turned out in force, and the 3:30 show didn't start until nearly 4. The 5:00 show started after 5:30, the 7:00 show began at about 7:45, which meant the evening's last showing didn't start until after 9:30. The audience, however, didn't seem to mind and were clearly there to have a good time.

By the time the film canisters were picked-up late Tuesday evening, more than 7,000 people had attended the scheduled 20 screenings. While that was a lot of money in the pocket of Sunn International, the Concord Theatre didn't do too badly. Theresa told me that the profit from concession sales had topped $5,000. That was considerably more money than the combined box office take and concession sales for the film that followed. *The Thief Who Came to Dinner* starring Ryan O' Neal and Jacqueline Bisset was, in Theresa's words, a Biblical disaster."

Theresa spruced up the theater in various ways during the 1970s. She painted quite a bit of the exterior a very bright yellow, which certainly made it stand out. I referred to it as "Doris Day Sunshine!" Unfortunately it also showed the dirt more easily necessitating a regular hosing down, which I offered to do a couple of times. She also put a nice rug in the upper lobby by the concession stand and drink machine. The area had been tiled for many years but the tile, no matter how many times you swept, vacuumed and washed it, always looked grungy. Theresa felt that if someone was going to want to purchase a concession item, one look at the floor would convince them otherwise.

The concession stand had a glass display case that had been filled with candy for many years, but Theresa felt it could be better displayed by having it on shelves at the back of the stand. It was more appealing when you saw the candy not through glass that had to be regularly cleaned and even then didn't show it off to the best results. Into the display case Theresa placed mementos that represented something to her or her family.

By this point in time, Theresa had pretty much decided that her permanent residence would be the apartment that was upstairs over the theater's long front lobby. The driving back and forth to Manchester was time consuming when there always seemed to be so much needing to be done at the theater. Theresa, who had loved to drive, never drove again after her long health crisis following the lawsuit several years earlier. Therefore, if she was going to spend much of her time living and working in the theater, she wanted to have around her some items that meant something to her and made it seem more like a home. Into the former candy case went cards, racing trophies belonging to her nephew, razor clam shells from a trip to the beach and a postcard that I had sent her in 1973 when I made my first trip to California. Because she didn't have the opportunity to travel any longer, she would live vicariously through my travels and the travels of other regular customers. When the theater closed in September 1994, my postcard was still sitting in that display case.

Lillian Garafoli, a Concord resident and longtime patron of the theater, would regularly try to lure Theresa to join her on one of her many overseas trips. While Theresa sometimes said that the temptation was great, she never went. To those who would ask her whether she had a desire to see the world, she would respond, "I've seen it all up there on the big screen from my seat here in the theater".

During the 1970s the day on which we would start a new feature attraction changed from Wednesday to Friday. More and more this was becoming the norm at theaters all over the country. In major cities it was often felt that if a film opened on Wednesday and was not a very good film, the reviews that would appear in the press on Thursday or bad word of mouth could kill the first weekend of business, which was very important to the opening success of a new film. By opening on a Friday, reviews might not appear until early the following week thus enabling the picture to have a good opening weekend.

Many of the major movie studios began to rely on television as a major tool in marketing their films. Previously, only Disney had utilized the tube for these purposes by way of the popular weekly Disney television series. In addition, actors and actresses selling their latest film would often go on Johnny Carson's late night program or stop by and chat with Merv Griffin or Mike Douglas.

Although film critics had periodically appeared on television to give their opinions of the latest releases, it was not until 1975 that millions began to sit down on a regular basis and listen to what they had to say. Siskel and Ebert began an amazingly popular partnership when their show debuted on PBS. For nearly 25 years the reviews by the pair would be oft-quoted and their "thumbs up and thumbs down" critiques would become part of the lexicon.

Several years later, in 1981, with the arrival of *Entertainment Tonight*, movies and show business would become almost as important, to some, as the news. *ET* as it quickly became known would breathlessly report on Monday what film had the biggest grossing weekend. Previously information and data such as that was generally reported only in the industry trade magazines and was not usually known by the general public.

While I sometimes watched *ET*, it wasn't until June 1983 that I realized how many others shared the habit. I was interviewed by reporter Catherine Mann for the program that aired on Monday, June 27. In the next two days, following the airing of the broadcast, no less than a hundred people remarked to me about having seen the interview. Many of them didn't strike me as someone who'd be watching an entertainment program.

In March 1979, the *New Hampshire Times*, a weekly paper published in Concord for about a decade and a half in the 1970s and 80s, did an extensive story called, *The Movies*. Writer Steve Taylor, a skilled writer who would later serve 25 years as New Hampshire's Commissioner of Agriculture, clearly did his homework in writing this piece. He extensively interviewed Barry Steelman and Theresa (off the record), about why films often stayed so long at theaters and why, at that time, Concord residents didn't always have the opportunity to see the latest film as soon as it was released.

On the cover of the issue was a picture of the exterior of the Concord Theatre with the marquee displaying the title of the feature then playing— *Warriors*. While there was an interior shot of the same film showing on the screen at the Concord Theatre, Theresa typically refused to allow her picture to be taken. There were four pictures taken at Cinema 93, which was showing a double feature in 3-D with a clearly enthralled audience decked out in 3-D glasses. Barry was also viewed working in the theater's projection booth.

The news story explained the "bidding system" that was in use for the awarding of a film title to a particular theater. It was noted that in December 1978 New Hampshire theater owners were offered the chance to bid on the Paramount release, *Star Trek* which was not even due to be released until December 1979, a full year later. Although bidding a year in advance was not the norm, it was often six months in advance of the release. This system forced theater owners to take huge risks, especially if there was not yet the opportunity to see the film you were bidding on or if you had to tie up money as an advance. There are so many instances in which you bid on a film title based upon the enthusiastic pitch of the salesman from that studio who is unlikely to ever bad mouth one of its titles.

The situation had improved, however, from what it had been in earlier years. Furthermore, with the road show concept of release no longer popular, few titles had to wait a year or more before making their Concord-area debut. There were increasing instances when a film would play "day and date" with its opening in Boston. Some titles still had to wait a few weeks and on some occasions Manchester still had clearance to play a particular title a certain number of days ahead of it reaching Concord. With Manchester barely 20 minutes away, a great many people chose not to wait for a picture to reach Concord and made the drive.

I recall an instance in 1975 when a very popular film never even played Concord. Columbia's *Funny Lady*, the very successful sequel to Barbra Streisand's *Funny Girl*, played in Hooksett at the Jerry Lewis Cinemas. It played for more than a month, never playing nearby Manchester. Theresa called the Columbia salesman to ask about availability for Concord and was told the film was not available.

It also became increasingly apparent in the 1970s that Concord audiences were more than eager to sample a wider variety of films—films and film styles that once upon a time would probably have not played the city. Among the new to Concord names that generated interest was the Italian screenwriter and director, Lina Wertmuller. She was the first woman director nominated for an Academy Award as Best Director and three of her titles played the Concord Theatre in the 1970s to surprisingly strong results.

The Seduction of Mimi, Swept Away and *Seven Beauties*—all shown in their own language with sub-titles, drew a whole different segment of the population to the Concord Theatre. Theresa continued to believe that the theater needed to show a variety of film types in order to continue to be relevant. Box office performance was often not the overriding concern. Instead, providing something that provoked interest and thought and something you would not always have the opportunity to see in Concord but would have had to travel to Boston to see. In the days before there were hundreds of cable channels or even video, much less DVD enabling someone the chance to partake in a veritable buffet of movies, the Concord and Cinema 93 opened eyes to what was out there.

Certainly Cinema 93 began moving from just commercial fare to foreign films, classic films from the past and in the process finding a devoted following among lovers of film. These were not only those who lived locally, but those who would journey from surrounding areas when Cinema 93 had a new picture that stirred their interest.

One of the titles that played Cinema 93 and drew me and Theresa was the comedy, *La Cage Aux Folles*. Cinema 93 had great success with this hilarious film and brought it back several times. Theresa even returned for a second viewing and I have rarely seen her laugh as hard as she did at this farce. Shown with subtitles, Theresa perfectly understood the French and it seemed to only delight her all the more. Tears poured down her face as she howled with glee at the on-screen antics.

A film that didn't delight anyone at the Concord Theatre was a wretched misfire entitled, *The French Woman*. A 1977 French film that had nothing to do with a latter film entitled, *The French Lieutenant's Woman*. Theresa watched *The French Woman* aghast, firmly holding her rosary beads throughout and half seriously telling friends that she was "going to hell" for playing this film. When the film would conclude each evening and the audience exit the theater, for the first time in her career Theresa would hide, too embarrassed to hear what they had to say. Many were outraged. The normally amiable Theresa was usually found in her seat in the lobby saying goodnight to those who had attended a movie and wishing them well and listening to their remarks. After *The French Woman* there was no Theresa. She asked me if I'd mind sitting in the lobby to make sure everyone left. I did and heard an earful.

The year 1977 marked the tenth anniversary of my starting my job at the Concord Theatre and while I no longer held a regularly paid position, I was still very much a part of the "Concord Theatre family." Whether I was working days for the State of New Hampshire or at Blue Cross and Blue Shield, Theresa and I talked daily and I was a regular fixture on weekend evenings in the theater.

During my coffee break at work on Monday, I would call Theresa prior to her making phone inquiries to salesmen from the various companies, to discuss anything I'd found out about a particular title that we should pursue. During my lunch break, I'd call for an update on her calls and right after work, I'd call again from home. When I was at the theater, I'd do whatever I could to help out and that involved everything from running to Filides Market on South State Street to pick something up for Theresa or dashing off to Diversi's Market to get something else. When I worked at the Endicott Hotel, which was almost across the street from the theater, I'd go across the street during my breaks much to the amusement of the "ladies of the night" who sometimes gathered, discretely, near the theater in the hopes of getting lucky with a departing patron.

In the spring of 1977 Theresa asked me to put together what I would consider an ideal schedule of films for the summer. What was expected to be a big hit and turned out to be a cultural landmark, *Star Wars* was to play Cinema 93. I took my time studying *Variety, Boxoffice Magazine* and several other sources before putting together a list of five titles. The titles were:

Annie Hall

Slap Shot

New York, New York

A Bridge Too Far

The Spy Who Loved Me

In making the selections, I tried to choose titles that would appeal to our regular clientele and also appeal to some of the tourist crowd that would surely be in the area. I told Theresa it was a "something for everyone" summer, freely stealing the title from an underrated but well-liked film we had played several years earlier.

The five titles pretty much filled out our summer schedule and at the end of the year when the top ten grossing films of the year were calculated, three of the titles I had selected were included on that hallowed list.

TEN BEST-GROSSING FILMS OF 1977
Title, studio, and domestic gross

1. *Star Wars* (20th Century Fox/Lucasfilm Ltd., $307,263,857)
2. *Smokey and the Bandit* (Universal Pictures, $126,737,428)
3. *Close Encounters of the Third Kind* (Columbia Pictures, $116,395,460)
4. *Saturday Night Fever* (Paramount Pictures, $94,213,184)
5. *The Goodbye Girl* (Metro-Goldwyn-Mayer/Warner Bros./Rastar, $82,000,470)
6. *A Bridge Too Far* (United Artists, $50,750,000)
7. *The Deep* (Columbia Pictures, $47,346,365)
8. *The Spy Who Loved Me* (United Artists, $46,838,673)
9. *Oh, God!* (Warner Bros., $41,687,243)
10. *Annie Hall* (United Artists, $38,251,425)

Slap Shot, a well-made and much-admired hockey film barely missed making the top ten and *New York, New York* directed by Martin Scorsese received kudos while the title song became a standard. The number 4 film on the list, *Saturday Night Fever* would become a huge hit at the Concord Theatre in late 1977 when it opened as our Christmas attraction.

The Concord Theatre, in the 70s, had the distinction of playing the Academy Award-winning Best Picture, for four consecutive years. *One Flew Over the Cuckoo's Nest* (1975), *Rocky* (1976), *Annie Hall* (1977) and *The Deer Hunter* (1978).

In terms of playing wildly popular films, 1978 would probably stand as the pinnacle in the Concord Theatre's history. Never before or since, did the Concord Theatre play six of the top money-making films of the year. The six titles played a total of more than 26 weeks. The six were *Grease, Superman, National Lampoon's Animal House, Revenge of the Pink Panther, The Deer Hunter* and *Halloween.*

HIGHEST-GROSSING FILMS OF 1978
Title, studio, and domestic gross

1. *Grease* (Paramount Pictures, $159,978,870)
2. *Superman* (Warner Bros., $134,218,018)
3. *National Lampoon's Animal House* (Universal Pictures, $120,091,123)
4. *Every Which Way but Loose* (Warner Bros., $85,196,485)
5. *Heaven Can Wait* (Paramount Pictures, $81,640,278)
6. *Hooper* (Warner Bros., $78,000,000)
7. *Jaws 2* (Universal Pictures, $77,737,272)
8. *Revenge of the Pink Panther* (United Artists, $49,579,269)
9. *The Deer Hunter* (Universal Pictures, $48,979,328)
10. *Halloween* (Compass International, $47,000,000)

Chapter Twenty-four

A COUPLE OF GENRES gained a certain level of respectability in the 1970s that went beyond the fans and aficionados of this kind of movie. Suddenly those who had dismissed the idea that they'd ever see a horror or sci-fi film, were standing in lines outside the Concord Theatre and theaters all across the country, waiting to be shocked or scared.

The Concord Theatre had been very fortunate to have played two sci-fi films in the late 60's that were critically acclaimed and became powerhouses at the box office. *Planet of the Apes* and especially *2001: A Space Odyssey*, appealed to far more than the youngsters and teens who in the past had been the dominant audience for a science fiction film.

Whenever a salesman would begin touting an upcoming feature, Theresa would ask what kind of movie it was. If the answer was science fiction, she'd immediately have visions of a string of badly made 1950s sci-fi films that played the theater. She once told me that her strongest memory of those films was the need to go inside and quiet the kids down that were watching the film, because they were raising such a ruckus.

In the 70s the Concord played several science fiction movies without a great deal of success. *Demon Seed* was a major failure while *Silent Running* received great reviews and was received enthusiastically by the several hundred who bothered to come out to see it. It lost money, however, as did *Logan's Run*, which didn't do badly but the terms were so excessive that barring a miracle, the Concord could not have seen a profit. *Coma* was based on a successful book but the majority of people who had read it felt that the movie didn't come close to capturing what they'd read or imagined in their heads.

Three science fiction movies released in the late 70s became huge successes, two of them critically as well as financially. They were *Superman* which opened in December 1978 as the Christmas attraction and remained well into January. The other title was the 1979 *Alien*, which came close to break-ing records and set a new bar for sci-fi. The third title was *Star Trek: The Motion Picture* which was the Christmas 1979 attraction. This was the film that Theresa had to offer a bid on almost a year before it opened. As the first big screen version of the cult television series, "Trekkies" were out in force for the first five days of the run. There were also plenty of curiosity seekers who decided to try out the film. Paramount, the releasing studio, had convinced Theresa that this was to be the "new *Star Wars*" but she didn't buy that line, fortunately. Too many viewers found it way too long and a little short on plot. Visually it was stunning. Future installments in the film series, which played at other local theaters did, in some instances do outstanding business, especially *Star Trek IV: The Voyage Home* which was released in 1986.

It would be 10 years before the Concord Theatre played another *Star Trek* motion picture. In 1989 we played *Star Trek V: The Final Frontier* but the response to the film, directed by cast member William Shatner, was tepid.

Superman was a film that was highly anticipated due to years of advance publicity surrounding the project and the casting of such well-known names as Marlon Brando and Gene Hackman. The critics were surprisingly kind to the film. Both Theresa and I had expected that it would not receive good reviews. Much of the charm of the film, in our opinion, was due to Christopher Reeve's outstanding performance as Clark Kent/Superman and the on-screen chemistry he shared with Margot Kidder as Lois Lane. There were lines onto Main Street for the first week and weekends contin-ued to be very strong, businesswise, for most of the engagement.

Concord audiences applauded and cheered the Man of Steel at several places of the storyline and there were many repeat viewers. However, there were also at least 15 to 20 percent who expressed disappointment. Their loudest carping went to the film's special effects.

It had not even been a year and a half since *Star Wars* forever changed the kind of special effects that audiences would demand from any high-budget special-effects project. *Close Encounters of the Third Kind* which had opened a year before *Superman* only reinforced that expectation of the awe factor. Audiences wanted to be stunned by what they saw on the screen and no longer would they willingly accept less.

The special effects in *Superman* were very good and a couple of years earlier would have been the chief talking point about the film. So much had changed and so quickly that the end result wasn't quite what some had expected. Furthermore, the build up to the movies release over the course of time had probably inflated expectations.

When *Alien* arrived at the Concord Theatre on July 6, 1979, we were not quite sure what to expect, although six months of exceptional reviews had certainly piqued our curiosity. The preview we screened for several weeks before the opening, however, seemed to be deliberately vague as though to create a buzz, and it certainly did.

On opening night, we sold out and once people were seated, they barely moved. It seemed as though they were collectively holding their breath. Generally you have audience members who visit the concession stand during the movie, at moments that might be deemed "slow" and you most definitely have those who need to visit the facilities. Throughout the lengthy run of *Alien*, this rarely happened. While people bought concession items on their way in, sales during the film were almost nonexistent.

During the 50s and early 60s, The Concord Theatre had periodically been stuck playing bad horror movies. Theresa referred to them as "schlock productions" and they never seemed to bring in much revenue. In the 1960s, the Capitol Theatre periodically played horror movies turned out by Hammer Productions in England. These titles, most often involving Dracula, the Mummy or Frankenstein, usually starred Peter Cushing and/or Christopher Lee. The Capitol would do very well with matiness on these films as youngsters in Concord would hurry to "The Cap," hoping to be scared.

American International Pictures (AIP) was famous in the 60s for the series of Beach Party films starring Frankie and Annette. However they also turned out some horror movies including new variations on Edgar Allen Poe tales. The stars of these films included Boris Karloff, Basil Rathbone and most especially Vincent Price. American International usually played at one of the local drive-ins, in particular the Sky-Hi in Boscawen.

During an dry period in 1971, Theresa listened to the entreaties of a salesman from American International and booked, for one week, the new title, *The Abominable Dr. Phibes*. It starred Vincent Price, and the business it brought in for the week was surprising. Even more importantly, the audience loved the film and came out telling Theresa how much they'd enjoyed themselves. When a sequel was produced the following year it didn't take much persuasion to get Theresa to say yes once again. Theresa let the AIP salesman know that if a third Phibes film was ever made to please let her know. There was no third film and the only other American International film we played was not a horror movie but simply horrible.

Bunny O'Hare co-starring Bette Davis and Ernest Borgnine was an embarrassing debacle, for the Oscar-winning stars and for any theater unfortunate enough to play it—to empty houses.

Because of the tremendous success the Concord Theatre had in 1974 with a run of *The Exorcist*, Theresa decided to try to book *The Omen*. The stars of the film were Gregory Peck and Lee Remick and the studio releasing it was 20th Century Fox. On Sunday, June 6, 1976, Theresa and I went to Manchester for a sneak preview of the film. Theresa noted that this type of film was usually not her cup of tea, but she watched the audience response, and it was electric. Walking out of the General Cinema at the Bedford Mall, she told me that she planned to call Fox the next morning and try to make a deal to get the film. We did not get the booking. That seemed to make Theresa more determined than ever to find a title that would shake-up an audience in the way *The Exorcist* and *The Omen* had.

On my birthday that year, Oct. 31, 1976, Theresa sent me on a scouting mission, to attend a special preview in Danvers, Massachusetts, for an upcoming release. The rep from United Artists was telling Theresa that the soon-to-be released film was going to "scare the bejeezus" out of anyone who went to see it. He'd seen it at a special screening and said he was still having nightmares about it.

The film's title was *Carrie* and it was based on a story by Stephen King, who was still in the early years of his megasuccess as an author.

I joined about 500 others on that Halloween evening and, for once, the hype for the film was not just an overly eager salesman trying to make a sale. Long before dozens of copycat horror thrillers dotted the landscape, *Carrie* stood out for the storyline, the acting and the chills it evoked. When I was returning home that evening, a little after 11, I made a beeline to the Concord Theatre and reported to Theresa what I had witnessed. On Monday morning, Nov. 2, she was on the phone with United Artists securing a deal to play *Carrie*.

Horror movies in the 70s did not necessarily open for Halloween, as is often the case today. Studios opened films when they felt they could secure the widest popularity or visibility. United Artists knew it had something special in *Carrie* and there was already talk about the possibility of acting honors for members of the cast.

Carrie opened on Christmas Day 1976, at the Concord Theatre and was a smash hit from the first showing. In those days before a shocking and surprise epilogue became almost mainstream with a horror movie, *Carrie* had one last thrill that never failed to startle audiences and set them screaming. I hadn't let Theresa know about that in advance and on the first night, she almost had a heart attack.

As usually happened during the early days of the film's run, the audience, in a rush to be the first out and beat the crowd, was already walking up the aisles as Amy Irving, on-screen, knelt to pay her respects to Carrie. As a result of those eager departures, some missed the moment when a hand comes out of the ground and grabs Irving's wrist. The hundreds still seated let out a loud scream, followed by nervous laughter. Theresa, sitting at the box office in the upper lobby heard several hundred people scream and thought something horrible had occurred inside. Fortunately I was standing there by the chopper and was able to tell her what had happened. Once she knew, she had a great laugh about it.

Four of the five best-attended horror movies in the Concord Theatre's history played during the 1970s. *The Exorcist, Carrie, Halloween* and *The Amityville Horror*. The fifth title played in the summer of 1980, so it almost qualifies as the 70s.

Halloween opened in only a handful of theaters in time for Halloween of 1978. It was a low-budget film and was not expected to be anything special. What ultimately sold it was word of mouth, probably the most important component in the making or breaking of a film.

During the remaining months of 1978 it built a reputation and a wave of curiosity throughout the country, gradually adding more and more theaters to its run. It finally made its debut in Concord on March 30, 1979. I think the delay in it reaching Concord only added to the pent-up desire for people to come and see it. It didn't matter that it was set at Halloween and playing during the early weeks of spring. It was a film people wanted to see and they did, some returning multiple times.

The Amityville Horror opened in August of 1979 and was another big hit, mostly due to the interest in the supposed real story about the house, which had been in the news a great deal. James Brolin starred along with Margot Kidder, who everyone had liked in *Superman* earlier that same year.

The *Dog Days of Summer* and the doldrums that can sometimes strike a theater in August, as the blush of the big summer releases begins to fade, was not evident while *Amityville* played. It was held-over for several weeks and although I recently watched it for the first time in decades and was somewhat disappointed, at the time it was a big success. True, the critics didn't take to it and it was no *Carrie* or *Halloween,* but sometimes you just want to sit in an air-conditioned theater and be scared.

By the late 1970s, the Concord continued to play a mix of popular Hollywood attractions and smaller films that drew an appreciative but smaller audience.

Chapter Twenty-five

BY THE LAST YEAR of the decade of the 1970s, the Capitol Theatre had ceased showing motion pictures, although there was an attempt in the 80s to revive films at the theater, often with double features of second-run titles. The Concord Theatre and Cinema 93 continued to show first-run movies with Cinema 93 occasionally showing an art film. Most of the time there were enough pictures to provide product for both houses. During the summer, due to the opening of the two drive-ins, it would sometimes become more difficult to get the better pictures. The Movie Centre in Hooksett continued to draw some business from the greater Concord area thanks in part to advertising in the Concord paper. The General Cinemas located at the Bedford Mall outside of Manchester, had reconfigured its two-screen complex into four screens, and due to the location in the Manchester area, sometimes secured film releases prior to Concord.

From time to time there were rumors and rumblings about a multiplex cinema coming to Concord but it always seemed to amount to nothing but speculation. Barry Steelman seriously investigated adding screens under the Cinema 93 name thereby enabling him to show art or classic films in one or more houses while playing new, first-run releases also.

The rumors about a multiplex opening turned to reality in early 1979 when it was announced that a four-screen complex was to be built on Loudon Road. There was a contest to name the cinema and there was excitement in Concord about the probable opening of the first new movie theater in Concord since Cinema 93 had opened its doors 12 years earlier.

Fortunately the new theaters, which were eventually called the Merrimack Cinemas, didn't open the doors until Wednesday, August 15, 1979. By opening at the end of the summer, the Concord and Cinema 93 were able to play many of the major summer releases without having them play the new theater.

The opening four features at the Merrimack Cinemas were: *Dracula* (Frank Langella and Laurence Olivier), *Meatballs* (Bill Murray), *The Main Event* (Barbra Streisand and Ryan O' Neal) and *Hot Stuff* (Dom De Luise). It also offered free popcorn and soda during the opening days and attracted sold out performances as well as its share of the curious who just wanted to take a peek.

Each cinema seated approximately 200 people, making each the smallest in the Concord area. As is often the case, however, there was a real fascination to see this new place in town. During the waning months of that summer, thousands made the trek up Loudon Road, parking in the large parking lot which, within two years, would become filled with pot holes and other hazardous irregularities.

During the next decade, the Merrimack would continue to be affectionately called the Merrimack Cinemas by locals. The theater would, however, have a variety of names as other companies bought it out. In the fall of 1982, Sack Cinemas out of Boston, purchased the theater and it became the Sack Merrimack Cinemas. Sack was a name well-known in Massachusetts and for over two decades had built a reputation for the quality of its theaters as well as the diverse product shown.

The Sack Merrimack later became Sony and then USA Cinemas and Lowes finally ending its life as Entertainment Cinemas. One thing never changed in any of these incarnations and that was the deteriorating condition of the parking lot. People joked that cars had their undercarriage decimated by one of the potholes. For some reason the parking lot was never overhauled and repaired.

As customers came in raving about the Merrimack, Theresa realized that after 46 years in the business, times were changing locally. The selection of product and the business style that she had been maintaining might begin shifting in favor of the new kid on the block.

There are a number of reasons that people like a multiplex cinema over a one-screen movie theater. Choice is the big reason. If you arrive at a multiplex uncertain as to what you are going to see, you can make up your mind when you get there from the four films showing. Even if you've made up your mind ahead of time, you can change it once you get to the box office.

In addition, should the movie you are want to see be sold out, you don't need to go home disappointed—an evening ruined, plans obliterated. You can simply make another selection and still see something. Very few people walk away from a multiplex if their first choice is full. At the Concord and certainly at Cinema 93, if you find you cannot get a ticket, you're left to walk away and hope to find something else.

A multiplex also has the ability to keep a movie for a lengthy period by moving it into a smaller auditorium, thereby enabling a new title to play in one of their larger houses should it be necessary. The Concord had recently played two films for long periods of time. *Animal House* had played for more than two months as had *10*. Both films still drew large crowds on the weekends but on some weeknights the attendance was sparse. Had there been a second screening room that was smaller, both films could have been moved into that space and a new movie brought in that would have, at least initially, drawn large crowds each night.

There is plenty of parking at the multiplex although Cinema 93 was also fortunate in having a huge strip mall parking lot available for moviegoers.

I have never figured out where hundreds of cars were parked when people would come to the Concord Theatre for an especially popular attraction. If we had 300-400 for the first show and an equal amount for the second, the second show crowd would arrive before the first show had finished. Some nights there were probably 200-400 cars from patrons of the Concord Theatre. While about two dozen could park in the Haggets parking lot, two buildings south of the Concord Theatre, there was limited on street parking, I guess the others parked either in the Capitol Shopping Center lot and walked up the hill or parked on surrounding side streets.

When I worked at the Concord, it seemed as though nobody expected to be able to park right at the door and I do recall some people walking from home to the movies thereby justifying the large popcorn they would purchase, as a reward for the hike. What I do not recall hearing were complaints about no parking being available. Perhaps the theater had been there for so many years that potential customers understood the parking situation or lack of.

That late summer when the Merrimack opened, the Concord Drive-In was continuing to play double features, especially family type films, and was doing very well with their program selections. The Sky-Hi was, more often than not, playing films designed for decidedly mature audiences. These double features had titles like *The Vixen* and *Russ Meyer's Beneath the Ultra Vixens*. The Sky-Hi would not survive too many more summers and would go the route of the Palace Theatre in Penacook and close.

In the meantime Arthur Dame was concerned as to how the arrival of the new cinemas would affect his business at the Scenic in Pittsfield. Some of his regulars were making a trip to Concord to check the new place out and with the long delay he had in getting movies—often anywhere from six months to a year—he was deeply concerned about his own theater's survival. The era of the neighborhood second-run theater was rapidly coming to a close throughout the country.

Chapter Twenty-six

THE CONCORD THEATRE would find itself, during the 1980s, in a definite minority as a downtown movie house. More and more downtown theaters throughout the country were shutting down or finding themselves being turned into something else. In Manchester only The Movies on Amherst Street remained as a downtown theater where once there had been almost a dozen. The Movies was the former Rex, later redubbed King Cinema, and despite having stadium seating, it had a difficult time getting first-run feature films that could fill those seats.

In Keene the Latchis closed and only the Colonial remained in the downtown district. Throughout the 80s the Colonial tried different formulas to bring in crowds—some successful and some not so. Fortunately it later became an important part of the Keene community after a major restoration. Now, with a mix of concerts, live performances and art films it thrives and like the Capitol Center for the Arts in Concord, it brings something special to the community.

Portsmouth would lose its last downtown movie palace in the 80s and even second-run theaters in New Hampshire's small towns and cities would close-up shop. The drive-ins, which had lost some of their novelty, began closing. The seasons during which they were open were often so short that developers began seeing the real estate they sat on as being more valuable for another use. The Sky-Hi Drive-In would close at the end of the 1983 season, and the Concord Drive-In would only hang on for one more year before closing in 1984.

A year hardly went by in the 80's in which Theresa was not approached by someone who was interested in purchasing the theater. Some wanted to utilize it for movies or some other performing venue. In some cases they simply wanted to tear down the building and use the valuable downtown lot for another purpose. One man from the North Shore in Massachusetts made no secret of his desire to turn it into a "Porn Palace!"

The city of Concord's downtown area would continue to see changes in the 1980s. F.W. Woolworth, the last of the three five-and-dime stores that had been an important fixture on Main Street, would shut its doors. All across the country these always reliable downtown mainstays were vanishing. Although Concord did not yet have a mall, other than the Capitol Shopping Center, malls were appearing nearby and shoppers were taking advantage of them.

While Concord shoppers had been making the quick trip to Manchester to shop at Jordan Marsh for several years and to frequently take in a movie at the nearby Bedford Mall, their options became even more enticing with the opening of the large Mall of New Hampshire in Manchester. It boasted scores of stores, including Filene's and Lechmere. Previously a local shopper had to journey to Boston or a surrounding suburb to enjoy these stores. Now they could do it in less than 30 minutes and with far less traffic headaches.

During the 1980s, Barry Steelman continued to skillfully walk a fine line between playing more commercial titles, often with tremendous success and more foreign titles, classic oldies or lesser-known films that deserved an audience. In many cases these more obscure films found that appreciative audience in Cinema 93's base of loyal followers, which continued to grow. I know that despite having been a regular attendee at Cinema 93 in the late 60s and 70s, I probably visited the theater more during the 80s than all the previous times combined.

Barry Steelman had an incredible gift for marketing his theater and was great at listening to what his customers said about films. You could purchase a membership at Cinema 93, and he regularly had flyers printed to promote upcoming films. Cinema 93 was definitely a destination stop in Concord and the credit belongs entirely to Barry. "I'm going to C-93 this evening" or "I'm going to Barry's" were remarks you regularly heard throughout the region.

In the fall of 1982 I approached Barry about playing a pair of Jeanette MacDonald films at his theater. I'd joined her fan club as the youngest member in 1963 and was P.R. director in 1982. Barry willingly listened to my pitch and immediately made plans to obtain two titles—*Rose Marie* and *Bitter Sweet* for a three-day booking in November. For my part I promised Barry I'd get a story in the Concord Monitor and go on a local radio program, "Coffee Chat," and talk up the films with host Gardner Hill. I likened Barry's enthusiastic response to my suggestion to the response Theresa had given Richard Blanchard a decade earlier when he'd approached her about playing *The Trojan Women*. Few if any chain theater managers would have given even passing notice to doing something similar.

Tom Keyser, a writer for the *Monitor*, did a nice half-page story on the upcoming films and I spent 25 minutes on WKXL promoting them.

Barry was satisfied enough with the turnout for the double feature. Many of those who attended had not been to a movie in years and some had never been to Cinema 93. Barry treated these new faces with the same degree of personal hospitality that was his hallmark.

In the year after the opening of the Merrimack Cinemas, I know that Theresa had more than a few sleepless night as she worried about how to fill a 52-week annual schedule of films. I would imagine that Barry experienced the same feelings. Theresa didn't consider going the route that Cinema 93 was pursuing with success, by diversifying her schedule with lesser known but acclaimed titles or with older films. The Concord had played several older classics in the 1970s without much success. The titles had included a pair of Charlie Chaplin classics at the time that he made a celebrated return to the United States. There had also been a couple of W.C. Fields films as well as the 1939 *The Hounds of the Baskervilles*. Theresa respected Barry's ability to play older, new and foreign titles to a very appreciative segment of the population. She didn't feel, however, that two theaters in Concord could follow the same formula with equal success.

The decades old system of showing movies with the use of two projectors and reel changes necessitated every twenty minutes began to change. The Concord Theatre had, for many years, utilized carbon arc lights with its two projector system. Theresa liked the sharp and clear image that was projected. Unfortunately at times the carbons would burn to the point where the picture would flicker and sometimes dim. In the early 70s she switched to Xenon lights which did not require the projectionist to watch the light as carefully and prevented the flicker and dimming problems. The Xenon lights were expensive—up to $1,000 apiece.

During the 70s a system utilizing a platter began to become increasingly popular. The platters held very large reels thereby relieving the projectionist from having to change a reel every 20 minutes or so. All reels were spliced together onto one platter and shown through one projector continuously. All the operator had to do was to press a button to start the film. No longer was it necessary for a projectionist to sit in the booth rewinding reels, lacing up the next reel and keeping a watchful eye on the cue marks. At the Concord Theatre, Theresa's youngest sister Laurie, was more often than not the projectionist. On her occasional night off, she was relieved by Lawrence Bunker or by her brother, Maurice.

Laurie held down a full-time job, five days a week, but possessed the same tireless work ethic that her sister Theresa had. Laurie never complained about spending her evenings in an often stifling hot projection booth. To her the theater represented a piece of her family. On weekends she could often be found skiing the slopes at Sunapee or nearby Pat's Peak, usually with her nephew Paul Constant.

During 1980 more than a handful of successful films arrived at the Concord Theatre, despite the arrival of the Merrimack Cinemas. Of the bigger box office performers, only a couple were especially good films, although the public certainly voiced their approval of some of the others by their large attendance. There were also more than a dozen disappointing films that drew little, while audiences continued to sample the goods at the Merrimack.

Probably no film that year generated as much good will from those who came and those who returned over and over again, as did *Somewhere in Time*. It wasn't a huge success in terms of the number of attendees, but few films have had as many repeat viewers as this film did. One Concord woman named Angela, attended every performance, arriving in the evening for the first show and remaining to see it a second time, each night it played.

Somewhere in Time starred Christopher Reeve, Jane Seymour and Christopher Plummer. There was also a performance by Teresa Wright, the Oscar-winning actress who had been one of the stars of *The Best Years of Our Lives*, the film that had launched Theresa's solo career at the Concord Theatre in 1947. *Somewhere in Time* had to do with time travel, five years before *Back to the Future* used a similar theme to enormous popularity as did a Francis Ford Coppola directed movie entitled, *Peggy Sue Got Married*.

Part of the film's success was no doubt due to the beautiful location used as part of the story. Mackinac Island in Michigan saw a tremendous increase in business as a result of the film and the way in which cinematographer Isidore Mankofsky photographed it. There was also a haunting musical score by John Barry, best known for his scoring of many of the James Bond films. Sergei Rachmaninoff's *Rhapsody on a Theme of Paganini* was also used to good effect.

There were virtually no concession sales during the run of this film but there were very audible sounds of crying. While I had not initially wanted to sit and watch the film, I finally decided to see it after seeing how many returnees we were getting. It was not difficult to get caught up in the emotion of the story.

The year's more popular releases ran the gamut from an adaptation of a Stephen King book to a comedy featuring a gopher and a movie about a couple of youngsters stranded on an island.

The Stanley Kubrick-directed *The Shining* with Jack Nicholson in the lead was a great hit with the public, although there was some grumbling about a few changes that were made for the movie making it different from the book. Nevertheless, it stayed for weeks and could have stayed longer but during the hot summer months it seemed as though there was more than enough film product to go around.

Two titles appealed to teens and a younger audience in the days preceding "The Brat Pack" and John Hughes' spate of movies that were already waiting in the wings in the early 80s. *Little Darlings* with Tatum O'Neal, Kristy McNichol and Matt Dillon was a surprise hit. Advance word had already prepared us for the response we received when we opened *The Blue Lagoon*. Theresa received a few angry calls from parents whose children had come to see the movie and may have slightly embellished what was actually seen on-screen. Theresa was strict when enforcing the rating for the film, before selling a ticket to anyone who might be too young.

A few years earlier Cinema 93 had seemed to do very well when it played *Smokey and the Bandit* at the height of the CB radio craze. When Universal really oversold the sequel, reuniting Burt Reynolds and Sally Field, Theresa was initially hesitant about playing it. She went ahead, after plenty of coaxing from Walter, and it proved to be profitable. The first week was actually a near sell-out at half a dozen showings but word of mouth made it quickly drop during the second week. *Caddyshack*, however, grew each week as word got out that the film was very funny. When we played the sequel in 1988, you couldn't give away tickets.

Interestingly during that summer of 1980, both Barry Steelman and I developed a "Hepburn Connection." Barry found himself working on a motion picture that was filming in New Hampshire. *On Golden Pond* was based on the successful play written by Ernest Thompson and starred Henry Fonda, Katharine Hepburn, Jane Fonda and Dabney Coleman. Barry was involved with a Concord film-related union and worked on the film for about 10 weeks. Cinema 93 would later be the first New Hampshire theater to show the movie, which proved to be a tremendous box office success. Nationwide, the movie was responsible for making a lot of people curious and interested in visiting New Hampshire. Henry Fonda picked up his only competitive Oscar for his performance and Katharine Hepburn won a record fourth Best Actress Oscar. I was fortunate to meet Miss Hepburn during the making of the movie and secure an autographed photo for Theresa in the process.

Miss Hepburn, and I was always told that she should be addressed in that way, and I had a mutual friend, the legendary "Hairstylist to the Stars," Sydney Guilaroff. Sydney had worked on nearly 2,000 films during a film career that spanned over 60 years. He had worked with "Kate" on more than a dozen films and they remained close personal friends. He once noted it took about 15 years before she allowed him to stop calling her "Miss Hepburn" and to call her "Kate."

Sydney arranged with Miss Hepburn's assistant/companion, Phyllis Wilbourn, to have me visit while she was in New Hampshire. From that visit we developed a good acquaintance. Miss Hepburn was not a big fan of giving out autographs and when I presented her with a picture and asked her to sign it, she was hesitant and fixed me with a look that made me feel I'd done something I shouldn't have done. It was only after I explained to her that it was for Theresa and told her a little bit about Theresa and her story that she seemed to relax and signed it in her customary fashion— "Katharine Houghton Hepburn".

"I love strong women, especially women who have had to fight for their place and achieve it," she stated in that unmistakable Bryn Mawr voice. Theresa was thrilled when I presented her with the photograph which I had framed for her.

Chapter Twenty-seven

DURING THE DECADE OF THE 1980S, Theresa had her faith tested on numerous occasions. Her eyesight began to fail noticeably. More and more she had to rely on her sister Laurie to take her places and to assist with some tasks that became difficult. Her failing sight also affected her ability to enjoy movies and with only a couple of exceptions to see sneak previews with me, she never again went to a theater, other than her own, to watch a movie. While she never bemoaned the changes that time was bringing to her and to her theater, there was sometimes a wistful or sad look that would briefly cross her face. Her faith became even more important to her.

Father Aimee Boisselle was the pastor of Sacred Heart Church on Pleasant Street in Concord. This was the church Theresa frequented, after the visit from the Pastor of St. John's at the time of *Valley of the Dolls* letting her know she was not welcome to worship at St. John's. Father Boisselle frequently visited the Concord Theatre and Theresa found herself taking the role of comforter to the priest who seemed to be in such emotional distress.

Sometimes Father Boisselle would arrive slightly inebriated and Theresa would call upstairs to her sister Laurie and ask her to prepare a cup of hot coffee and bring it down. She'd give it to Father Boisselle and softly talk to him about his troubles and about their shared faith. When he'd leave an hour or two later, he always appeared to be in better condition, physically and emotionally, and was walking more steadily. Sadly the demons that tormented him only got worse with the passage of time and he resigned in 2002.

Theresa rarely if ever passed judgment on anyone. While she might express disappointment in something that happened or in the way that someone had behaved, she strived to be a completely accepting person.

When playing the Eddie Murphy comedy *Trading Places* in 1983, a husband and wife, who'd periodically come to the Concord Theatre over the years, stopped by one evening to express their opinion about the current film being shown. I was in the concession stand restocking the shelves at Theresa's request and couldn't help but overhear their tirade.

"Why are you playing another of those Eddie Murphy darky pictures? What's wrong with you, Theresa? Aren't there enough decent pictures you can play?"

Theresa maintained her composure while she explained that she tried to cater to every taste in film when making her selections. She also confided to the couple her opinion that she thought Eddie Murphy was especially good in *Trading Places*.

Clearly this wasn't the answer they were seeking and they continued complaining about not only the film but how "blacks" (not the word they used) are taking over the Concord community. They added, "It's bad enough we have the Bacons and their rugs here," referencing a local rug company that had been owned by a black family for many years.

Theresa sat up straight as she stated, "I buy the rugs for the theater from Mr. Bacon and he also cleans the rugs. He is an excellent businessman and as for the color of his skin, I've never noticed!"

The couple stormed out vowing they would never return for another movie, and to the best of my knowledge they never did.

Similar rage was directed at Theresa when she played a 1982 film drama and later played a film musical that had been widely acclaimed.

Making Love from 20th Century Fox was the story of a seemingly happily married man who falls in love with another man. Considered very adult and controversial in its time, it starred Harry Hamlin, Michael Ontkean, Kate Jackson and Wendy Hiller. The film leaned toward a soap opera style and was not successful at the box office.

One scene in particular raised quite a ruckus from the audience at the Concord Theatre. When Ontkean and Hamlin share a kiss, there were loud boos, hisses and a variety of sounds expressing distaste as well as quite a few walkouts. A night didn't go by in which one of those walkouts didn't stop at the box office and tell Theresa, in no uncertain terms, what they thought of the movie and her theater playing it. "You know what happened in Sodom and Gomorrah, don't you?" was one especially harsh critique directed at her.

Despite the presence of Julie Andrews, *Victor/Victoria* was not without its share of detractors. Julie Andrews received an Oscar nomination for her performance as a woman pretending to be a man pretending to be a woman. The Blake Edwards musical was enjoyed by many. The film received seven Academy Award nominations. None of that mattered, however, to several dozen ticket buyers who demanded their money back or could not understand how actors like James Garner and Alex Karras could have agreed to appear in something so "degenerate." Theresa always listened to what a customer had to say and never argued with a customer whose opinion might differ from hers. Refunds were given out liberally.

Interestingly, the 1935 version of the same story entitled, *First a Girl* starring Jessie Matthews and released by Gaumont British Pictures, had also played the Concord Theatre at the time of its release. It raised no eyebrows in the Capital City and was, in fact, one of the best-received British-made films to play the Concord at the time.

After nearly 50 years, Theresa had learned to let a dissatisfied customer vent. A few years earlier when Cheech and Chong's first film, *Up in Smoke,* had played at the Concord, some of the customers were outraged by the film's content and subject matter. Several customers, however, exclaimed as they left the theater that it was probably the "coolest thing they'd ever seen her play . . ." She would smile, nod and thank them for coming.

The 1980s were also filled with a great many "event" films as well as summer blockbusters designed to bring in hundreds of millions at the box office. *Indiana Jones* made a big splash on the silver screen in 1981 and the popular character would return. Also during the 80s there were two more *Star Wars* features as well as *Ghostbusters*. Arnold became a big star while Sylvester Stallone kept alive his character of Rocky and added Rambo to the mix. Freddie Krueger came back over and over as did Michael and Jason, and John Hughes found the perfect formula that appealed to millions of teens.

On Golden Pond when it finally opened enjoyed a lengthy and deserved run at Cinema 93. *Stir Crazy,* a late 1980 release, played the Concord Theatre in early 1981 and was welcomed by fans of Gene Wilder and Richard Pryor. Their prior teaming in *Silver Streak* had enjoyed a successful Concord Theatre run several years earlier.

Probably the biggest hit for the Concord in 1981 was *Arthur* starring Dudley Moore and John Gielgud in his Oscar-winning role. The Concord Theatre audiences howled with laughter at Moore's antics and the film stayed for many weeks. Runner-up was that summer's James Bond hit, *For Your Eyes Only*, helped by a top-selling title song by Sheena Easton. It was the first Bond film to play the Concord since 1977 and from the size of the crowds, Bond, in the person of Roger Moore, still had some life left in him.

The rest of the year was a little spotty with titles like, *All the Marbles, Friday the 13th—Part 2, Southern Comfort, Tattoo* and a repeat double bill of *Airplane* and *S.O.B.* resulting in some evenings when nobody bothered to show up. For every successful title, there were no less than half a dozen that didn't generate much interest. The Christmas picture that year was a comedy entitled, *Neighbors* with John Belushi and Dan Akyroyd. The film marked Belushi's final role in a movie, as he died a couple of months later. It did about 1/20 of the business done by Belushi's big-screen breakout role three years earlier in *Animal House*.

Despite a running time of three hours and 15 minutes, *Reds* did tremendous business when it played in early 1982. The story seemed to genuinely interest the Concord audience and with only one evening performance, the film actually sold-out three or four times. No doubt the stars of the film—Warren Beatty, Diane Keaton and Jack Nicholson—helped create an interest, but the fact that many people sat there without leaving there seats, for the entire picture, reinforced the reality that Concord audiences wanted to be offered a variety of film types and would support those choices if presented with them.

The Concord also played *Prince of the City* and *Ragtime*, each of which had running times exceeding 2½ hours. Although they did not have the drawing power of *Reds*, each was well-received by more than respectable crowds.

During 1982 the three most popular releases, amidst a dozen or more titles that barely warrant mention, were *An Officer and a Gentleman, 48 Hours* and the John Huston directed screen version of *Annie*. *Officer* played for the longest period of time with *48 Hours,*" which was the Christmas attraction for 1972, a close second. *Annie* came in third and easily was the year's winner with regard to the number of children's tickets that it sold. Theresa actually enjoyed playing afternoon matinees for *Annie* since it had been a while since a film had warranted such showings. I took the afternoon off from my job at Blue Cross and Blue Shield on a couple of days to help out with crowd control and manning the concession stand. As we watched a steady stream of children come out to the concession stand during the movie, I told Theresa that "in my day" we had bought our concession items when we came in. We then sat and watched the movie without budging from our seats. How times had changed.

The year's biggest debacle was a so-called comedy entitled, *Jekyll and Hyde: Together Again* with *Monsignor* and *Heidi's Song* tied for second place.

After not playing a Disney release for decades, several Disney films proved to have varying degrees of success. The national reissue of *Alice in Wonderland* brought lots of people while the more mature, *The Devil and Max Devlin,* opened and closed without anyone seeming to notice it had been there. The best-received Disney release at the Concord Theatre for the decade was *Splash* in 1984. The romantic-fantasy with Tom Hanks, Daryl Hannah and John Candy, hit a bullseye. It proved to be another example of drawing an audience that had rarely if ever been to the Concord Theatre. Four years later Hanks would have another mammoth hit at the Concord with the opening of *Big.* That one did so well that both Theresa and I wondered why it hadn't been snatched by the Merrimack Cinemas. In the mid-80s the Merrimack added two additional screens to its facility, bringing the total to six and effectively grabbing the majority of the largest money-making films. Not as successful for Hanks during the summer of 1985 was a film entitled, *The Man with One Red Shoe* which disappeared from the Concord's screen quickly.

The Omen trilogy ended with the disastrous *The Final Conflict* and it also appeared that the public's love affair with Neil Simon had, at least, temporarily abated. *Only When I Laugh,* despite getting some critical approval and award nominations, played to mostly silent audiences and a great many walk-outs.

Four smaller pictures released in the 1980s with very reasonable terms in their contracts, earned the Concord Theatre more profit than a lot of films that drew lines stretching outside the lobby doors and spilling out on to Main Street.

Educating Rita (1983), *Fright Night* (1985), *Brazil* (1986) and *Murphy's Romance* (1986) were all extremely well-liked by local audiences during their runs and had received nods of approval from discerning critics. The Terry Gilliam-directed *Brazil* brought in many of his fanatics, with several returning to see the movie five or six times. There was even applause at the picture's conclusion.

Michael Caine and Julie Walters co-starred in *Educating Rita* which played in November of 1983. The film received three Oscar nominations including Caine and Walters for Best Actor and Best Actress. James Garner received his only nomination as Best Actor for *Murphy's Romance* co-starring Sally Field. It was such a popular movie that we attempted to hold it over without success. The limited number of prints available had been promised elsewhere.

If I were to compile a list of the top six horror movies to ever play the Concord, *Fright Night* which played in the summer of 1985 would come in a strong sixth. It was within 150 attendees of pushing fifth place *The Amityville Horror* out of that slot. Theresa didn't normally go to see a horror movie, however the rep from Columbia urged her to attend a sneak preview of their planned release. She and I went to a screening in Massachusetts. She was having some eye issues at the time which made it difficult to clearly see the film. However, she loved the sound of Roddy McDowall and Chris Sarandon's voices and the very enthusiastic response from the audience at the preview. She booked it and didn't regret it. Critic Roger Ebert noted in his review of *Fright Night*, "*Fright Night* is not a distinguished movie, but it has a lot of fun being undistinguished." The thousands who poured into the Concord Theatre during the run of the film, seemed to agree with Ebert's assessment.

The Christmas release for 1983 was probably the most poorly received film to ever play that coveted spot, although a few other titles from both the recent past and waiting in the future, could give it a run for the money. No matter how bad the quality of the films might have been during the fall months, it was not unreasonable to think that you could count on the

Christmas release bringing a bit of holiday cheer. In 1983 it was a little gem entitled, *Two of a Kind*. The stars were John Travolta and Olivia Newton John who five years earlier had packed the theater with their hit, *Grease*. When the second-run films that were played in the weeks before *Two of a Kind* (*War Games* and *The Big Chill*), make twice as much as a first-run film, you know its trouble. The most talked about films of that season were filling the coffers of the Sack Merrimack Cinemas.

I had just left a 14 month post as a manager of the Sack Merrimack Cinemas when the holiday films moved in. In November of 1982 I was offered a management position at the theater and after a lengthy consultation with Theresa, accepted it. Theresa's rave reference had gone a long way toward making Mr. Reis, the district manager, offer me the job.

Theresa and I agreed that we would not discuss any matters that might cross some clearly defined boundaries. I received permission from Mr. Reis to continue helping out at the Concord Theatre on my two evenings off. I didn't discuss with any Sack management individuals what the business at the Concord was like and vice versa. My departure in December of 1983 was solely due to my wanting to return to the level of help I had provided Theresa before taking the position.

Working for Sack provided me with insight into how the movie exhibition world was changing. The bottom line at Sack was profit and keeping costs down. While Ken Drum, the other manager, and myself were treated respectfully, it was a far cry from the more interpersonal relationship Theresa and I had built over 15 years. I did learn how to run the new platter system and was able to sing the virtues of such a system to Theresa and her sister Laurie.

"TT, imagine how much more time Laurie would have to do other things and not be tied to the two projectors in the booth?"

My favorite part of working at Sack was the staff. Some were already there when I started but I also had a hand in helping to hire a great many individuals. Most were students at Concord High School and the job was a source of income for them. However, I was a little in awe at the work ethic that most possessed and how determined they were to represent the name Sack in the best possible way. A few I remain in touch with but many of them are names that I'll never forget. Mitch, Kim, Chris, Vince, Christine,

Gretchen, David, Dennis, Dan, Karla, Pat, Mary, Sean, Wayne and so many others. What's really missing in many of today's multiplex cinemas is the kind of personal touch that we were all able to convey as a team. I'm not sure how much of that was due to anything I brought with me as a result of the years I'd spent at the Concord Theatre or what had regularly drawn me to Cinema 93, but I'd like to believe that those experiences helped.

Chapter Twenty-eight

THE KARATE KID IN THE SUMMER OF 1984 brought the same response from an audience that had greeted *Rocky* almost a decade earlier. Although attracting a much younger crowd than *Rocky*, the enthusiasm was unbridled. Columbia hadn't been sure how the film would go over initially, so Theresa's deal with them was fair in the negotiating world of the mid 1980s. The concession stand, in the meantime, could barely keep up with the demands of the seemingly ravenous customers.

Sally Field's second Best Actress Oscar was for *Places in the Heart*, which had a long and successful run at the Concord in 1984. Jeff Bridges earned an Oscar nomination for the Christmas attraction that year—*Starman* but the competition from the Merrimack and a good comedy at Cinema 93 entitled, *Micki and Maude* kept a lot of people away. Both *Starman* and *Micki and Maude* were Columbia releases. Theresa was upset about what she referred to as "shenanigans from the salesman for Columbia." I do not know what transpired. What I do know is that Theresa wrote a letter of apology to Barry Steelman with regard to some kind of misunderstanding that took place while negotiating for the Columbia releases. It wasn't until years later, however, that I found out that the letter had not been mailed. Theresa had given it to her sister with instructions to take it to the post office. Knowing the contents, her sister made a decision that it should not be sent. I wish she'd given it to me to mail, because I would most certainly have sent it since it was what Theresa wanted.

The Breakfast Club opened on Feb. 15, 1985, day and date with its release at more than 1,000 theaters nationwide. Thousands came to see this teen comedy and most of them were first-time visitors to the Concord Theatre. An oft-heard phrase was "My parents" or "my grandparents used to come here . . ."

The pickings were rather lean throughout much of 1985. *Private Function* was a funny British release with Maggie Smith but nobody showed up and *The Emerald Forest* didn't bring in much of a summer crowd. Business only got a jolt toward the end of the year. *Mask*, with Cher starring, drew good business and a lot of positive remarks. *Jagged Edge* with Jeff Bridges and Glenn Close also did well although it remained for way too long and toward the end of the run there were plenty of weekday evenings when nobody showed up.

Sylvester Stallone did bring Rocky Balboa back to life in late 1985 and he returned to the site of his first fight which had taken place at the Concord Theatre. *Rocky IV* was the film's title this time around. During the first week we actually thought it might do better than the first film but after a near-record first week, business subsided, although it remained good through-out the run. This picture also overstayed its welcome, having opened in November and remaining until January. Theresa rationalized that it was better to keep the film than to try to fill out the schedule with titles like *Tuff Turf* and *Heaven Help Us*, two 1985 films that had played to virtually no audience. The night *Rocky IV* opened it played to a total of more than 800 people total between the two evening showings. On its last night, there were less than a dozen sitting quietly in the audience.

Theresa, Laurie and I had developed a habit of dining at Howard Johnson's on Wednesday evenings. The restaurant would be gone within a couple of years but from those dinner/talks, Theresa made a pitch for several film titles that would help make 1986 a little more stellar.

Those three, the most popular films to play the Concord Theatre in 1986, were all aimed at the burgeoning teen market and there wasn't a special effect in sight.

Pretty in Pink, The Karate Kid Part II and *Stand By Me* each played for many weeks and at year's end Theresa noted that the total grosses on those three pictures combined, almost equaled the total from the other dozen or more films that had played throughout the year.

The Karate Kid Part II did about 20 percent more business than the original film had done two years earlier, and that in itself was unusual. Once again the "house rocked" with the sounds of a very excited crowd. Of course the terms for this one were much steeper than for the first and in 1989, the terms for *The Karate Kid Part III* were astronomical. Sadly, the third time was not the charm and we paid dearly for that.

Pretty in Pink wasn't in the blockbuster league with *The Karate Kid Part II*, but few films were. The Molly Ringwald starring romance did bring in a lot of the same crowd that had enjoyed *The Breakfast Club* the year before. It also sold more tickets than the previous film had by holding up throughout the run and not falling off as is a more typical pattern. *Pretty in Pink* also resulted in a response Theresa had rarely had in her more than 50 years at the theater. A group of teenage girls who had come to see it more than once, jointly got together and sent a nice letter to Theresa telling her how much they'd enjoyed their visit to her theater, which had been their first.

Based upon a Stephen King novella, *Stand by Me* attracted a great many males in their teens as well as King fans and those remembering their youth in the late 50s. It had the longest run of any motion picture that played the Concord during 1986. It stayed for nearly two months although it was only being shown at 7 p.m. during its last weeks. There were a great many return viewers.

When the follow-up attraction to *Stand By Me*, *The Name of the Rose* did some of the worst business in the theater's then 53-year history, Theresa channeled her *Butterflies are Free* days and brought *Stand By Me* back for a one-week engagement. On a second run, it brought in more than triple what *The Name of the Rose* had brought in.

The Morning After was the Christmas attraction. It starred Jane Fonda and Jeff Bridges, Fonda received an Oscar nomination for her role. The people who attended seemed to like it, although there were some who were irate that Theresa was playing "that Jane Fonda traitor." Cinema 93 was playing *King Kong Lives* and, as usual, the Merrimack had six first-run hits playing extended runs. On New Year's Eve 1986, a gentleman from the North Shore region outside Boston stopped in to see the movie and talk to Theresa.

He offered her $300,000 cash, for the whole "kit and caboodle" as he phrased it. Theresa asked him what he wanted it for and his response was, "Not sure yet but I am working out some ideas."

Theresa thanked him for his interest, even giving him a free popcorn to enjoy during the movie. On his way out after the film, he stopped to speak with her again and she let him know that she had thought it over and was not interested in selling. He looked surprised at her quick response and told her the site would make a great adult cinema.

Acting as though she'd not heard what he said, Theresa continued, "That's not to say I'll never say no to selling the place. My eyesight isn't what it used to be but at 73, I think I still have a few more years here before I stop."

While he promised to stay in touch, Theresa said, several years later, that she'd never heard from him again and wasn't even sure if he had been serious.

As 1987 started she did confide in me that she was having to put more and more of her own money into keeping the theater going. Since she didn't travel or take vacations or spend much on herself, she felt it was a worthwhile expenditure for the time being.

Several years earlier, in October 1983, and while marking the theater's 50th anniversary, Theresa had told *Concord Monitor* writer Tom Keyser she planned to keep going, "As long as I can get pictures, the best pictures I can to satisfy the people. I've got my aches and pains, but I can put up with them. My doctor says it's good for me to do this kind of work."

Theresa liked Keyser. She liked his style of writing and enjoyed anything he wrote for the *Concord Monitor*. He'd done another story in 1978 about the theater and Theresa had briefly overcome her reticence to have her picture taken, and posed in conjunction with the story. At the time she told Keyser that she planned to spend many more nights selling tickets at the theater adding, "When you retire, you might as well bury yourself."

Ishtar was probably the worst film that flickered on the Concord Theatre's screen during the entire year of 1987. A lot of talent was involved in the comedy film alleged to have cost $50 million to make. Warren Beatty and Dustin Hoffman headed the cast, but the result wasn't funny, it lacked action or even a coherent storyline. The critics trounced on it and the people of Concord showed good taste in shunning it, too. Theresa said a lot of rosarys to make up for the lack of people in the theater.

Mel Brook's *Spaceballs* did well enough to hold it over, but Timothy Dalton's debut as 007 in *The Living Daylights* was almost in a league with *Ishtar*. Rabid Bond fans loved Dalton's take on James Bond but fans that had grown used to Roger Moore's wittier portrayal, didn't like their agent being tougher. Neither *The Big Easy* nor *The Big Town* brought in big business. In September Theresa and I traveled to a sneak preview in the hope of finding something more appealing. We sat near the front of the theater so Theresa could see better but she assured me that she could listen to both the movie and the audiences response and know whether it was good enough to play.

The film was *Baby Boom* starring Diane Keaton and was partially filmed in Vermont. The preview audience loved the picture and it played the Concord for several weeks generating the best business of 1987 up to that fall play date. Although millions claimed to have read the book by V.C. Andrews on which the movie was based, *Flowers in the Attic* came in a close second behind *Ishtar* as the biggest bomb of the year.

In light of the disappointing ticket sales for 1987, Theresa and Laurie were even more hopeful that the Christmas release would not turn out to be another *Two of a Kind* or *Neighbors* but something approximating the business that had been done five years earlier by *48 Hours*.

Opening at 677 theaters nationwide on Christmas Day, *Broadcast News* from 20th Century Fox was the kind of Christmas gift Theresa said she liked to open. Directing his first film since the Oscar-winning *Terms of Endearment* four years earlier, James L. Brooks assembled a great cast and made a film that thousands poured in to see. William Hurt, Holly Hunter, Albert Brooks and Jack Nicholson played their roles to perfection. Nothing all year came even close to drawing the kind of business *Broadcast News* drew and Theresa told Laurie that she had a good feeling about 1988. She was right.

Chapter Twenty-nine

BROADCAST NEWS NOT ONLY CONTINUED to draw big business well into January, it also created an energy in the Concord Theatre that had been dormant for a while. Seeing lines stretching down the lower lobby and out the doors into the cold January evening felt good. Even more importantly, those exiting the theater had clearly enjoyed the film. Word of mouth was a huge asset.

Although the film earned numerous awards and was nominated for multiple Oscars including Best Picture, winning none, it didn't seem to matter to the public. They enjoyed what they saw, and Theresa was very hopeful of continuing the upbeat trend with her next scheduled film.

Moonstruck was seen by nearly as many paying customers as had come to see *Valley of the Dolls* exactly twenty years earlier. There was a party atmosphere about seeing the movie and Theresa was delighted to dust-off the "Sold-Out" sign one more time. If *Broadcast News* was the appetizer for a dinner, then *Moonstruck* was the main course. Departing audience members were effusive in their praise and Theresa was beaming, easily looking twenty years younger than her 74 years.

Theresa often had to use a magnifying glass while intricately making the ads for the *Concord Monitor*, but there was a giddiness about her as she selected just the right picture or quote to use when designing an ad for *Moonstruck*. When she'd complete her creation, she would stick it in an envelope and hand it to me, asking me to drop it through the slot at the *Monitor* on my way home later that evening. The *Concord Monitor* offices on North State Street were about a block away from the Concord Theatre.

When the next attraction, *The Last Emperor* opened to more big business and remained for weeks, Theresa checked her back records and noted that we'd not done this level of business on three hits in a row in

13 years. Not since early 1975 when we played *The Towering Inferno, Young Frankenstein* and *Lenny*. Ultimately the trio of *Broadcast News, Moonstruck* and *The Last Emperor* bested the 1975 films in the number of tickets sold.

While there were certainly the usual mix of films that didn't interest many and a few we'd expected to do well on but didn't (*Bright Lights Big City* is an example), 1988 turned out to be the most profitable year for the Concord Theatre since 1980. At the top of the list for popularity was *Big* with Tom Hanks and *Die Hard* with Bruce Willis. In most cities these hits played at a multiplex but fortunately for Theresa, 20th Century Fox awarded them to the Concord Theatre.

When the top moneymaking films of 1988 were announced, the Concord Theatre had played two of the top-ten hits. Competing with seven other screens in town, Theresa felt that she had done quite well. During the next five years, however, not a single film that played the Concord Theatre would figure as a top-ten moneymaker.

HIGHEST-GROSSING FILMS OF 1988
Title, distributor, and domestic gross

1. *Rain Man* (United Artists, $172,825,435)
2. *Who Framed Roger Rabbit* (Disney, $156,452,370)
3. *Coming to America* (Paramount, $128,152,301)
4. *Big* (20th Century Fox, $114,968,774)
5. *Twins* (Universal, $111,938,388)
6. *Crocodile Dundee II* (Paramount, $109,306,210)
7. *Die Hard* (20th Century Fox, $83,008,852)
8. *The Naked Gun: From the Files of Police Squad!* (Paramount, $78,756,177)
9. *Cocktail* (Disney, $78,222,753)
10. *Beetlejuice* (Warner Bros. ,$73,707,461)

Twentieth Century Fox had been pleased with the huge grosses for *Broadcast News* and were already talking to Theresa about the Christmas release for 1988.

The usual fall lapse did hit but Theresa was not discouraged and took it philosophically. The year had been such a good one that she knew there would be a slew of underperformers. The most surprisingly of those was the Francis Ford Coppola directed, *Tucker: The Man and his Dream* with *Jeff Bridges*. *Bat 21* and *1969* didn't do well and the Thanksgiving release,

Cocoon: The Return, a sequel to the successful 1985 film, was strong for the first week but fell off by more than 75 percent during the second.

Opening on Dec. 23 at more than 1,000 theaters, *Working Girl* proved to be the perfect capper to a dazzling year. It brought in even more customers than had enjoyed *Broadcast News* a year earlier during the Christmas-New Year's holidays.

Cinema 93's Christmas release was the very popular, *The Naked Gun: From the Files of Police Squad,* the first in a series of comic/spoofs starring Leslie Nielsen. Cinema 93 continued to offer a varied and always interesting selection of films. That fall I'd especially enjoyed *Crossing Delancey* and *84 Charing Cross Road.* I had even stopped in at the Concord the following evenings to tell Theresa about the films. While we often discussed the movies I'd seen at Cinema 93, Theresa never asked how many people had been there and I never volunteered that information. We both felt it would have been inappropriate. That didn't stop a small local faction from sometimes taking sides and debating as to which theater was better—Cinema 93 or the Concord.

There were people I knew who felt it would be below them to attend a movie at the Concord. "We'd rather drive to Manchester than support that place," they almost sneered. When I asked why they felt that way, they didn't provide any real reason. I loved going to Cinema 93 and even enjoyed an occasional foray to the Merrimack Cinemas where I had worked.

In November of 1988 we brought *Die Hard* back for a one-week return after *Bat 21* failed to hold up. On the opening night a man arrived and asked Theresa, "Are they biting tonight?"

Theresa wasn't sure what he'd said and asked him to please repeat himself.

"Are the rats biting tonight," he bellowed, in a voice that could be heard inside the theater.

He quickly showed Theresa the heavy boots he had on and added, "They'll never be able to bite me through these!"

Theresa didn't say anything other than "enjoy the show," her customary greeting after someone had purchased a ticket. However, after he went inside she told me that after more than 50 years of hearing remarks like that, "it doesn't get any easier".

I had heard all the rumors and rumblings about rats at the Concord

Theatre since long before I had started working there. When my parents first moved to Concord in May of 1948, they were also warned by new friends they met. Of course none of these so-called "caring" individuals had ever seen a rat at the Concord Theatre, but a friend of a friend of a friend had warned them.

My father worked on the road Monday through Friday and was not home until the weekend. My mom, being new in the community, spent a lot of time going to the movies during the week. One evening she'd go to the Capitol Theatre, the next evening to the Star and the next evening to the Concord. She never had any trepidation about going by herself to the Concord Theatre. Urban legends, however, continued to follow the theater throughout the decades and continued even after the theater had closed.

A friend I had gone to school with spoke with me years after the Concord Theatre had shut its doors. He knew I'd been associated with the theater for many years and felt he owed an apology to someone. He seemed genuine in what he said.

"We used to spread all that shit about the rats because it was cool to talk that way and when we said we went there, everyone thought we were so brave. When you'd ask a girl out and say you were going to the Concord, they'd be all scared and nervous and make you promise to take care of them. They'd practically sit on your lap and would squeeze your hand throughout the movie, and that wasn't a bad thing."

I would give no credibility to those who would announce, "When I went to *Star Wars* at the Concord Theatre, there were rats running around. *Star Wars* never played the Concord Theatre, nor did any other title in the series. More often than not, the title of the film someone was attending when they swear they saw a rat, never appeared at the Concord Theatre.

While I cannot attest to the entire 61-year history of the theater as a movie house, I can unequivocally state that during the 27 years in which I was associated with the theater, there was never a rat or even a mouse sighting nor any evidence that vermin were present. Knowing Theresa as well as I did, I know she was emphatic about keeping the theater clean and making sure that the best conditions possible existed for her paying customers. She was always honest and forthright with me and would have told me about any such problem, whether current or in the past.

The building was old. The interior of the theater was deliberately in dark colors to prevent any distraction that might have lessened the sharp and clear images projected onto the screen. Providing the best sound and picture quality for her patrons topped Theresa's list of what made a theater special.

From time to time Theresa would still muse about doing some major renovations although ultimately she'd revert to a version of what she had told writer Keyser in one of her interviews with him.

"Oh, I have heard people call it an old theater, but they don't say it in a bad way. We keep it up, like putting in new rugs and repainting now and then. I wouldn't want to fix it up all modern. You might call me old fashioned but I like this theater."

Fortunately, a great many people shared Theresa's opinion about liking the theater and even decades after it closed, they retained those affectionate memories.

Sitting in her office in New Hampshire in the summer of 2018, Executive Assistant Lynn Colby recalled her many visits to the Concord Theatre. "Nothing but happy memories cross my mind when going into that theater. The smell of the FRESH popcorn popping and the two ladies all dressed up in their finest clothes; the smell of the theater itself was like my nana's basement and the chairs were covered in leather. I saw many a great movie in this theater . . . and I am so very fortunate to know that it once existed as so many of you reading this book did not have this wonderful memory."

When the State Theatre (aka Queen Cinema, Cine 1 & 2) shut its doors in the 70s and was doomed to be demolished, Theresa was offered a good deal for the purchase of 499 of the more than 2,000 seats in the building. She gave it serious consideration for a couple of weeks before deciding against it. Before reaching her decision, she walked through her entire theater—up and down each row—testing every seat to determine whether or not they were still solid. Although they were original seats from 1933, none were found to be damaged or falling apart. As a result she declined the seat offer and never considered replacing the seats again. She and Laurie, however, frequently replaced filling and made minor improvements as necessitated by the passage of time.

Between the conclusion of the successful run of *Working Girl* in January

1989 and the opening of the 1989 Christmas attraction on Dec. 8, 1989, stretched a year that was not especially momentous for the Concord Theatre. There were less than a handful of films that could be called "boffo" to use vernacular from Variety. Most tended to range from "tepid" to "so-so" although several were critical successes and enjoyed by a small but enthusiastic audience.

Karate Kid III was the biggest disappointment in light of what the first two entries in the series had done. It was quickly replaced by *Weekend at Bernies* which didn't duplicate its national success in Concord. *Friday the 13th Part VIII* was awful but *The Abyss* from director James Cameron, which opened on Aug. 9, at least stopped the flow of bad films. While nowhere near the blockbuster 20th Century Fox had touted it as being, August business on *The Abyss* was good and word of mouth was positive enough to keep it running for several weeks.

The Fabulous Baker Boys with Jeff and Beau Bridges as well as Michelle Pfeiffer, was one of the few pictures that was held for an extended run. Despite being considered a box office failure in many places, *Communion* had some genuinely rabid fanatics who came back for repeated showings. Based on a book by Whitley Strieber and starring Christopher Walken, a lot of people who attended stated they'd come from Keene, Claremont, Laconia, and even Berlin to see the film. Apparently it had not played in wide release and they had read the book and wanted to see the film. Six years earlier we'd played *The Hunger* based on another Strieber book and while that was moderately more successful than *Communion*, we had once again seen a lot of Strieber admirers.

True Love won several awards at film festivals but barely attracted 100 people during its entire week run. *The Bear*, however, turned out to be a big surprise. The Concord Theatre ran Saturday and Sunday matinees to almost full houses and concession sales were probably higher for that one picture than the combined sales for every other picture that played in 1989.

Thousands of people, myself included, crossed the Merrimack River to Cinema 93 during the summer of 1989 to see *Dead Poet's Society*. The film was loved by just about everyone who saw it and stayed at C-93 for several months. After telling Theresa about the film, in detail, she said it sounded as though it would be a film she'd enjoy. She added, however, "But my eyes are getting so bad and not seeing clearly would frustrate me and ruin my enjoyment."

A great deal of anxiety was gripping the downtown community in Concord during 1989 as construction began on the first enclosed mall to be built in the area. The Steeplegate Mall, which would open in mid-1990, would boast some 50 stores including four anchor stores. The impact on Concord's downtown was expected to be considerable. In particular, Sears, which occupied a large space across the street from the Concord Theatre, would be one of the anchors. Another anchor would be J.C. Penney. Although they had moved several years earlier from their popular downtown location to a spot on Fort Eddy Road, Penney's still seemed nearby. Steinbach's, a department store located in the Capitol Shopping Center, only a block east of the Concord Theatre, was also planning to be an anchor.

Steinbach's was descended from one of Concord's most beloved downtown stores, Harry G. Emmons. Emmons had been located for decades on North Main Street and was noted for its quality, staff, and the pneumatic tubes that whizzed throughout the store, sending money to the credit department and returning change back to the clerk to give to the customer. Harry G. Emmons became simply Emmons when it relocated in the early 60s to the Capitol Shopping Center, later becoming Howland's and eventually Steinbach's.

For many store owners, 1989 might be the last time that thousands looked to downtown Concord when making their holiday purchases. Theresa commented that although she couldn't clearly see the Sears store across the street like she once could, there was always a warm and comforting feeling in knowing that Sears was there as it had been as far back as she could recall.

"Point Break," which played in the late summer of 1991, was enthusiastically received by film fans. (Photo courtesy of Michael Von Redlich.)

Chapter Thirty

THE WAR OF THE ROSES was the holiday feature that helped to usher in 1990. Thanks to the star power of Michael Douglas, Kathleen Turner and Danny DeVito, it was an enormous success, running well into January. Although there would be four more holiday pictures at the Concord in the future (1990-1993), none would draw the same level of business that *Roses* did.

One of the most visible signs of a changing world was the paucity of large ads in the newspaper for movies. Once upon a time there were often enough large ads to just about fill a page, especially during the time of the year when the drive-ins were open. By the 1990s, the ads were tiny and most people relied on the listing of theaters and films being shown. I missed the larger ads and had often made a decision on what I went to see based upon them. More and more people were making decisions on what to see based upon extensive television advertising or from what they'd see or hear on the increasing number of entertainment-based television programs.

The months between the end of the run of *The War of the Roses* and the December 1990 opening of the holiday release, *Edward Scissorhands*, was not exactly a film lover's paradise at the Concord Theatre. Certainly a handful of movies received great critical acclaim (*Enemies: A Love Story, Glory, Miller's Crossing* and *The Krays*) but despite the kudos produced varying degrees of business. Most of the titles like *Quigley Down Under* and *The Predator 2* should have been left in the film cans.

Cinema 93 had a huge success in the early months of 1990 with the Oscar winner, *Driving Miss Daisy* which stayed around for a long time. Folks crossed the river to take in a slew of great films at C-93 in 1990 including *My Left Foot, Tie Me Up, Tie Me Down,* and *Cinema Paradiso*.

A great many Concord movie fans had enjoyed *The Gods Must Be Crazy* when it played at Cinema 93 several years earlier. In 1990 the unnecessary sequel, *The Gods Must Be Crazy II* played a short run at the Concord with a total of less than 300 attendees during the run. *I Love You to Death*, and *Stanley and Iris* were also enjoyed by a few people and for the May 25, 1990, opening of *Mountains of the Moon*, the Concord Theatre's ad announced:

ENJOY OUR NEWLY

ENHANCED

PROJECTION SYSTEM ON

THE AREA'S LARGEST SCREEN

The Concord had switched its decades old projection system of two projectors for the platter system thanks to the efforts of Mert Tolman and his son Tom. They made available the system that had been used in Franklin's Regal Theatre. For those who had been operating the projector, including Laurie, Mr. Bunker and once or twice in recent years, Theresa's brother Maurice, the freedom the platter afforded them in the booth was a joy. In the summertime when the added heat from the two projectors had made the booth almost intolerable, the change was even more appreciated.

The summer releases in 1990 brought in the worst crowds in years. *Ghost Dad* demonstrated that Bill Cosby's television popularity did not translate to the movie screen. *Ford Fairlane* went completely unnoticed and *Longtime Companion*, while well-made, was clearly not an escapist summer release for locals or for tourists. Two years earlier, *Young Guns* had done well during the summer of 1988. *Young Guns II* did not repeat that business in the summer of 1990.

The biggest summer hit in 1990 was *Flatliners* with Keifer Sutherland and Julia Roberts heading the cast. It actually brought some lines with it, something that was becoming an increasingly rare sight.

At Christmastime, Tim Burton's *Edward Scissorhands* starring Johnny Depp and Winona Ryder and featuring Vincent Price in his final big screen performance, brought a large crowd of teens and those in their early 20s. Theresa was surprised that none of her regulars, who frequently saw just about everything the theater played, showed up. Despite steep terms for the film, it showed a small profit which is more than most of the films that played in 1990 had done.

From there things went way downhill. *Havana* starring Robert Redford was an abysmal dud!!! Theresa, however, had not lost her sense of humor, comparing it to the similarly titled, *Cuba* that had played about a decade earlier and to equally bad results.

"Cuba" had starred Sean Connery who might qualify as the winner of an award for having starred in more box office flops at the Concord Theatre than any other actor in the years of 1960 to 1990. In addition to *Cuba*, Connery had driven away moviegoers with *Zardov, Shalako, The Name of the Rose* and numerous non-Bond roles he had essayed in the 1960s. The film that followed *Havana, The Russia House* in which Connery costarred with Michelle Pfeiffer, continued that trend.

Fortunately for the theater, "Darling of the Box Office" Julia Roberts was the star of the next attraction, *Sleeping with the Enemy*. It brought in more customers than any picture that had played the Concord since *The War of the Roses*.

In the meantime, Cinema 93 was having one of the biggest, if not the biggest box office success in its history. *Dances with Wolves* which opened at the end of 1990 would continue playing through the winter and spring. It seemed as though every person living in the community went to see the film.

The summer season roused a bit of interest with *Point Break* starring Keanu Reeves and Patrick Swayze. It was the most popular summer film in 1991. Tourists as well as area residents came out to enjoy the story and exciting cinematography. In second place was *Hot Shots* and a close third was *Dying Young,* which did well only because it starred Julia Roberts. Theresa joked that *Highlander II: The Quickening* failed because of Connery's guest appearance in the film. Theresa genuinely liked Connery as an actor but outside of playing Bond or the father of Indiana Jones, many of his films had failed to generate much excitement when they played the Concord Theatre.

Paradise slipped in and out without being noticed while *Little Man Tate* had a small but very enthusiastic audience that, in many instances, returned for a second visit, bringing family or friends who'd not seen the Jodie Foster directed story. Bette Midler finally made her first appearance at the Concord Theatre in 20th Century Fox's *For the Boys*. Midler's comedies and dramas for Touchstone had mostly been booked at the Merrimack

Cinemas where they did very well. *For the Boys* wasn't a big hit, but a surprising number of Theresa's "regulars" showed up to see it and were vocal about the film and its star.

Cinema 93 had a couple of popular films in the fall/holiday period including the remakes of *Cape Fear* and *Father of the Bride*. Meanwhile, 1991 ended with the Concord playing *Bugsy* starring Warren Beatty and his soon to be wife, Annette Bening. It was critically lauded and nominated for many awards. It didn't come close to bringing in the business that *Reds* had brought in nearly a decade earlier, but it sure beat *Ishtar*.

Theresa's youngest sister Laurie became ill in the last weeks of December 1991. There had been some periodic health issues during the last half of 1991, but Laurie continued to work her full-time day job for the New Hampshire Department of Employment Security. Each evening she was in the booth at the Concord Theatre and whenever she had some spare time, she went skiing.

She died on Jan. 28, 1992, at the age of 66, having worked until seven days earlier.

Arnold Rocklin-Weare, her supervisor at Employment Security, told the *Concord Monitor* right after her passing how Laurie had brought popcorn from the theater whenever any of the 30 office workers—or their family members—had a birthday. "She never, in 10 years, forgot anybody's birthday," he recalled.

Each day Laurie had walked to church on her lunch break to attend a noontime mass and during her afternoon break would pull out a booklet and rosary and say the rosary. Rocklin-Weare also remembered, "She always walked faster than anyone else. You couldn't keep up with her."

With the sister she had virtually raised since Laurie was barely two years of age gone, Theresa sought comfort in prayer, seeking counsel from Father Boiselle, who officiated at Laurie's funeral mass on Feb. 1, and by working. Theresa refused to close the theater telling the *Monitor*, "I've got to keep busy."

As the oldest, Theresa had always assumed that she would be the first to go, although she sometimes said she'd like to live to be 100. She had been the source of strength and guidance for her family since the late 1920s and that role, in some ways, fulfilled her even more than her "marriage" to her theater.

Hardly any of the film titles that decorated the marquee at the Concord Theatre during the remainder of 1992 warrant a mention. Those that were worth viewing were more often than not repeats of titles that had played elsewhere. *Howard's End* and *Enchanted April* were good films that brought in more revenue in a repeat than most of the first-run films brought. Even more importantly, they satisfied moviegoers. Both, however, had played at other theaters for their first run. I was living in Los Angeles and working in CBS Television City at the time. What I should have done was to return to Concord and to help out during what was obviously a trying and difficult time. Theresa and I talked on the phone, weekly, and I continued to prepare detailed listings of forthcoming films. In retrospect I can see that my presence would have provided a small measure of comfort.

Rapid Fire with Brandon Lee and *The Gun in Betty Lou's Handbag* did so badly that Monday through Thursday evenings Theresa only played one evening show at 7 p.m. Equally bad, from a box office perspective, were *Wind, Hellraiser III, Zebrahead* and probably the nadir of Anthony Hopkin's career, *Efficiency Expert. Night and the City* may have had a cast led by Robert DeNiro and Jessica Lange, but that didn't stir any local interest. Woody Allen's *Husbands and Wives* came out at the same time as allegations were being made against him and probably doomed that film. *Twin Peaks: Fire Walk* with Me brought out fans of the former cult favorite and *School Ties* did okay. *Toys* the Christmas attraction with Robin Williams brought the lowest holiday grosses since the 1960s.

Cinema 93 used good marketing tools to continue drawing loyal audiences including a strategy of only charging $3.50 on Wednesdays in September. Titles like *Glengarry Glen Ross* and *Of Mice and Men, Sneakers* and *Distinguished Gentleman* also kept the lights on. I know that during that year away, whenever I'd visit Concord, Cinema 93 seemed to always have an interesting film playing and I visited there several times.

When I returned home for the holidays, I spent an evening decorating the theater's lobby area, as I had been doing for decades. When I tossed some of the items away because they were looking frayed and tired, replacing them with newer items, I was hopeful that they'd be usable for another decade or more. Theresa however noted, "Their time has passed and maybe it's passed for me and this theater. Maybe we're just getting too old and frayed around the edges."

A year prior to closing, the Concord Theatre qui-etly marked 60 years of film exhibition.

Chapter Thirty-one

IT SAID SOMETHING about the state of the movie business when *Unforgiven*, the Clint Eastwood directed Best Picture Oscar winner, in a second run engagement was the second most successful film to play the Concord Theatre during 1993. The most popular film was *The Crying Game* and, indeed, during its run it almost seemed like the good old days for the Concord. The lines were out the door and down the street and several performances managed to even sellout.

Excessive Force, a New Line release that cost $13 million to make, only took in a little more than a million at the box office. Nobody showed up at the Concord for three of the seven days in which it ran. *Splitting Heirs,* a British comedy starring Rick Moranis, Barbara Hershey, Catherine Zeta-Jones and John Cleese didn't do much better, although the people who did come laughed. Coming off her great success in the comedy *Sister Act*, Whoopi Goldberg and Ted Danson co-starred in the third most-popular film to play the Concord in 1993, *Made in America*.

It was during the run of *Made in America* that Theresa agreed to an extensive filmed interview for a project entitled, *A Century of Motion Picture Audiences in Northern New England*. Although still reluctant to be photographed or filmed, she felt comfortable enough with Eithne Johnson. Theresa's eyesight had failed to such a degree that she was unable to successfully view the finished project but listening to it, she thought it had gone well. When telling me about it, she acknowledged, "I sounded as though I knew what I was talking about."

The Beverly Hillbillies with Jim Varney of *Ernest* fame assuming the role that Buddy Ebsen had made famous opened in November. After a couple of nights of listening to the film, Theresa concluded that she had preferred the old *Ma and Pa Kettle* movies she'd been forced to play 40 years earlier.

"At least the audiences laughed at them," she concluded, noting the silent crowds that were attending *Hillbillies*.

A repeat of *Age of Innocence* only proved the point that everyone who wanted to see this well-crafted film had seen it during its first-run. In December business got so bad that she closed the theater Dec.ber 12-16. With the Steeplegate Mall doing very well, there was a shortage of downtown shoppers. "There's no one to stop in impulsively, like they used to when they wanted a break from the shopping frenzy," she noted.

Theresa Cantin had no idea as 1994 began that it would be the last year her beloved Concord Theatre would be open. As had become the custom, the theater's lobby was decorated for the holiday season and Theresa greeted her customers with a "Merry Christmas" or "Happy Holiday" and wished them the best for 1994. A number of her loyal regulars from many years past, dropped off remembrances for her or baked just a little something extra because they knew she enjoyed an occasional sweet. As she had done since 1967, my first Christmas working at the theater, my mom put together a box of her homemade cookies of every variety, for me to bring to Theresa. Theresa was always pleased with herself that she made the box last until "Little Christmas," Jan. 6.

While the movie that was continuing its run, *Tombstone*, wasn't exactly her cup of tea, she was pleased by the comments from a largely male audience. She was also happy to be playing another film from the Disney studios, this time from its Hollywood Pictures division. She felt reasonably certain the film would go at least three weeks, and concession sales were brisk. It was not unusual to make three or four batches of popcorn on any given evening.

Her next attraction, from Warner Brothers, made her regret her decision to not extend *Tombstone* for one additional week. The new title, *M. Butterfly* starring Jeremy Irons did not find an audience in Concord. She had been told it would do the kind of business that *The Crying Game* had done a year earlier and she had believed the hype. *The Crying Game*, a year earlier, had brought lines out the front door, *M. Butterfly* played to less than a total of 500 people during its one-week run.

While the next feature, *Shadowlands* did not shatter records, it was well liked. Anthony Hopkins and Debra Winger starred and Winger was even nominated for an Academy Award for her performance. Business actually improved each day that the film ran, indicating positive word of mouth. Unfortunately another booking precluded a continuation of the run but Theresa was able to request and be granted an option to bring it back for a week at a later date.

What followed would prove to be the most successful film to play the Concord Theatre in 1994. While not quite in the league of *The Crying Game*, *The Piano* created quite a stir during a run of almost a month. It was already being acclaimed and was nominated for multiple awards and honors. Directed by Jane Campion and starring Holly Hunter and Anna Paquin, it never sold out but opened with about 400 in attendance between the two showings and barely dropped off. Comments were so positive that Theresa began to feel optimistic about the future of the theater and the ability to get enough product to keep the house open.

Cinema 93 had some strong films during the winter/spring season including *Grumpy Old Men*, possibly the most successful of the many pairings of Jack Lemmon and Walter Matthau, and *In the Name of the Father*.

Shadowlands returned for a week in March and the business was more than respectable. *The Piano* came back the following week after winning several Oscars including Best Actress and Best Supporting Actress honors. Those wins actually resulted in the strongest attendance on a Saturday evening for the year.

The House of the Spirits from Miramax looked promising on paper. It had a $40 million-plus budget and a dream cast. Meryl Streep, Jeremy Irons, Glenn Close, Winona Ryder, Antonio Banderas and Vanessa Redgrave. It was based on a popular novel and was touted as a German-Danish-Portuguese period drama. What it actually proved to be was 140 minutes of tedium for most audiences. So many people headed for the doors during the film that you'd have thought a fire drill had been called. Some of those who remained actually dozed off during the film and had to be awakened when it was over. The terms to play it had been stiff and the film had to remain for longer than was warranted by the business. On the last night, nobody showed up.

If possible the next film to grace the screen, *With Honors*, was even worse. The so-called comedy/drama starred Brendan Fraser, Joe Pesci,

Patrick Dempsey, Moira Kelly and even featured Gore Vidal. While it opened day and date and in the midst of a major television push, Concord audiences didn't feel it was worth the trip downtown to not laugh. A moderately good-sized crowd did chuckle and even laugh uproariously at the next picture.

The Concord Theatre played its first John Waters film when *Serial Mom* opened in May. Starring Kathleen Turner and Rikki Lake, the dark comedy drew a diverse audience including people who had clearly never stepped foot in the Concord Theatre. One woman even asked Theresa, "How long have you been here?"

Several years earlier Theresa had tried to get the popular John Waters film *Hairspray* but had not been able to book it. Waters' style of filmmaking was far removed from what Theresa normally enjoyed but in 1981 she had gone to Cinema 93 to see *Polyester*, a Waters' directed film starring Divine, and had enjoyed it more than she'd expected to.

Polyester featured a novelty known as Odorama. Upon purchasing your ticket you were given a scratch and sniff card with 10 numbers on it. At various times during the film, a number would flash on the screen and you'd scratch and sniff the corresponding number on your card. Theresa had read about this gimmick in the trade papers and was intrigued.

It was one of those evenings when nobody had showed up for the Concord Theatre's feature film and impulsively Theresa asked me to join her and Laurie for the second evening showing at Cinema 93 of *Polyester*. Barry looked just a little surprised when we walked in since he probably wouldn't have expected Theresa to be attending that particular film. The three of us had a great time, scratching, sniffing and enjoying the silliness of the whole enterprise.

When *Sirens* opened at the Concord in early June of 1994, Theresa remarked to me with regard to the slow business, "This picture would be perfect for Barry's theater. I bet he'd do a really good business with his people." *Sirens* starred Hugh Grant and Sam Neill and was a Miramax release, clearly aimed at the art house market. Toward the end of the short run, Theresa wondered whether she should contact Barry and discuss some kind of collaborative effort. I urged her to talk with him and explore options since it seemed that the days of the small independent movie theater would continue to be a struggle. There were also whispers that yet another multiplex might be coming to Loudon Road in Concord in the future.

Cinema 93 played several popular commercial films during the summer season including *Renaissance Man, I Love Trouble* with Julia Roberts and Nick Nolte, and *Angels in the Outfield.* The Merrimack Cinemas now going under the moniker of Lowes, continued to snatch up the bulk of the major moneymakers as had been expected.

Wolf, a Mike Nichols-directed film starring Jack Nicholson, Michelle Pfeiffer and James Spader, opened on June 17 and played for four successful weeks. Nicholson had done well for the Concord Theatre in the past, especially in two enormously popular films—*One Flew Over the Cuckoo's Nest* and *The Shining.* He came through again with this decidedly different role for him. With school out and some travelers on the road, business was good during the mid-week and very strong on the weekends. While there were no lines heading up Main Street as in days of old, the film played very well. That could not be said for *The Shadow* which arrived on July 15 for two weeks of bad business.

The picture clearly cost a great deal to make as was apparent from the production values. Alex Baldwin also did a great job in the title role. There just didn't seem to be any local interest in seeing this character brought to the screen, after lying dormant for so many years. What had been meant to begin a series of films failed to ignite.

Late July was probably not the ideal time to play a film like *Widow's Peak* which opened on July 29. This gentle, well-acted and beautifully photographed story would probably have found more interest in the fall. It wasn't necessarily a film for the summer crowd looking for escapist entertainment or splashy special effects. Filmed on location in Ireland, the film starred Mia Farrow, Joan Plowright and Natasha Richardson. Writing in the *Chicago Sun-Times,* critic Roger Ebert noted that the film "uses understated humor and fluent, witty speech; it's a delight to listen to, as it gradually reveals how eccentric these apparently respectable people really are."

With very limited sight still remaining, Theresa did indeed relish listening to the film during its run, although when looking at the box-office receipts, she once again noted, without sarcasm or bitterness, that the picture would probably have drawn bigger business with "The Cinema 93 crowd."

The summer season at the Concord would wrap with *Andre* from Paramount Pictures. Based on a popular book which was based on a true story, the film was set in Maine although filmed in Vancouver and Mississippi. Andre had been a seal that would return each year to Rockport, Maine, to a young girl who loved him. It was the first out and out family film that Theresa had played in quite a while and she was hopeful it would bring in the family trade. Sadly, it instead brought with it the end of an era.

Chapter Thirty-two

FRIDAY EVENING, AUG. 19, 1994, was like so many other evenings for me. A new film was opening at the Concord Theatre, and since it was the first night and Theresa was hoping for a good turnout for the first show, I had offered to come down and help out as needed.

As I had thousands of times in the 27 years with which I'd been a part of the Concord Theatre, I walked to the theater on the route that had always worked the best for me. Down Academy Street and then a left on Cambridge, a right onto Spring and then a left at Center. I'd walk Centre to Green, turning right and then making a left onto Park Street where I'd walk until I reached the State House Plaza. I'd cut across the Plaza and take Main Street, crossing over Capitol, School, Warren and finally Pleasant. From there it was barely a block, and the whole trip took about 12 minutes, 15 minutes if I paused to check out any store windows. I made it a habit of standing and admiring the displays in the windows of Endicott Furniture, Theresa's next door neighbor.

That evening Main Street seemed eerily quiet but then in the latter part of August that was sometimes the case. Many locals took vacations the last two weeks of August, and Friday night was no longer the hubbub of activity and shopping that it had once been. There were now empty storefronts and less retail businesses. Across the street from the Concord, the Sears building still loomed but it was no longer the center of shopping it had been for many years.

When I reached the door of the Concord Theatre, I pulled out my key. As you faced the theater there were three doors. Only one, the door on the far left, had a lock that a key would fit in, and I unlocked that door and stepped inside. As was my habit, I removed what we called "the hook" from the middle and far right door. The hook was a heavy rubber tube through which ran a chain and two spikes one on each end. These were slipped into the two doors and held them, in my opinion, more securely than any lock.

I began walking up the long lobby, pausing to close the door on the old ticket booth which continued to sit where it had at the front of the lobby, for decades. Curious customers often opened the door a bit to peek inside and see what might be kept in there. When they realized it was only the letters that were used on the marquee, they usually went away disappointed, often leaving the door ajar.

I stopped to turn the lights on in the lower lobby and noticed that one was burned out. While there I checked the men's room to make sure there were adequate toilet paper and paper towels and that everything had been flushed. Next I went into the switch room to reach up and push the lever upward to turn on the power to the upstairs projection booth. I then turned on the light inside the auditorium, both the ceiling lights and the smaller lights that illuminated the walls, and finally I turned on the ceiling light in the upper lobby where I then returned.

The ladies room received the same once over I'd had already given the men's and I adjusted the red curtains that led into the auditorium, stepping inside to make sure none of the interior lights had burned out. I also made sure that the large industrial air conditioner was turned on and that the large fan located in the back of the auditorium area, was turned on. This ensured that the cooling provided by the air conditioner was being dispersed throughout the theater.

The steel door that covered the concession stand was then rolled open and secured with a latch. In 1994 it seemed like the easiest thing to open that door. Thinking back to 1967, I had thought at the time that I had better embark on a weight training program if I expected to open the door on a regular basis.

The light switch for the concession stand was then turned on and I perused the shelves of candies wondering which I'd like to enjoy that evening when Theresa inevitably asked me if I'd like to have some candy. The warmer in the popcorn machine was the next thing to be put on so that the fresh popcorn Theresa would make that evening would stay hot. Theresa and her sister Rena came down the stairs within minutes, Theresa carrying the trusty cardboard box that contained the bills and change for the evening's business as well as a roll of tickets. Rena headed right to the concession stand where she began restocking the shelves. Twizzlers were the first order of business since their supply was almost depleted.

Customers started to trickle in about 20 minutes before the show was scheduled to start at 7. Theresa said she'd hold the show a few minutes if a lot of last-minute stragglers were coming in. There was no short subject or cartoon nor was there a trailer or preview since she didn't know what the next attraction was going to be. She said she'd know more after the first weekend of *Andre* when she could gauge how long the picture might hold.

Less than 100, about half of them children, attended the first showing of *Andre*. Lured by the delicious smell of the popping corn, however, more than 80 popcorns were sold not to mention dozens of candy bars. "Maybe we'll make something on concession during this film," Theresa stated.

I was scheduled to leave on Saturday morning for a two-week business trip to Los Angeles and after the show had begun and I'd used a sweeper to clean the upper lobby's rug from the fragments of popcorn, I told Theresa I would see her in two weeks. She squeezed my hands as she wished me a safe and good trip. I still recall how cold her fingers felt and almost said something but didn't. I didn't know at the time that I would never see her again.

Walking home on the same route from earlier that evening, I paused for a few minutes on the State House Plaza and watched dozens of bats flying and swooping around the State House dome, clearly attracted to the light. I thought it was beautiful to see and noticed that there was just the hint of a chill in the air as summer began to wind down. I also could not shake a sense of melancholy.

When I returned to Concord two weeks later, I drove by the theater on my way home from Manchester's airport, to see what was playing. Seeing *Andre* still on the marquee made me optimistic that perhaps business had been good after all and that Theresa had decided to hold the film for another week. I showed up the next evening to find the doors locked and the lights out and a homemade sign on the door stating, "No showing tonight".

The next morning I called Theresa on the phone and she told me that business for *Andre* had been terrible and that she couldn't get another booking right away. "I think we're going to be closed until Sept. 16." There was never to be another picture.

Andre was not intentionally planned as being the last film to play the Concord Theatre. For a while, Theresa believed that there would be a new film booked and actively pursued that possibility. She was especially interested in playing the upcoming Warner Brothers remake of the classic film, *Love Affair*. It was scheduled to be released in the latter part of October and starred Warren Beatty, Annette Bening and Katharine Hepburn, in what turned out to be the final motion picture of her career. Beatty and Bening had drawn good crowds to the Concord a few years earlier in *Bugsy*.

Love Affair was awarded to a different theater and when Theresa called to let me know what had happened, there was, for the first time, a sense of resignation in her voice. I assured her there would be other films that we could go after but the spark that had driven her for so many years, especially in the time since Laurie's passing, didn't seem to want to glow.

We continued to talk, almost weekly for a while, but Theresa always sounded tired. In December a short piece ran in the *Concord Monitor* headlined, "Curtain may be closing on Main Street theater." The story noted that Theresa had no plans to reopen the theater and that the property was for sale, according to Gene Blake, Concord's health and licensing officer.

The marquee on the theater continued to read:

TRUE STORY IN MAINE

ANDRE

AT TWO PM

In May of 1995, Steve Rothenberg who is currently CTE director at Concord Regional Technical Center, wrote a very funny tongue-in-cheek story for the *Concord Monitor* asking why, after more than eight months, *Andre* remained on the marquee. The story, entitled, "Ring the curtain down on the last picture show" expressed his frustration at seeing the film name continue to appear stating, "I cannot bear it any longer. It has exhausted my ability to suppress its triviality."

It would be more than a year before not only *Andre* but the entire marquee would be removed after having provided a downtown landmark for nearly 50 years.

In June of 1996, a transformer fell through the sign and nearly hit a pedestrian. The City of Concord informed Theresa that something had to be done about the marquee.

Monitor writer Ben Schmitt reported that Theresa considered having the sign repaired but upon determining what the cost would be, hired a private contractor to have it removed. Theresa noted to the reporter that

"Things can't last forever, I suppose" and the removal of the marquee accelerated the downward spiral of Theresa's health. She never regained her stamina or the drive that had been integral to her success as a businesswoman.

I was reminded of the story by O' Henry called *The Last Leaf*. A critically ill woman sees a plant outside her window shedding its leaves. She believes that when the last leaf falls, she will die. As long as the marquee hung from the front of the Concord Theatre, there was a possibility that another film might be shown. With the marquee gone, that possibility seemed to be lost.

Theresa and I continued to talk throughout 1997, but more often than not the calls were short because Theresa was tired. In the fall of 1997 I was able to briefly generate some interest from her about the possibility of selling the theater to an interested buyer. I arranged to have Jeff Larrabee talk with Theresa. There was a hope that she would sell the theater to him, enabling it to be renovated and brought up to code and then have it leased to Barry Steelman.

Theresa was upbeat when I talked with her about that possibility and you could hear a renewed sense of hope in her voice when she said, "I'd love to see it open again and Barry at the helm." She paused for a moment and then added, "If only I could see."

Her eyesight had further worsened until she could barely make out shadows and her days were spent in prayer or warmly recalling decades of interacting with a public whose loyalty was unquestioned.

Unfortunately any new plans were not to be and on Thursday, Feb. 19, 1998, at Elliot Hospital in Manchester, Theresa took her leave from the physical suffering that had been such a part of her life for so many years. Her brother Maurice had passed away in September of 1997 and her sister Rena would live until November 5, 2000.

Father Boisselle conducted the services on Monday, Feb. 23 at Sacred Heart Church and Theresa was buried in Mt. Calvary Cemetery in Manchester, returning home to the city in which she was born and the place where she had first found her love for motion pictures.

The *Concord Monitor* paid a fond tribute to Theresa with a story entitled, "From front row, Cantin saw world change." Sarah M. Earle was able to warmly capture some of the reasons that Theresa and her theater had played an important role in the local life of Concord and its residents.

A longtime regular at the theater, Superior Court Judge Vincent Dunn noted, "She was a very affable and friendly person, and it was a nice thing to go and watch a film there." In all the years I was associated with the theater, Judge Dunn missed very few films and always elicited a big smile from Theresa when his tall frame would approach the box office.

Barry Steelman tipped his hat to his "competitor" and stated, "She's got to garner your admiration for having the will to be in a fairly rough business for that period of time. I think there is some kinship between what she was trying to do and what I'm still trying to do."

Cinema 93 closed that June and Concord suddenly found itself without an independent movie theater for the first time in sixty-five years. There was not even a theater in Manchester or any of the immediate surrounding towns that showed more specialized motion pictures. The discerning moviegoer had no choice other than renting or purchasing a video. Fortunately Barry Steelman was soon able to relocate his thriving video business to Pleasant Street in downtown Concord. Even better was that the location for Cinema 93 Videos was the Star Building, formerly the Star Theatre.

A decade after closing, the front of the theater still looked as though it might be ready to greet anyone interested in buying a ticket. (Photo courtesy of Tony Schinella.)

Barry Steelman looks out over the auditorium of the Concord Theatre from the stage several years after its closing. He was hoping to be part of a restoration effort. (Photo by Dan Habib, courtesy of the Concord Monitor.)

Chapter Thirty-three

IN THE YEARS AFTER THERESA PASSED AWAY, less and less people asked me about the years I had spent at the Concord Theatre. I was increasingly surprised at the growing number of individuals who never even knew that a bustling movie theater had once been a centerpiece for that block of downtown real estate. Theresa's nephew, Paul, sold the building and although there were brief rumblings about the possibility of it being reopened as a theater, with a new configuration, nothing happened.

Barry Steelman pondered making a return to the kind of cinema he had made available, locally, at Cinema 93 and there was considerable enthusiasm. The enormous cost of bringing the Concord Theatre up to code and doing the needed improvements ultimately made it an impossibility and so the theater sunk into the recesses of a dwindling number of memories. I never forgot, however, and whenever the opportunity presented itself, chatted at length about the history of the theater and the people associated with the Concord Theatre.

Red River Theatres opened its doors several years into the new millennium, on the site of the old Sears Building. Fortunately Barry Steelman has a major presence at the new three-screen theater featuring stadium seating and the kind of film programming that a growing number of locals wanted. Red River became a destination for lovers of film.

In 2011 my autobiography was published and became a number one best-seller. Featured prominently within its 536 pages were stories about the Concord Theatre. Tony Schinella, editor of the fledgling *Concord Patch*, encouraged me to write blogs about Concord's richly diverse history. I listened to him and wrote about our community. Among my best received blogs were those about the Concord Theatre.

With the encouragement of Felice Belman at the *Concord Monitor*, I did an extensive piece about the theater in early 2014. Entitled, "Let's Bring the Concord Theatre Back to Life," it became one of the paper's 10 most-read pieces that month. I found myself the recipient of dozens of emails from people who had equally fond remembrances of the Concord Theatre and its place in Concord. For me it was especially gratifying to know that it wasn't merely my own sense of warm nostalgia for the years I'd been there, but that it had obviously left a mark on others as well.

The City of Concord marked its 250th birthday in 2015. While there was a great deal of recognition for the city's past as well as for individuals who had made contributions toward making it a great place to live and work, Theresa Cantin and the Concord Theatre were sadly absent from any mention. A book entitled *Legendary Locals* highlighting past and present role models as well as movers and shakers, didn't even see fit to mention Theresa.

It troubled me because for more than six decades she had been a promi-nent part of our city. She fought against many odds in order to bring the best possible films to the Concord. Although born in Manchester, Concord became her adopted home, a place where she not only conducted her own business, but a place she lived for most of her adult life. Sadly she didn't even seem to rate a footnote in the various tributes paid to Concord on the occasion of its 250 celebration.

Finally, as much out of frustration as anything else, I offered to do a free talk as part of the 250th celebrations. "Concord Chats," one of many programs held at Red River Theatres, was interested in having me do my talk there. The date selected was Thursday, Nov. 19, 2015, and an appreciable crowd filled the theater's screening room.

A handful or more of those in attendance had personal recollections of the Concord Theatre. Family members who had owned Star Hot Dog on Pleasant Street recalled the lines stretching past their business on those cold January nights in 1968 when *Valley of the Dolls* was playing. For many others who bombarded me with questions, this was all new to them and after my talk was completed, I noticed a great many stroll across the street to the deserted theater and peer inside the windows staring at it with a new found respect. It was no longer just some deserted downtown building.

I wrote additional blogs and pieces about the theater and I did another talk about the theater's history in January of 2017, for the OLLI (Osher Lifelong Learning Institute) Program at Granite State College. The classroom was filled to overflowing. The question-and-answer portion of the program took over a half hour, as former customers of the theater as well as those who only knew it as "that old downtown building" finally had the opportunity to get some answers.

Coincidentally, there were forces already at work behind the scenes, determined to bring new life to the Concord Theatre.

Within the Concord community, the name Steve Duprey gets an immediate response whenever he is mentioned or talked about. I had first met him in the 1970s when he was spending time with Martha Levensaler. Martha's mom and dad, Dorothy and Whitman, were close friends of my parents. I also knew their daughter Cindy. Dot and Whit owned the downtown mainstay, The Concord Camera Store. Steve was barely out of his teens but he left an immediate and lasting impression. He seemed focused, intelligent, charming and seemed to possess a desire to accomplish something meaningful with his life. Although I didn't talk with him again, other than saying hello when he'd see a movie at the Concord Theatre, I left that initial meeting with a feeling that he was someone who would be heard from in the future.

A mere glance at his resume solidifies the facts of his life, to date. Elected to the New Hampshire House of Representatives at the age of 19, a graduate of Cornell, a lawyer, a businessman, a real estate manager, a developer and a visionary. That barely touches the surface of what he has and continues to accomplish. As with any successful person, some people like him and some don't. What is clear, however, is his commitment to trying to make a difference and to standing by his convictions. Some communities would move mountains to have someone like Steve Duprey believe in them the way in which he believes in Concord. Always ready to listen to a differing opinion, he patiently and factually explains the reasoning behind decisions he makes or projects that he undertakes.

After the piece I wrote appeared in the *Concord Monitor* several years ago, I heard from Steve. For some years he had been trying to purchase the theater from the Aznive family that had bought it from Theresa's family. Steve didn't want to see the building lost forever. He recognized the historic value of the property, not just because of the movie theater that had been on the site but also the building's place in the community dating back to its days as the Norris Bakery in the mid-1800s.

In June of 2018, Steve shared some of his memories of the Concord Theatre with me, in an email that is a perfect example of both the man and the businessman.

> I always got a kick out of talking with the Cantins before the shows. When I started attending the theater in the late 70s and 80s the building was well past its glory years and it had the distinct odor of mildew and must. Every now and then a bat would make its way through the theater for extra entertainment!
>
> But when I bought the theater and started to think about how to reuse it I got to learn of the incredible story of these two women, what pioneers they were in a totally sexist and male dominated business, how hard they worked, and what courage it took to stand up to Joseph Kennedy. I never knew that about them all those years I attended shows. Their story is inspirational.
>
> And I also got to learn about the Norris bakery that preceded the theater, making biscuits for Union troops. It is pretty cool to go in the theater and see an old oven door from those days.
>
> I am really excited to bring back this theater. It will help Concord further cement our reputation as the cultural center of NH, will add life and people and shoppers and diners to Main Street, and will also be a big boost to the Capitol Center for the Art, an organization that is special and one I had been involved with since it started.
>
> Plus, I love the fact we will have a great old fashioned colorful neon theater sign out front."

Steve Duprey was instrumental in making the Capitol Center for the Arts (CCANH) a shining jewel in not only the local community but in the state. The center is a beautifully run facility that annually presents hundreds of stage and screen presentations to enthralled audiences numbering in the hundreds of thousands. I've been fortunate enough to work with them in bringing half a dozen artists to the area for benefit concerts. In each case, the artist has been in awe of both the facility and the amazing ability of the staff to coordinate all aspects of a production for maximum quality for both the performer and the audience.

Because of the great mix that is presented at the CCANH, they have been attempting for some years to find a way to create additional performing space for more intimate offerings that do not require the main theater with its large capacity of more than 1,300 seats.

Clearly the planets were aligned when Steve Duprey and the Capitol Center for the Arts joined together in an effort to bring the Concord Theatre back to life.

News of this joint effort first came to public attention in February of 2017. The plan announced immediately caused a great deal of curiosity and fascination within the Concord area. The plan discussed came with a very stiff price tag and lesser efforts involving other projects have often come to naught. I was thrilled, hopeful but cautious in my optimism. It was a tremendous undertaking and would necessitate an enormous fundraising effort if it were to be done correctly. On the plus side were the track records of the Capitol Center and most definitely Steve Duprey.

Several months later, Steve arranged for me to visit the closed theater. Almost 50 years to the day I began working at the Concord, and almost 23 years since I walked out the door for the last time on Aug. 19, 1994, I went inside again. It was an overwhelming experience. A few days later I wrote about it for *Concord Patch* in a blog:

> It seemed eerily right that my first visit to the Concord Theatre since it closed in September of 1994, would be almost 50 years to the day that I started working there. That first film had been *Caprice* starring my friend Doris Day and Richard Harris. She'd warned me against seeing it in a letter written some weeks earlier, but I was there on opening night and left with a new job. I remained there, doing various functions including assisting Theresa Cantin, the theater's owner, with film bookings, until the last picture show, *Andre*, based on a true story about a young Maine girl and the seal—Andre—who returned yearly.
>
> On Friday, June 30th, thanks to Steve Duprey and his assistant, Christie, I joined WMUR's Kristen Carosa and her cameraman, in a trip back in time. I really didn't know what to expect, fearing the worst after more than two decades of the theater sitting very quietly and unobtrusively on South Main Street.
>
> When I first walked in I felt the tears welling. After all, I'd walked through that door and down that long lobby thousands of times during the 27 years I was associated with the Concord Theatre. However, I quickly noted the still standing remnants from those days when thousands had purchased tickets.

The original ticket booth, where we stored the letters to go on the long gone marquee, is intact as are many of the art deco lights and fixtures. The huge sliding door that we would open nightly to reveal the concession stand appeared intact and the seats, dating back, when cinemascope movies became the new wave, replacing the theater's original 1933 screen, doesn't seem to glitter like it did when the images of everyone from Clark Gable to Elizabeth Taylor to Brooke Shields and Jack Nicholson brought audiences unforgettable films but it still felt like "The Concord!"

When the theater opened in 1933, Theresa was 19 years of age and when it closed she was weeks away from her 81st birthday. She was there every night and was proud of the fact that she cared about her audiences—whether they liked a film, what they wanted to see, if the presentation—sound and picture quality—were up to a standard. She listened telling me once that the theater opened during the darkest days of the Great Depression and it was important that she help audiences forget the pain and anguish that surrounded their lives on a daily basis. Everyone was treated equally—whether you were a surgeon at Concord Hospital or worked in the local Five and Dime—she cared and wanted you to have a good experience at the movies.

She regularly sent me to screenings of upcoming films so that we could jointly determine the best films to bid for and even when I was in Basic Training in the Navy at Greats Lakes, Illinois, I called her collect, twice a week, to talk about upcoming films.

The upcoming plans that Steve Duprey and the Capitol Center for the Arts have announced for the Concord, bode well for all of us living in Concord. It not only saves a nice piece of our history but it will provide all of us with a new venue for the increasingly diverse arts and entertainment scene in Concord. I've spent the better half of the last quarter century trying to keep the memory of the Concord Theatre alive. It was a community gathering place and you'd never know who you might meet or chat with. Jackie Onassis showed up one night in the 1970s and I'll never forget then Governor Meldrim Thomson arriving one evening with his wife Gale to see the musical version of "Tom Sawyer" starring Johnny Whittaker and Jodie Foster.

I'd heard so many remarks about the Governor—pro and con—and felt a bit intimidated as I handed him his popcorn. However, when he came out after the film, he excitedly told Theresa, how much they'd loved the film and that "Hollywood should make more movies like that. . . ."

By the time I departed the theater on Friday I can only describe my feelings as comparable to those I felt, as a youngster, on Christmas Eve as I went to bed anticipating what I'd find under the tree the next morning. Something truly wonderful is about to unfold and I am hoping that everyone in Concord, whether you have a special memory of the Concord Theatre or not, will want to be a part of this wonderful new chapter.

Chapter Thirty-four

I CONTINUED MY TALKING ENGAGEMENTS with a renewed sense of hope, optimism and purpose. Clearly this was a result of my visit to the theater. An event that was held outside the theater for INTOWN Concord provided me the opportunity to meet Joe Gleason, the assistant executive director at the Capitol Center for the Arts. Joe had arrived in Concord with his family after the Concord Theatre had closed. However, he was really interested in the theater's past. He also had an indefatigable way of bringing the future plans for the theater to startling life when he would speak before a group.

At the INTOWN Concord event, I provided a capsulized history of the Concord Theatre and then Joe shared the future plans for the site. Prior talks that I'd given alone had usually ended with some in the audience feeling a sense of sadness due to the theater being closed. However, once I teamed with Joe and he would bring his natural buoyance to discussing the next chapter, attendees were left with the same optimism I was feeling more and more with each day.

Joe and I talked to hundreds of people. We did a presentation at Goodlife and for the LINEC program at New England College. We also did a well-received evening at the Concord Public Library. Far more rewarding than the applause that would often ring out, were the questions from the audience and their obvious pleasure in knowing the theater's story was not yet over.

On Wednesday, May 30, 2018, Joe Gleason met me at the theater's front door. I had asked to be able to go inside one last time before the noise of construction and the hubbub associated with restoring the Concord Theatre was to begin. I wanted to be able to walk around the still familiar place, knowing that the next time I am there, I'll more than likely be in awe and amazement at what has been accomplished. While I had gone inside a year earlier, for the first time in nearly 23 years, it had been a rather hurried and short visit. I wanted time to say a proper farewell to the old Concord Theatre.

It had been cleaned out considerably since my previous visit eight months earlier. Some walls and fixtures had been removed, but it was still the Concord Theatre. The hook that once secured two of the three front doors was long gone, replaced by modern locks, but the box-office still sat there, minus the marquee letters but seeming as welcoming as it always did. The long lobby, although a bit frayed around the edges, could still clearly have held several hundred patrons anticipating what would unfold for them once they bought their ticket and went inside to find a seat.

The recessed area where the concession stand welcomed those who appreciated fresh-popped corn, still seemed to beckon, even without shelves lined with dozens of varieties of candy. The enormous sliding door that would roll open and closed looked as though it would still work. There was no longer an inviting display case showing off personal memories, nor was there the scent of candy waiting to be devoured. The popcorn machine, capable of making the best popcorn I'd ever had, had popped its last kernel and was long gone.

The thick red velvet curtains leading into the auditorium that I opened and closed thousands of times were still the originals and, although a bit dusty, had withstood the decades in which they'd hung there. What stories they could tell of people coming in and out, looking forward to what movie they would see or as they left, feeling either satisfied or disappointed. Even after more than half a century, I was still surprised by the first glimpse of the auditorium as you entered and how vast it seemed to be. From Main Street, looking at the theater, you don't expect it to be more than a couple of hundred seats. Like Doctor Who's Tardis, however, the interior is far bigger than the exterior would indicate.

Joe and I walked up and down the aisles heading toward the stage. I told Joe stories about the large screen doors I would put in place at three of the exit doors after the last evening show in the summertime. This would air the place out overnight. Up close from the footlights, the screen actually looked to be in pretty good condition for having hung around since 1953. I listened as Joe explained what would be replaced, what would be changed and how many new opportunities the end result would provide for audiences seeking something different.

I'd not been upstairs since prior to the theater closing. As we walked up the old wooden steps, Joe solicitously told me to watch my step. He even offered to pull out a flashlight to help us find our way. I told him I could go up and down those stairs with my eyes closed. I'd done that thousands of times, often carrying canisters of film reels to and from the projection booth. It seemed so familiar going up those steps one more time that I almost expected to find TT or Laurie at the top of the steps.

There was little in the booth to indicate what a hub of activity it had once been. The projectors and the platter were all gone. The slots where the reels would go were empty and only a few strips of film still littered the room. I'd never seen it empty and it seemed so small and unimportant although the view, looking down into the auditorium, impressed me as much as it ever had.

What had once been Theresa's office now sat filled with pieces of furniture and fragments of a life that had once shone like a beacon of light. That light was the lady who worked late into the night, sitting at a desk and balancing books and ledgers and trying to figure out what movie to next book. There were a couple of old antique adding machines on the floor as reminders of the work entailed in keeping a business alive and thriving.

The rest of the second floor was silent with few traces of the people who had filled it for so many years with the joys, sorrows, laughs and tears that made them a family. Leaning against a wall was a chart designed by Theresa's legal team for that long ago suit to get a fair share of good films for the Concord Theatre. Even to someone not familiar with the movie industry machinations, it was obvious from looking at the chart that the Concord Theatre was receiving less than 20 percent of the product available during a time period in the 1950s.

One of the questions I put to Joe was what this project meant to the Capitol Center for the Arts. His response was clearly reflective of the spirit that has infused the CCANH since it became an important part of our community.

The CCA's mission is to "inspire, educate, and entertain audiences" and "serve as a resource and gathering place for the community at large." As the community has grown and changed over time, so too has the CCA. Several years ago we made changes to our 44 South Main Street facility to allow for smaller productions in what we call our Spotlight Café. The existing facility has been maximized for use but unfortunately the configuration of the available space limits the types of smaller productions that we can bring in while still operating the large 1,304 seat Chubb Theatre. When the opportunity came along for us to have a truly separate second venue we recognized the potential to further expand our programming and move some of our existing smaller programs into the second venue. This frees up prime dates on our Chubb Theatre calendar to bring more large productions to town and gives us the ability to more effectively program artists that are not ready to perform in the big theatre. With a nearly 300 seat capacity projected for the renovated Concord Theatre this size venue will be more cost effective to bring in smaller shows and artists that don't have the following to fill the larger theatre. The smaller size of the Concord Theatre will also allow us to provide a lower cost option to community groups when they need a smaller space for their functions.

I was curious as to what kind of response the CCANH had received from the residents of Concord and the surrounding areas that make up much of their audience.

People in the community have been receptive to our plans for the renovation of the Concord Theatre. In the early stages of the project we had to do a fair bit of explaining about how the building renovation was being handled. To be fair, in the early part of the project there were many unknowns, not the least of which was what exactly was the relationship between the developer (Steve Duprey) and the CCA. To complicate things, there were several available tax credit programs which could be used to help fund the project and these programs had conflicting requirements for ownership. Explaining these details to prospective donors was a bit of a challenge which got easier over time as the details of the project began to crystalize. In a nutshell—Steve Duprey is acting as developer on behalf of the CCA which will own and operate the new venue.

Joe's endless enthusiasm for the project made me wonder how others associated with the CCANH feel about taking on a new project.

While some staff are naturally more involved in the project than others, we have made a point of soliciting input on the design and build out of the project from all of our staff at CCA. As a result, we are all feeling a sense of ownership in making this project a success. Without a doubt, there will be challenges ahead but being part of a project from the early stages through completion is an experience all of us at the CCA are excited to be a part of.

As we walked back down the stairs and returned to 2018, I didn't feel as sad as I had feared. Sure, I'd have liked nothing better than to have one more chat about movies with Theresa or to once again open those red velvet curtains leading into the auditorium to allow a new audience to go inside to experience a movie. I realized, however, that Theresa would probably nod in agreement with all of the great plans afoot for her theater and be happy that audiences will once again stroll up that long lobby to experience some magic.

The Capitol Center for the Arts arranged to make available to anyone who was interested, the 499 seats in the Concord Theatre's auditorium. There was no cost. All you had to do was to show-up on Saturday morning, June 16, 2018, and take a seat or two or three.

I arrived about an hour after the designated time and found that virtually every seat had been taken. I was gratified that so many people had shown up because they wanted to have a little piece of history in their home. I selected two seats.

As I walked down South Main Street carrying them to my car, I found myself chuckling a little bit. I remembered what Theresa would often say to someone stepping up to the box office to purchase a ticket on a night when the performance was sold-out.

"I'm sorry, but all our seats are taken," she'd remark.

By noon on June 16, 2018, they really were all taken.

After 25 years, The Concord Theatre will reopen in the summer of 2019 as Bank of New Hampshire Stage. (Dennis Mires, Architect)

Epilogue

THE ENDING TO THE STORY of the Concord Theatre has not yet been written. In the late summer of 2018, I was invited to a press conference at the Concord Theatre. The occasion was the announcement that thanks to the generosity of Bank of New Hampshire, the new venue is to be called Bank of New Hampshire Stage. On hand was Paul Falvey, president and CEO of Bank of New Hampshire. Bank of New Hampshire is a longtime supporter of the Capitol Center for the Arts. Falvey noted during his speech, "We've been supporting them since 1967. This is quite an exciting project for us to support and to continue our relationship with the community."

As he looked around at the theater's walls he noted, "To think, all of this could have gone away."

Although the name of the theater will change, the structure will remain as a place where people can go to be entertained.

Theresa Cantin spent most of her life practicing humility. That quality was one of the reasons she was reluctant to grant interviews to the various media. Her theater was her job and she gave more than 100 percent to it, each and every day for more than six decades. She would, however, be the last person to even remotely think of herself as any kind of trailblazer, and yet she was. Women certainly owned businesses and did well at it. Often they owned and operated clothing and apparel stores, markets and other enterprises. However, the world of movie theater ownership was not open to women. As a result, Theresa was often belittled, dismissed or tolerated, even after she had proven her mettle as a businesswoman.

For me, one of the most rewarding aspects of the talks I have done about the Concord Theatre, was hearing from those who remember Theresa. They've shared stories about their warmly remembered experiences at the

Concord Theatre over the decades. Many of those stories resonate with me because they represent the woman I was fortunate enough to call a friend.

Longtime Concord resident and former business owner, Catherine Pappas, attended the talk that Joe and I gave at New England College. She clearly loved the stories we shared and afterwards shared a few of her own. She'd spent many an hour from the time she was a teenager at the Concord Theatre. Theresa Cantin had been the face of that theater for as long as she could recall.

Theresa's nephew, Paul Constant, who lived with his parents upstairs in the apartment over the theater's lobby, recalled his aunt in July of 2018.

> TT was an amazing woman. She taught me how to survive, treat everyone as I would want to be treated and how to succeed in life. I think of her every day. I named my boat TwoThumbs Up. As you know she loved to listen to Siskel & Ebert. I carry a silver dollar in my pocket every day in memory of her. One that she left me.

I asked Paul, who I've known since that first day in June of 1967 when I started work at the Concord Theatre, what his favorite memory of TT was.

> My favorite memory of her is when they would get all gussied up to go to the opera. That is what she enjoyed most.

Finally, I inquired as to how he had felt being a part of a family-run business.

> Being part of a family business was definitely a positive experience for me, it taught me the value of team work and how to be chief cook and bottle washer. We all did whatever it took to be successful and for that I am most grateful.

I don't pretend to say that this story is the definitive book about the history of motion pictures within the Concord area. I am hopeful, however, that it will provide an overview of how important the movies were to generations of Concord residents. I am also hopeful that the story of Theresa Cantin and her theater will provide insight into how far we have all come in perceptions and acceptance in the more than 85 years since she first sat in the box office.

Today we hurry into a multiplex, often not noticing who is selling us the ticket or the popcorn and other concession treats. It's a much more impersonal experience. Staffing at movie theaters changes frequently.

Fortunately Red River is a reminder of what was once the norm in our city. Barry Steelman, each time I see him at Red River, evokes warm recollections of all those great movies that played Cinema 93. The Capitol and Star Theatres had their own cast of characters. These were all the people who shared the same vision that Theresa Cantin held to. Make the moviegoing experience a complete experience for your customer.

The Tickets Tell the Tale

A MOVIE'S POPULARITY is determined by various factors. Critical acclaim, awards won or the number of tickets sold or what it takes in at the box office. With a major change in the release pattern of motion pictures, from the 30s into the 70s, 80s and 90s, the measure of a film's success during its run at the Concord Theatre is more easily defined by the number of tickets sold during its run. In the 1930s a film might only play for two or three days and sell-out during that run whereas in the years beginning in the 60s, it might play multiple weeks, thereby attracting vastly larger numbers.

The most tickets sold for a film title in the Concord Theatre's 61-year history was for *Valley of the Dolls*. The 1967 20th Century Fox Release, which opened in Concord in January of 1968, sold just over 15,000 tickets during its run.

Below are the most attended films in various genre. The year listed is the year in which the film played the Concord Theatre and not necessarily the year the film was initially released.

MUSICALS
1. *Woodstock* (1970)
2. *Grease* (1978)
3. *Saturday Night Fever* (1977)
4. *Billy Rose's Jumbo* (1963)
5. *Thoroughly Modern Millie* (1968)

COMEDIES
1. *Animal House* (1978)
2. *10* (1979)
3. *Young Frankenstein* (1975)
4. *Arthur* (1981)
5. *Trading Places* (1983)

HORROR
1. *Carrie* (1976)
2. *Halloween* (1978)
3. *The Exorcist* (1974)
4. *The Shining* (1980)
5. *The Amityville Horror* (1979)

SCI-FI
1. *Alien* (1979)
2. *Star Trek* (1979)
3. *Superman* (1978)
4. *2001: A Space Odyssey* (1969)
5. *Planet of the Apes* (1968)

TEEN
1. *The Karate Kid 2* (1986)
2. *The Karate Kid* (1984)
3. *Stand By Me* (1986)
4. *The Blue Lagoon* (1980)
5. *Pretty in Pink* (1986)

STARRING JOHN WAYNE
1. *Rooster Cogburn* (1976)
2. *The Quiet Man* (1952)
3. *The Alamo* (1961)
4. *McLintock* (1963)
5. *The Cowboys* (1972)

ROMANCE
1. *Moonstruck* (1988)
2. *Big* (1988)
3. *Working Girl* (1988)
4. *Splash* (1984)
5. *Annie Hall* (1977)

ACTION
1. *Die Hard* (1988)
2. *Rocky* (1977)
3. *Rocky IV* (1985)
4. *The Towering Inferno* (1975)
5. *Rocky II* (1979)

MY NAME IS BOND
1. *Thunderball* (1966)
2. *The Spy Who Loved Me* (1977)
3. *For Your Eyes Only* (1981)
4. *Goldfinger* (1965)
5. *Dr. No* (1963)

DRAMA
1. *One Flew Over the Cuckoo's Nest* (1976)
2. *Network* (1977)
3. *The Crying Game* (1993)
4. *Lawrence of Arabia* (1964)
5. *The Ten Commandments* (1958)

FAMILY
1. *The Black Stallion* (1979)
2. *Breaking Away* (1979)
3. *Around the World in 80 Days* (1958)
4. *Pinocchio* (1954 Disney reissue)
5. *Lilies of the Field* (1964)

Oscar Gold

The Academy Awards have always been considered a barometer by which to judge the value of a film or performance. Whatever their flaws—and there are many including popularity and jockeying for an award—being able to tout your film as an Academy Award winner can lead to increased box-office revenue and prestige.

The Concord Theatre was fortunate through the years in being able to play a number of films that took home an Oscar in various categories. Some of the notable winners in the Best Film and Best Foreign Film are listed here.

1946 *The Best Years of Our Life* (Best Picture)
1956 *Around the World in 80 Days*
1961 *West Side Story*
1962 *Lawrence of Arabia*
1963 *Tom Jones*
1965 *The Shop on Main Street* (Best Foreign Language Film)
1966 *A Man for All Seasons*
        A Man and a Woman (Best Foreign Language Film)
1971 *The Garden of the Finzi Continis* (Best Foreign Language Film)
1974 *Amarcord* (Best Foreign Language Film)
1975 *One Flew Over the Cuckoo's Nest*
1976 *Rocky*
1977 *Annie Hall*
1978 *Deer Hunter*
1979 *The Tin Drum* (Best Foreign Language Film)
1987 *The Last Emperor*

Memories of the Concord Theatre
Robert Pingree

Robert Pingree first taught film as a graduate assistant at Rutgers University in 1967. In 1971 he created the film study course at Concord High School and taught multiple sections for 33 years. He was also a film critic for the Concord Monitor and in retirement, he has offered enrichment courses at OLLI (Osher Lifelong Learning Institute) in Concord during the past eight years.

A WHILE AGO ON FACEBOOK someone on the site devoted to recollections of Concord asked, "Who remembers the rat theater?" I responded with one word: "Canard." This fairly esoteric word, derived from the French for duck, is defined as "a false or unfounded report or story, esp. a fabricated report. In today's parlance, fake news.

But it is one of the first things I heard about the Concord Theatre shortly after arriving here in 1970. For the record, I never saw a rat there.

I did see movies, at first just for pleasure and later for profit, when I began reviewing for the *Concord Monitor*. The city had four theaters in 1970, each with only one screen. The Capitol, which was to become the Capitol Center for the Arts, was on Main Street, as was the Concord. Cinema 93 was located in what was then known King's Plaza, now the site of Bed, Bath, and Beyond and the post office. The drive-in off Manchester Street completed the picture. There was not yet a multi-screen facility on the Heights. Since only the drive-in showed double features, one any given night residents had a choice of five movies during the summer, three the rest of the year.

The Concord had its share of hits in the 70s. There I saw Christopher Reeve debut as Superman, and Howard Beale, the mad prophet of the airways, exhort people to get up, go to their windows, and shout their displeasure with the state of the world. Marty Feldman instructed Gene Wilder to "walk this way" in *Young Frankenstein*. And the theater had highly successful runs of two successive Oscar winners, *Rocky* and *One Flew over the Cuckoo's Nest*.

In 1980 I started reviewing. The second piece I wrote was for a blessedly forgotten movie entitled *Cuba*, with Sean Connery as a mercenary come to help train Batista's army. My first sentence: "In 10 years, if I am doing a column on the worst films of the decade, I hope someone will remind me that I spent part of the evening of Jan. 29, 1980, watching *Cuba*." This did not endear me to Ms. Cantin, who told me when I returned on my next assignment that she was reluctant to let me in.

She did, however, and I hope that many positive reviews over the next four years brought an increase in viewers and profits. The Cutters of Bloomington, Indiana, in *Breaking Away* were certainly well-liked, and perhaps some people agreed with my praise of *For Your Eyes Only* as "the perfect summer entertainment." I tried to spur interest in a revival of Fellini's *Amarcord*, an unusual piece of scheduling at a time when foreign films were rare in Concord, by calling it "ecstatic and elegiac, rollicking and gentle, jubilant and poignant." *Southern Comfort*, with National Guardsmen set upon by murderous Cajuns in a Louisiana bayou, was "a solid adventure story," and I commented on its ability to involve an audience member to call out "Do it! Do it!" when a character shouts "Kill him! Kill him!" to another.

Looking back at my reviews, I am most pleased by two of them. *The Competition* was a small film about two people vying for the top spot in a piano competition and "grudgingly, hesitantly, but believably" falling in love along the way. The screenplay gave its three principal characters—the two pianists and the teacher of one of them—"distinct and credible personalities, and Amy Irving, Richard Dreyfuss and Lee Remick flesh them out with charm and conviction." Alas, Netflix doesn't seem able to put it into my mailbox.

Fortunately, I own other film. Sidney Lumet's *Prince of the City*, nearly three hours long and with a large cast of characters, about whom your feelings are likely to be conflicted, was probably not very popular. Lumet's *Serpico* had given us Al Pacino as a cop who blows the whistle on his crooked colleagues. In *Prince of the City*, it's Treat Williams as Danny Ciello, but, unlike Frank Serpico, he is corrupt himself. I watched the film again two years ago, and I agree with my original assessment: "I know of no picture which explores complex ethical questions about loyalty, honor and justice with comparable depth and maturity." For me, it is the greatest of cop movies.

All in all, the Concord Theatre was a good place to see some fine films.

Movie Musicals at The Concord Theatre
Jim Webber

Jim Webber, who has directed plays and designed sets for more than 50 productions in the central New Hampshire area, has lived in Concord since 1967 when he began seventh grade at Rundlett Junior High School. His memories of late 1960s and early 1970s movie musicals helped to inspire his theater work in Los Angeles and when he returned to New Hampshire in 2004.

I WAS RAISED a good St. John's Church Catholic and since I was also a stepchild, that meant being quiet and well-behaved and staying out of the way as much as possible. That is probably why I fell in love with musicals, because the characters were so exuberant and expressive and so much the opposite of me and people in my life. My most formative movie experiences were seeing Julie Andrews in *Mary Poppins* (Rte. 3 Cinema, Chelmsford, Mass., now gone) and in *The Sound of Music* (Gary Theatre, Boston, now gone). Though my fondness for Ms. Andrews was, perhaps, as much for her creative child rearing techniques as for her exuberance. The music, color and magic of both films made a huge impression on me. It also made a huge impression on some gentlemen over 3,000 miles to the southwest, in the board rooms of the Hollywood movie studios.

In 1965, *The Sound of Music* not only saved 20th Century Fox from bankruptcy (mostly caused by the disaster that was *Cleopatra* two years earlier), but provided them with cash to sink into more movie musicals, which were expected to reproduce the smash box-office bonanza that was *The Sound of Music*. Every studio jumped on the bandwagon and four or five years later, each released a string of big, expensive musicals, most all of which did poorly at the box office (if not exactly reproducing the disaster that was *Cleopatra*). We'll recall that in 1969 and 1970, the hippies had come and gone and the antiwar movement was in full swing. Mass-market taste had jumped the generation gap and a hit movie looked much like *M*A*S*H*. Widescreen costume musicals were decidedly not hip anymore.

Not one movie studio remained unscathed by their unwise investments. Even Columbia Pictures, which scored with Barbra Streisand in *Funny Girl* and a British co-production, *Oliver!* (which won an Oscar for Best Picture), later dumped their profits into a disastrous musical remake of *Lost Horizon* with a full cast of non-singers and lost its money.

For some reason, the Concord Theatre was able to take in some of these straggling, struggling musicals, and give them a temporary home as they made their way from the under-performing reserved seat engagements in the big cities to strip mall cinemas and small-town theaters before heading back to cold storage vaults to await being cut to accommodate the commercials on the CBS late movie.

Going back further in time, my first movie at the Concord Theatre was when I did not live there, but was visiting my stepmother's family (who did). To shoo us out of the house when my widower dad was dating my soon-to-be stepmom, my brother and I were given some change to go and see Jimmy Stewart in *Mr. Hobbs Takes A Vacation*. Alone. He 11 and I was seven. (It was 1962.) My only memories are of the bouncy background music (Mancini) and that Jimmy Stewart snarled and delivered lines out the corner of his mouth as though he thought they were funny. They probably were, but I was seven.

Our family moved to Concord in December of 1967. Just in time for *Camelot*. (I was 12 and *Valley of the Dolls* was out of the question.) We had the record album of the *Camelot* soundtrack already. Even then I thought Richard Harris was a bit full of himself, but I liked Vanessa Redgrave's comic bits in *Take Me To The Fair*. Even at that age, I found the movie itself disappointing with long, mushy love montages and strange hippie-like costumes which seemed desperately contrived to appeal to a younger audience. (Did I think this at age 12? Yes!)

Around that time, I began to have some impressions of the Concord Theatre. I liked the art deco light fixtures and the designs on the wall panels, and especially the tile floor in the front lobby and the old box office booth in the center of it. (My memory of it is that it was rarely used, but that is because in later years you bought your tickets at that counter near the refreshment stand.) My stepmother had told me about going to the movies downtown in the war years when she was in high school and I think I attributed a good deal of (imagined) WWII nostalgia to the theater—people bundling up in cold weather, going on dates and waiting in long lines to see—what—*Casablanca*? Very likely.

And thus began my few years of seeing Hollywood second-era musicals at the Concord: *Half A Sixpence* with Tommy Steele, a British coproduction of Mr. Steele's stage hit. The story seemed thin to me and Tommy perhaps not quite handsome enough for the movies, but the dancing was great fun. I was learning something about British musicals (expect lots of Cockney "charm.") *Finian's Rainbow* with Petula Clark and Fred Astaire (and more Tommy Steele)—made on a budget but with a verve and spark missing from many other more expensive movies—and a great Burton Lane—E.Y. Harburg score. Dated. Odd. But not without charm. I think I attended on the night of the first moon walk—obviously *Finian's Rainbow* was more important, at least to me.

Goodbye Mr. Chips, a rather intelligent musical with Petula Clark and Peter O'Toole, was missing several songs when it played Concord, at least they were on the soundtrack album. I was not sure if songs were cut from the film before the big city engagements or afterwards. Years later, when I saw the video, that had been restored. Not a memorable score, but a very good, very touching film and O'Toole was wonderful. *Sweet Charity*, was perhaps the sexiest G-rated movie I had ever seen, with the naughty "dance hall hostesses" and the inferred premarital sex. (Shocking!) Bob Fosse's first movie got slammed by critics, but even then I thought I had never seen dance numbers better choreographed, shot and edited. Shirley MacLaine was no singer, but very good in the role and Chita Rivera blew me away. I had never seen such theatricality and assurance in a performance. I still can't understand why she did not do more films. The downbeat ending was a shock, I recall. The ending of "Fiddler on the Roof" shocked me more, but the ending of *Charity* was pretty rough, when her straight arrow boyfriend dumps her at the altar and she heads back to midtown with a battered suitcase.

Paramount Pictures was the studio that crapped out at the bottom in the neo-musical marathon. *Paint Your Wagon*, *Darling Lili* and *On A Clear*

Day were all conceived as three-hour "roadshow" movies with reserved-seat engagements and intermissions. When the singing Clint Eastwood/Lee Marvin musical *Paint Your Wagon* tanked, the studio took *Darling Lili* away from comedy director Blake Edwards and re-edited the Julie Andrews WWI spy-musical-comedy-romance and released it to mixed reviews and no business. Barbra Streisand was filming her third big musical *On A Clear Day You Can See Forever* under *Gigi* director Vincente Minnelli when the Paramount brass told them to cut an hour out of the Alan J. Lerner musical and somehow make it work. By 1970, everyone knew the era had passed and only the Streisand fans lined up for tickets to *On A Clear Day*. Such a strange movie, modern-day Barbra had no visible means of support (like Marlo Thomas in *That Girl*), but wore up-to-the-minute Park Avenue fashions. The movie seemed to have no contact with the real world beyond a sound stage, but for some reason a "campus protest" was shoehorned into the proceedings. Her love interest, French star Yves Montand, was too old and sleepy to make any romantic chemistry work, but nevertheless, Barbra was fun—if a bit obsessed with her fingernails and her wardrobe. It's a terrible movie, completely unbelievable on any level, but Lerner's lines were mildly amusing and Minnelli's compelling visual sense made it oddly hypnotic. (Apparently the creators of the original Broadway show were all getting shots from Dr. Max Jacobson, doctor to the stars. Shots of cocaine, apparently. Even seeing the movie, this comes across…)

In 1971, MGM released its last "MGM Musical"—a British co-production called *The Boy Friend*. The property was a 1950s spoof of a paper-thin 1920s British stage musical. When it was done in New York in the early 50s, a very young Julie Andrews played the lead. (Later, in 1967, Julie did a movie called *Thoroughly Modern Millie*, a spoof of American silent movies from the 1920s. No connection.) When British director Ken Russell filmed *The Boy Friend* he decided to pretend it had been a real 1920s stage musical, now struggling on in the provinces, performing to thin audiences in a crumbling music hall in an English coastal town in the 1930s. A Hollywood movie mogul comes to see the show and (on occasion) imagines what his version of a Busby Berkeley-type movie version would look like. Some of the other characters have moments where they imagine what various musical moments would look like to them as well. (And you thought *On*

A Clear Day was strange …) Needless to say, it was a crazy movie. Not only did you see the thespians act out *The Boy Friend* on their creaky stage with clunky scenery, you witnessed all their backstage intrigues, affairs, jealousies, plots and technical snafus as well. Plus the fantasy sequences. There was a lot going on. Nobody went to see it. Not even for Twiggy, who was not bad at all.

When I went the Concord Theatre to see the film on a Sunday night, I went to an early show with a friend from high school (I was sixteen.) There were two other people in the theater. We thought the movie was hilarious. After the first show ended, the other two people left. We stayed to see it again. No one else came in. And we went back two days later to see it again on a week night. Even today, it remains one of my favorite movies and I drag out the DVD to watch it once a year. A great, sprawling show business spoof, way before the days of *Waiting for Guffman*. (Interesting fact: the sets for the movie *The Boy Friend* were all designed by Julie Andrews' first husband, Tony Walton, who had done sets for *Mary Poppins* for Disney. Most of his other design work was for the stage.)

After I went to college in Boston, I did return now and then. My only other real Concord Theatre memory was seeing *Saturday Night Fever* (Paramount came back with a vengence in 1977) on opening weekend in Concord. The days of slow release and big city build-up delaying small-town engagements for months and years was over. The studios pumped all the publicity into the national press for one mega-opening and the movie opened everywhere at once with thousands of prints being exhibited across the country simultaneously. The theater was packed and rocking to the 4/4 disco beat of Bee Gees. Times had changed. Again.

Movies Influenced Me
Tony Schinella

Anthony "Tony" Schinella has spent most of his life in the Concord area. A graduate of Concord High School, he has worked extensively in the area of media, including radio and news. For many years he was the editor of Concord Patch and had a front-row seat to the Concord community. Presently he works for the State of New Hampshire.

MOVIES HAVE PLAYED A ROLE in nearly everyone's lives including creative people in the city of Concord. Whether it was an edge-of-your-seat thriller, an emotional drama that moves to tears, or a sidesplitting comedy that is viewed multiple times, movies—film, cinema, flicks, whatever they have been called during the course of the history of moving pictures—have been a great and often, inexpensive escape for many.

My earliest memories of cinema in the city harken back to the early 1970s when movies primarily played at three theaters: The Capitol Theatre (now, the Capitol Center for the Arts), Cinema 93, and the Concord Theatre. Movies also played at the Concord Drive-In, but I only remember seeing a movie there on one occasion. I think it was a Chuck Norris double-feature.

At the time, the city was a bit of a mundane, Rockefeller Republican, bedroom community; residents lived a relatively sheltered, boring life. It was nothing like it is today.

Children (including me) were sometimes dropped off at a Disney matinee at the Capitol while parents ran their errands. In many ways, as bad as things may have been for a lot of people at the time, a matinee was like gold for kids—a couple of hours with a movie, some previews, and a small box of popcorn.

The screens were massive compared to our tiny televisions. Somewhat forgettable but silly and innocent films such as *Son of Flubber, No Deposit, No Return,* or *The Love Bug,* and later, *Escape to Witch Mountain* and *The*

Bad News Bears, offered the most ridiculous and unimaginable stories that fully came to life before our very eyes.

The Capitol stopped showing movies around the mid-1970s, so most of my memories of movies revolve around the Concord Theatre and Cinema 93.

At the Concord Theatre, old movie placards of yore hung in the long entryway. I recall exchanging pleasantries with the ladies who owned the theater; they always gave kids a sly once-over—especially if they thought you might be too young for the movie that was playing. The theater was a bit dank and dusty and, after a while, you came to learn where the uncomfortable seats were (stay away from the front, left hand side rows). But we cherished it.

When Bookland, the popular downtown Concord bookstore, began carrying *Variety*, I bought it every week, just to find out what was coming soon. It as well as *Billboard* were required reading for me, an education in all that was going on in the film and music businesses.

My early interest in horror movies turned to comedies and ridiculously dumb high school flicks like *The Last American Virgin*, *Meatballs*, *Fast Times at Ridgemont High*, and later, *Caddyshack*, which I still try to watch at least once a year (the first night *Animal House* played in the city, at the Concord Theatre, it sold out).

I was a huge fan of the previous Rocky films and not just because I am mostly Italian but due to the underdog spirit of the films, especially the gritty original; it was easy to relate to much of what the character experienced. Many pooh-pooh the Rocky series because Sylvester Stallone has churned out many money-making sequels (recent offerings, *Rocky Balboa* and *Creed*, are standouts, actually). Customers, though, loved the third film, which earned about $270 million at the box office. People forget that the original film won Best Picture, Best Director and Best Film Editing Academy Awards and had seven other nominations. It also won the Best Motion Picture Drama Golden Globe in 1977. Stallone's personal story of how he got to the point of Rocky, languishing in shitty acting roles and life situations all because he had a dream, makes the first film all the more important to cinema history today.

The last film I recall seeing at the Concord Theatre is another of my all-time favorites: *Pretty In Pink*, the John Hughes movie starring Molly Ringwald, Andrew McCarthy, James Spader and Jon Cryer, which played at the theater in early 1986. My girlfriend at the time, Deana Edmunds, and I went to the early showing on its first night. Not unlike *Rocky III*, there weren't many people in the audience, which was OK, since we snuck in beers and made a night of it.

There are so many memorable lines in the film including Cryer's character Duckie's classic, "Blane?! His name is Blane?!? That's not a name, it's a major appliance!" and Iona, played riotously by Annie Potts, "I swear my thighs went up in flames," after getting a kiss from Duckie. The film earned more than four times what it cost to make, about $40.5 million, at the box office (or $93 million in 2018 dollars), and every time I watch it, I think back to that first time seeing it at the Concord Theatre.

A life-altering moment that summer brought me to realize some of my own perceived failures which, being so young at the time, weren't quite accurate. I also had a desire to be more than who I was at the time—something that seems so irrelevant, in the scheme of things, today (Let life be what it is and live every day to the fullest, were tenets I would come to accept).

That moment prompted me to dream big, again, and up and move to Boston, where I would attempt to do everything that I'd ever dreamed of wanting to do. My love of film went with me and, thankfully, there were many great movie houses and an endless selection of films to see, too.

Those influential early days of attending movies at places like the Concord Theatre, thankfully, made me what I am today. They helped me build a career in media—radio, print and online—as well as create news videos and short films and be as creative as I possibly could be.